Winner of the *Child* magazine Book Award for Excellence in Family Issues

"Hewlett's book is one of the most thoughtful and provocative analyses to come along about what is wrong with American policies toward families."—*Washington Post*

"A convincing and foreboding picture of this country's treatment of children."—*Boston Globe*

"Pick a page, any page, of this book and learn one grim fact after another to support Sylvia Ann Hewlett's thesis. . . . She demonstrates exhaustively that neglect is producing a generation unprepared to compete in today's global economy. . . . Mercifully, she [also] offers remedies."—*Baltimore Sun*

"A powerful, solidly documented study . . . citing stunning statistics."—*Publishers Weekly*

"A powerful, extensively researched and often shocking book that explores the plight of a vast number of our children today."
—*Library Journal*

"A searing critique of the American family, our corporate leaders and public officials. Much can be learned from this compelling, well-documented study."—*Kirkus Reviews*

"Hewlett doesn't only wring our hearts . . . she tries to wring our pocketbooks as well. And she makes some very good sense."
—Christopher Lehmann-Haupt, *New York Times*

"Hewlett's moving description of the cost of neglecting our children can guide our nation to a better day, when we will all benefit from putting our children first."—Senator Bill Bradley

"Very accessible and utterly convincing. . . . In this landmark study, Hewlett takes a hard-eyed, bottom-line-oriented look at the increasingly fractured lives children are being forced to lead."—*Booklist*

"Hewlett has launched an all-out indictment of how we, as a society, fail to adequately care for our children, and warns that continued neglect will drag down the entire nation." —*Chicago Tribune*

"A hard-hitting, thought-provoking study on the way America provides for its children."—*Parenting* magazine

"As a society, we have children but are unwilling to provide for their futures. *When the Bough Breaks* is a good place to start to understand what is at stake and what should be done."—Lester C. Thurow, Dean, Alfred P. Sloan School of Management, M.I.T.

"This fine book provides a powerful examination of the many ways our public and private policies undermine the successful development and education of children. The conclusion is inescapable. Unless we invest more wisely in our children today, the nation's economic and social futures are in jeopardy."
—Owen B. Butler, retired chairman, Procter & Gamble, and Chairman, Committee for Economic Development

"If this powerful account of America's neglect of its children doesn't move us, then nothing will. *When the Bough Breaks* tells a shameful story. It must be read."
—Albert Shanker, President, American Federation of Teachers

When THE Bough Breaks

The Cost of Neglecting Our Children

Sylvia Ann Hewlett

HarperPerennial
A Division of HarperCollins*Publishers*

A hardcover edition of this book was published in 1991 by Basic Books, a division of HarperCollins Publishers.

First HarperPerennial edition published 1992.

Designed by Ellen Levine

Library of Congress Cataloging-in-Publication Data
Hewlett, Sylvia Ann.
    When the bough breaks : the cost of neglecting our children / Sylvia Ann Hewlett. — 1st HarperPerennial ed.
        p.   cm.
    Originally published: New York : Basic Books, 1991.
    ISBN 0-06-097479-6 (paper)
    1. Child welfare—United States.   2. Children—United States—Social conditions.   3. Children—Government policy—United States.   I. Title.
    [HV741.H48   1992]
    362.7′68′0973—dc20   91-58461

92 93 94 95 96 CC/RRD 10 9 8 7 6 5 4 3 2 1

For Shira, Lisa, David, and Adam, with love

Contents

Preface

This book has two roots.

My volunteer work with homeless children in New York City and Westchester County changed my consciousness in profound ways. Touching, holding, comforting these outcast kids as they dealt with their gratuitous agony ignited my anger and seared my soul as nothing else ever has. These children provided me with a reservoir of passion that fuels this book, and I am permanently in their debt.

A second inspiration flowed out of the business community. For several years in the mid-1980s, I was the executive director of the Economic Policy Council and headed up a study panel on how corporations might help bridge the work/family divide. During the life span of this project, I spent hundreds of hours pursuing reluctant business leaders, telling them over innumerable power breakfasts that they needed to get up to speed on work/family issues and put some support policies in place. Mostly it was an exercise in rejection. Powerful executives just didn't get the connection. How could these "soft" women's issues be worthy of serious time or attention?

Then, in 1988, everything changed. Looming skill shortages and a prospective heavy reliance on women and minorities did wonders to concentrate the corporate mind. The number of companies interested in family supports quintupled overnight, and I got upgraded from breakfast to lunch. That was when I decided there was a need for this book. I wanted to push and prod our political leaders and have them shout from the rooftops the good news: in the 1990s, conscience and convenience will come together. As this century fades, doing what is right by our kids will also be good for the bottom line. The aching pain of our children might well be cured if only we can harness the energies of enlightened self-interest.

A word about what this book does and does not do. In the following pages, I look at the world from the child's point of view. My driving purpose is to chronicle the plight of America's children; to show how and why our attitudes and policies have tilted against young people; and to demonstrate why we must create conditions under which all children can flourish.

This book does not present the adult perspective. It does not seek to explore, for example, the complicated trade-offs women face between earning power and parenthood, nor does it analyze the special problems of the impoverished elderly. These issues are alluded to insofar as they intersect with the welfare of children, but they are not dealt with in their own right. Other books, including my 1986 book *A Lesser Life,* focus on these topics and give them central attention.

I make no apology for adopting the voice and vantage point of children. In 1991, they are the least heard and the most seriously disadvantaged group in our population. Besides, if we continue to squander our children, we will incur huge costs in the quality and possibilities of our own adult lives. Child neglect diminishes our potential—and our humanity.

As is true of much of my recent writing, this book represents a coming together of the personal and the professional. It therefore gives me particular pleasure to acknowledge the extensive help I have received from family, friends, and colleagues.

My grestest debt is to my husband, Richard Weinert. I am grateful for his practical help with the "second shift," for the insight of his ideas and the clarity of his critical responses. But, most especially, I am grateful for his unfailing, loving support during the draining months I spent wrapped up in this book.

A special word of thanks is due to our children—Shira, Lisa, David, and Adam. Their generous love has buoyed my spirits and replenished my energies at critical junctures over the last three years. Together they have taught me much about joy, responsibility, and commitment, and much of the fierce attachment I feel to the themes of this book flows out of my love for them.

I am indebted to many others. My agent, Molly Friedrich, guided this book through its birth pangs with skill and judgment and continues to give me extravagant amounts of time and friendship. I am deeply grateful. My editor, Martin Kessler, carved out large chunks of his precious time to help shape the bones of this book. I thank him for challenging and honing my ideas and for sustaining me through the agonies of redrafting. Peggy Shiller provided invaluable research assistance throughout the life span of this project. She vested extraordinary, careful energy in this book and I give her my thanks. Phoebe Hoss, Linda Carbone, and Jen Fleissner at Basic Books contributed valuable editorial help, and Marthe

Abraham and Marie Sauveur Fils played critical roles on the home front. Few authors receive such generous support and I am extremely appreciative.

My largest intellectual debt is to David Blankenhorn, Jean Elshtain, Mary Ann Glendon, Rosabeth Kanter, Pete Peterson, David Popenoe, and Ed Zigler. In conversation and through their written works, they enriched and informed the arguments in this book and I am pleased to pay tribute to their scholarship. I would also like to thank Charles Perrow and Forrest Church for thoughtful comments on a draft of the book.

Maria and Roy Brown, Murray Cohen, Charles Frank, Loretta and Murray Haimes, Abby Hirsch, Peter and Kay Leslie, Janet Lever, Mary and Roger Mulvilhill, Madeleine and Pat Oden, René and John O'Leary, Silu and Marcello Olarte, Ernest and Rebekkah Remo, Eleanor Sebastian, Joan and Michael Spero, Thelma Weinert, and Marcia and David Welles gave generous amounts of support, advice, and affection. I thank them all.

I also wish to acknowledge all the experts I talked with. Scholars, business executives, journalists, government officials, labor leaders, and hundreds of parents around the country gave freely of their time and energy. I am particularly grateful to Ann Bedsole, Peter Bell, Andrée Aelion Brooks, Gretchen Buchenholz, John Buehrens, Dagmar Celeste, Lynette Friedrich Cofer, Candace de Russy, Frank Doyle, Vicki Ford, Dana Friedman, Geraldine Greene, David Gutmann, Sandra Hamburg, Bob Holland, Maisie Houghton, Alice Ilchman, Arlene Johnson, Kathy Lord, Nita Lowey, Marie Mackee, Ray Marshall, Sandra Maxwell, Jeanne North, Catherine O'Neill, Doug Phillips, Rennie Roberts, Rosalind Rosenberg, Carol Sanger, Ted Shatigan, Al Shanker, Jack Sheinkman, Ruth Spellman, Sandra Stingle, Art Strohmer, Claudia Wallis, and Barbara Whitehead.

Most of all I want to thank the kids I interviewed. Over the last three years I have criss-crossed the country from Tallahassee to Trenton, from Watts to White Plains, talking to and just being with children. In a profound sense they made this book possible and I am extremely grateful to them. Shira Weinert and Jenny Golden were particularly insightful and helped me conceptualize the problems of middle-class kids, and the homeless children at the Prince George Hotel in Manhattan and the Coachman Hotel in White Plains contributed significantly to my understanding of what it means to be young and poor in this society. Hundreds of children contributed their voices to this book. I cannot thank them all in person but I would like to pay tribute to the following young people: Irv Davis, Ivanne Deneroff, Jenny Fielding, Jonathan Hirsch, Erin Hollingsworth, Caitlin Johnson, Elizabeth Kunrath, Susan Lee, Margaret Munzer, Jenny Pommiss, Kaia Stern, Lisa Weinert, and Michael Welles.

Finally, my heartfelt thanks go to my mother, Jean Hewlett, and my late father, Vernon Anthony Hewlett. They gave their best energies to their six daughters and any perspective I have found is grounded in the family they created.

Bronxville, New York
February 1991

Rockabye baby, on the treetop
When the wind blows, the cradle will rock
When the bough breaks, the cradle will fall
And down will come baby, cradle and all.

Prologue

Fractured Childhoods

Fatima, age six, sank her teeth into my upper arm. "Let go!" I said sharply, trying to stay calm. "That hurts." She peered up at me, her black button eyes bright and challenging. She bit down again, this time much harder. "Fatima," I said slowly and deliberately, "if you don't let go, I will never let you brush my hair again." The threat worked. Fatima slowly let go. She spent a minute looking with pride at the teeth marks and small drops of blood on my arm and then quickly snatched the brush from inside my purse, plunked her frail six-year-old body on my lap, and started to stroke my hair with care and tenderness.

We had known each other only an hour, but I already knew that Fatima loved brushing and braiding my hair. My first thought was that long, straight hair was different and therefore interesting to this small black child. But I soon realized that her fascination with the activity had much more to do with

Fatima's desperate need for any form of physical intimacy. Biting, braiding, pinching, and cuddling all helped fill the void in a way that games and storytelling didn't. And with Fatima's short attention span—she found it impossible to concentrate on Candy Land for longer than three minutes—playing board games was a painful business.

Ernie, the large, genial man who ran the services in the Prince George's ballroom for the Children's Aid Society, filled me in on the family background before I left the hotel that day.

Fatima had four siblings, two older, two younger. Between them these children had three fathers, none of them currently on the scene. According to Ernie, their mother, Regina, was "totally out of it." She spent most of her waking hours servicing her crack habit, "weighed at most ninety-five pounds, and jangled all over." The children rarely made it to school, as their mother had a hard time getting them down to the hotel lobby in time to catch the school bus. Instead, they spent their days drifting around the hallways of the hotel. The oldest, Tyrone, a boy of ten, already spent much of his time on the streets.

The Prince George Hotel, where Fatima lived, was, in 1988, a welfare hotel populated with some 800 homeless families.[1] Located on Madison Avenue at 28th Street in Manhattan amid quiet residential streets, publishing houses, and coffee shops, it was an oasis of noise and action in a genteel part of town. There was always plenty of commotion in front of the Prince George. Mothers and children hanging out, joking and bickering with one another. Toddlers in strollers, babies straddling most women's hips. Circling the edges were a few men, some of them sharply dressed. They seemed to be sizing up the women, hoping to strike a deal for either drugs or sex.

Every Tuesday afternoon in the summer of 1988, I edged warily through this small crowd on my way to my duties in the ballroom. I was one of several volunteers from my church. Each of us spent three to six hours a week helping these homeless hotel children with their schoolwork, playing "educational" games, or just giving individual kids some special attention.

I always dreaded entering the hotel. The guards were invariably hostile, pushing you about with rough hands as they searched you, keeping you waiting for twenty minutes as they checked identification. Besides which, the entrance of the Prince George Hotel was a menacing place. Violence was pervasive; small ugly incidents were constantly erupting on the steps or in the lobby and hallways. I never learned to deal with these well—and neither did many of the luckless residents.

I remember one such ugly incident. It was a beautiful summer's day in early June. Due to the warm weather the hotel steps were particularly crowded, and I stood in line waiting my turn to go through the revolving door. "Shut your fucking mouth," one mother bellowed a few feet to my right. I jumped nervously, wondering whether she was yelling at me. But she grabbed a three-year-old boy and started slapping his face, quite viciously, I thought. The boy thought otherwise. "It don't hurt, Mom," he crowed between each slap, goading her on. "You goddamn brat!" screamed his mother, and set to work with a series of more powerful blows. I winced as blood started to leak from the boy's mouth and, taking advantage of a gap in the crowd (people had moved to the side to get a better view of the standoff between mother and son), quickly scuttled into the hotel to fetch a guard—who, after surveying the scene, shrugged his shoulders and walked away.

A kid with a bloody face was small potatoes by Prince George standards. Just that month there had been two homicides and five drug-related knifings in the hotel that I knew of. All these welfare hotels in midtown were immensely violent. In one particularly tragic case at the Martinique Hotel a baby girl had been found dead in a hotel room. When she died, this ten-month-old weighed less than seven pounds. The proximate causes of death were premature birth, poor nutrition, and an intestinal infection. The underlying reasons ranged from poverty and homelessness to parental neglect. A few weeks after the baby's death, her big brother, eight-year-old Brian, dictated a poem:[2]

When our baby die we start to
sit by the window. We just
sit an' sit, all wrapped up
quiet in old shirts an' watch
the pigeons. That pigeon she fly so
fast, move so fast. She move nice.
A real pretty flyer.

She open her mouth and take in
the wind. We just spread out crumbs,
me and my brother. And we wait.
Sit and wait.
There under the windowsill.

She don't even see us till we slam
down the window. And she break.
She look with one eye.
She don't die right away.
We dip her in, over and over,
in the water pot we boils on
the hot plate.

We wanna see how it be to die
slow like our baby die.

Children's Images of Life Inside the Welfare Hotels

I showed this poem to one of the social workers at the Prince George. Her reaction was bitter: "We are breeding expensive killers in these homeless hotels and no one seems to care." An understandable response given the fact that in 1988 New York City was spending more than $2,000 a month to house Brian's family in a squalid welfare hotel.

* * *

The same summer that I played Candy Land with Fatima at the Prince George Hotel, I spent a lot of time talking with Becky Kraus,* a much more privileged New York youngster. On Tuesdays, after my stint at the hotel, I would often take a cab uptown and join Becky on the Upper East Side for a late afternoon chat over tea or cappuccino. She had a summer job at a Benetton shop and got out of work at 5:30 P.M.

Becky had elegant taste, and we generally met at Island, one of those chic cafés on Madison Avenue in the nineties. It was hard not to be aware of the stark contrasts of New York City. Island was an air-conditioned haven of hand-painted tiles and angel hair pasta, a place where everyone's voice was full of money. But just three miles south on the same avenue was the Prince George Hotel with its garbage-strewn hallways, blood-spattered carpets—and 1,400 homeless children. I sometimes told Becky of my afternoon's activities, which ranged from setting roach traps in the hotel ballroom to delousing Fatima's hair. "Weird" was Becky's usual comment; I might well have been talking about some strange tribe in Outer Mongolia.

When I became acquainted with Becky in the summer of '88, she had some good reasons for being self-absorbed. An attractive sixteen-year-old, tall and graceful with spiked auburn hair and a small, heart-shaped face, Becky carried herself with confidence and poise. But appearances are deceptive: all was not well in Becky's life. Her problems, though clearly different from those of Brian or Fatima, were hardly less serious.

According to Becky, the problems began when her parents

*A pseudonym.

split. She was six months old. Her Mom took off with a new boyfriend, taking her baby with her. Becky didn't see her Dad after that until she was seven years old. She has spent most of her childhood living a precarious existence with her mother, who now earns $28,000 a year working as a paralegal in a midtown law office—a salary that doesn't buy a whole lot in Manhattan.

As Becky explained: "We have always been real low on money. My Mom went back to school when she was thirty so that she could make some kind of a living for us. But things have been tough, making ends meet. We live in this tiny apartment, and my Mom sleeps on the couch in the living room. Some weeks we eat rice and beans three nights in a row because it's, like, the cheapest food you can get."

I found this hard to believe. Becky attended one of the most expensive schools in Manhattan—annual tuition $8,000 or thereabouts—and just this past summer had spent four weeks in Europe with her father.

"Oh, I know what you're thinking," said Becky, responding to my skeptical expression. "It's true, my Dad has money, and he now pays for the big items—school, vacations, a few clothes, that kind of thing—but on a daily basis we have to get along on my Mom's salary, which is kind of small. It's hard to figure out what my social status is. I mean, sometimes I feel I belong to the jet set, summering in Europe and all that, but mostly I feel poor. I guess I don't fit in anyplace." Becky's laugh was thin and brittle. "Imagine telling my friends at school that Con Edison just disconnected the electricity because the bill hasn't been paid in months. The stuff that goes on in my house! Sometimes I get embarrassed in front of the walls because I don't want anyone to know how we live.

"But don't get me wrong," she said quickly, wanting to demonstrate loyalty. "I know how hard my Mom's worked to provide for us. She's done the best she could. My God, I was so proud of her when she graduated college and got this legal job—so totally impressed with her! I thought she was the most incredible woman in the world." Becky paused and sighed. "But I don't know that our life together got any better. You see, when she took this job in midtown I became a latchkey kid, and I hated it. Our building doesn't have a doorman in the afternoons, and it really scared me to come home to an empty apartment. A big fear was having a robber come in my bedroom window. We live on the second floor and it could happen easily. I got very pudgy, because I would come home and eat. I would let myself in, go straight to the refrigerator, and make big, fattening snacks. Great globs of ice cream, whole packs of cheap cookies, that kind of thing. I would eat and watch TV. That way I could kind of smother my fears."

"You must have been so pleased when your Mom got home," I offered hopefully.

"I guess so," said Becky dubiously, "but she would be irritable and I would be resentful—we mostly fought."

"What exactly happened when she came through the door?"

"She'd come in, drop her stuff, and walk the dog—or yell at me for ten minutes and then go walk the dog. She would always find fault: 'I do everything, you do nothing' kind of routine. She always thought that I should have washed the dishes or made dinner or whatever.

"After chewing me out, she would generally go and pick up some supper. Then she would get on the phone with a beer and yatter away with a girlfriend. I used to like that because she left me alone, and I would take my food and watch television some more. Mom never told me to do my homework, and it mostly didn't get done." Becky looked dejected remembering those scenes.

"I feel badly now. I guess I didn't realize how totally worn out she was just making a living. But back then when I was twelve or thirteen, I was so wrapped up with my own difficulties I couldn't be bothered with her problems. I just blamed her for this crummy life we were leading. I didn't want to deal with her. I mean if she made a big effort and said, 'How was your day, honey?' I'd snap back, 'Oh, leave me alone!' I liked the weekends she worked better than the weekends she didn't. When she was at the office on Saturdays, all kinds of kids would come to my apartment and we'd experiment with stuff."

"What kinds of stuff?"

"Well, in sixth grade everyone got started with alcohol and cigarettes, then we got into drugs and making out with boys. You know, the usual kinds of things."

The next time I saw Becky she had been doing some thinking. "You know all that money pressure? The stuff we were talking about last time? Well, I think I can deal with those kinds of problems pretty well. What really depresses me about the divorce is that it's left me looking after my Mom."

"What do you mean?" I wanted to understand.

"It's hard to explain." Becky paused, searching for the right words. "But when you're a single mother, it is almost impossible to maintain that line between being a parent and being a pal. It's kind of tempting to lean on your seven- or ten-year-old daughter, to dump all kinds of stuff on this kid because she is the only person around. But if you do this, if you turn your child into, like, your best friend, you deprive her of what she needs in a parent. I know it sounds strange, but I have never thought that my mother could protect me—in fact, even as a little kid, I felt all kinds of pressure to protect *her!*

"I remember when I was about seven, my Mom was going out with this totally crazy guy, Jim. Well, Jim was scary, he did coke and other serious stuff. We were with him on and off for three years. Well, one day he came back to his apartment and found someone had broken in (looking for drugs or something), and an antique vase and some other valuables had gotten broken. His first reaction was to accuse my mother of doing these things. He went berserk, hitting her and cursing her out. I felt that I had to help, so I ran up and started screaming and pounding on him. I only reached his chest so I didn't make much impression. But then he got angry with me. He grabbed my wrists and twisted them real hard behind my back. I was in serious pain and terrified. I thought he was going to kill me. But my Mom just froze, she didn't lift a finger to help me—just, like, crouched in a corner waiting to see what he would do next. Well, I was lucky; in the end he just kicked me away and stomped out of the apartment."

"What did your Mom do afterward?"

"She was a mess. She cried and apologized and seemed so upset that I felt guilty, totally guilty—as though I had failed in taking care of the situation! I mean, just think about it, at age seven I thought I was supposed to be the adult." Becky looked disgusted.

"No kid deserves to grow up with a mother all over the map. All it means is that you don't get to have a parent. I mean, my childhood's over. She missed it and so did I. . . ." Becky's voice, high and bitter, trailed off.

Just before Christmas, Becky sent me a poem she had written; she said it was the story of her childhood. It was called "Mother to Mother":

> You never protected your child because maybe
> love would walk out the door.
> I needed it,
> I knew
> and I was seven.
>
> You never realized how dangerous it was
> to cry to your child.
> It singed me,
> but I was strong
> and I was seven.
>
> You never stopped shaking until I took
> your hand.
> I was your Valium,
> I felt it
> and I was seven.
>
> I was your mother
> and I knew it.
> You were thirty-one
> and I was seven.

It's all too easy to dismiss the stories of Fatima, Brian, and Becky as far-out tales from the lives of embattled New Yorkers. When we pick up the newspaper and read distressing articles about homeless or battered children, we sigh and feel badly for a moment or two. Then we turn the page and look for some news that is more upbeat or mainstream. For it's very tempting to handle bad news about children as strictly someone else's problem. Babies are born dead, but generally these are poor, black babies. Divorce can be devastating, but the worse casualties are someplace else. Everyone knows that New York City is a zoo! We see these as serious problems, even painful problems, but they don't belong to us. We try to convince ourselves: as long as we're not poor or black, as long as we don't live in the inner cities, our children are safe.

We are, of course, dead wrong.

Few families can escape the neglect that threatens to overwhelm children in contemporary America. Two-thirds of black babies are now born to single mothers, and many of these women find it impossible to provide shelter or safety for their children.[3] Fifty percent of the children in Becky's generation are dealing with the fallout from their parents' divorce, and almost half of these children lose contact with their fathers.[4]

Fractured childhoods are no longer the exception but the rule. Deprivation and rejection dominate the lives of children not only in New York City but in cities and towns across the country, among both the poor and the middle class. Child neglect on this scale has frightening implications for society. If we take good care of children, they will add to the productive capability of the economy. If we fail to look after our children, they will drag this nation down. In the words of Lyndon B. Johnson: "Ignorance, ill health, personality disorders—these are destructions often contracted in childhood; afflictions which linger to cripple the man and damage the nation."[5]

When the bough breaks the cradle falls, and more than just baby comes tumbling down.

1

A Matter of National Survival

Across the face of America, children are failing to flourish. Rich kids, middle-class kids, poor kids—all deal with risk and neglect on a scale unimagined in previous generations. Problems of poverty, divorce, out-of-wedlock births, absentee parents, latchkey kids, violence, and drugs are no longer confined to the ghetto. They reach deep into the mainstream; they belong to "us" as well as to "them." Child neglect has become endemic to our society, and childhood is now "far more precarious and less safe for millions of America's children."[1] In the words of a 1990 National Commission, "never before has one generation of American children been less healthy, less cared for, or less prepared for life than their parents were at the same age."[2] According to an index that measures the social health of children and youth, the well-being of children has declined dramatically over the last twenty years. In 1970 the index stood at 68; by 1987 it had plummeted to 37.[3]

The Facts of Child Neglect

Most of us know that it's rough out there. Children are not doing well in late-twentieth-century America. But few of us realize how bad things have become. Consider the following:

- 20 percent of all children are growing up in poverty, a 21 percent increase since 1970.[4]
- 330,000 children are homeless.[5]
- the rate of suicide among adolescents has tripled since 1960.[6]
- 42 percent of fathers fail to see their children in the wake of divorce.[7]
- 27 percent of teenagers drop out of high school.[8]

Children in America are at much greater risk than children elsewhere in the advanced industrial world. Compared with other rich countries, children in the United States are much more likely to die before their first birthday; to live in poverty; to be abandoned by their fathers; and to be killed before they reach the age of twenty-five.[9] Although the United States ranks No. 2 worldwide in per capita income, this country does not even make it into the top ten on any significant indicator of child welfare.

The problems of our youth range from elemental issues of health and safety to more complicated issues of motivation and performance. We cannot ensure the safety of children on the streets or in our homes. Each day in the United States an average of ten youngsters are shot dead.[10] In New York City two children die each week as a result of abuse inflicted by a parent or some other close relative.[11] Nationwide, the incidence of child abuse has quadrupled since 1975.[12] A child is safer in Northern Ireland than in America.[13]

Nor can we keep our children healthy. Infant mortality in the United States places it twentieth in the world, behind such countries as Spain and Singapore.[14] Increasingly, millions of American children are failing to receive immunizations that can protect them against polio, measles, and mumps. A black baby born in the shadow of the White House is now more likely to die in the first year of life than a baby born in Jamaica or Trinidad.

On the educational front the news is even more grim, since underachievement and failure are now widespread. An October 1988 ABC News Special entitled "Burning Questions: America's Kids: Why They Flunk" opened with the following dialogue:

INTERVIEWER: Do you know who's running for president?
FIRST STUDENT: Who, run? Ooh. I don't watch the news.
INTERVIEWER: Do you know when the Vietnam War was?
SECOND STUDENT: Don't even ask me that. I don't know.
INTERVIEWER: What side won the Civil War?
THIRD STUDENT: I have no idea.
INTERVIEWER: Do you know when the American Civil War was?
FOURTH STUDENT: 1970.[15]

These are not students from some inner-city ghetto. The children featured in this program attended middle-class high schools in Bridgeville, Pennsylvania, and Pine Bluff, Arkansas. But despite the mainstream contexts, these youngsters are not learning a whole lot in school. Across the nation, combined average Scholastic Aptitude Test (SAT) scores have fallen 70 points since 1963.[16] Experts say that only half of high school students are performing even moderately well, and many of their problems seem to be rooted in the family. According to Mary Futrell, president of the National Education Association, "children are enrolled in school and then are ignored or abandoned by their parents. . . . With so many single parents and so many families with both parents working . . . there is no one around to make sure kids are doing their schoolwork."[17] As Futrell points out, three out of four parents never visit their child's school.[18]

American kids are at or near the bottom in most international surveys measuring educational achievement: seventh out of ten countries in physics; ninth out of ten countries in chemistry; and tenth—dead last—in average mathematics proficiency. In a recent study by the International Association for the Evaluation of Educational Achievement, American ninth-graders tied with Singapore and Thailand for fourteenth place in science.[19] The United States does do well in one area, though: it ranks No. 1 in the percentage of thirteen-year-olds who watch five or more hours of TV every day.[20] The typical eighth-grader now spends four times as many hours watching TV per week as on homework.[21]

It's not just math and science skills. American high school students seem to know very little about the world they live in. In a poll ABC News conducted for its 1988 program, fewer than half the students knew what apartheid was, and nearly 70 percent hadn't heard of Chernobyl, the worst nuclear accident in history. One student thought it was Cher's last name!

A Comparative Perspective

We think of America as a child-centered nation. We like to boast that our children are cherished, protected, nurtured, and offered a field of opportunity unmatched elsewhere in the world. We see ourselves as valuing children to a fault—indeed, we brag about "spoiling" them.

Close inspection reveals a much less comforting reality. Over the past twenty-five years, slowly but relentlessly, American society has been tilting in an ominous new direction—toward the devaluation of children. "There has been an alarming weakening of a fundamental assumption, long at the center of our culture, that children are to be loved and valued at the highest level of priority."[22] In the public sphere, our policies display a weak and eroding commitment to children. We slash school budgets, build "adults only" housing, and deny working parents the right to spend a few weeks with their newborn babies. In 1987 less than 5 percent of the federal budget was devoted to programs that benefit children—one-fifth the amount we spent that year on persons over sixty-five.[23] Up until thirty years ago, most Americans would have considered it unthinkable that "the resources we invest in the beginnings of life might be dwarfed by the resources we consume at the end of life."[24]

The other rich democracies continue to give children much higher priority. Great Britain, France, Sweden, and Canada spend two or three times as much as the United States on families with children[25]—which helps explain why so many more American than European or Canadian children live below the poverty line.

The Twin Deficits

This *resource deficit,* this failure to invest public money in our children, is aggravated by a growing *time deficit.* Over the last decades there has been a sharp decline in the amount of time parents spend caring for their children. According to economist Victor Fuchs, children have lost ten to twelve hours of parental time per week since 1960.[26] Parental time has been squeezed by the rapid shift of mothers into the labor force; by escalating divorce rates and the abandonment of children by their fathers; and by an increase in the number of hours required on the job. Today the average worker puts in six hours more per week than in 1973.[27] This reduction in parental time has had an extremely negative impact on children. As we shall discover in chapter 3, the research shows that unsupervised "latchkey" kids are at increased risk of substance abuse, and that children with little or no contact with their fathers are unlikely to perform well at school.[28]

One thing is sure: our failure to invest either public resources or private time in the raising of children has left many families fragile and overburdened, unable to do a decent job in raising the next generation. True, some children continue to be raised in supportive communities by thoughtful, attentive parents, but the larger fact is that the whole drift of our society, our government policies, and our private adult choices is toward blighting our youngsters and stunting their potential. An anti-child spirit is loose in the land.

Repercussions in the Economy

We are only just beginning to realize that this swelling tide of child neglect "has potentially disastrous consequences not only for the individual child but for society as a whole."[29] *Business Week* warns us that corporate America is starting to be "haunted" by society's underinvestment in children and the deteriorating quality of our human resources. Chemical Bank must interview forty applicants to find one who can be successfully trained as a teller. And in 1988 IBM discovered, after installing millions of dollars' worth of fancy equipment in its Burlington, Vermont, factories, that it had to teach high school algebra to workers before they could handle the new technology.[30]

The United States is facing nothing less than "a monumental mismatch between jobs and the ability of Americans to do them."[31] On the supply side of the equation, companies face a shortage of workers and a shortage of skills. On the demand side, they face growing competitive pressures and the need for a more highly qualified work force.

The baby boom generation is aging. For twenty years the labor supply was pumped up by the high birth rates of the 1946–63 period. But the last members of this demographic bulge are now straggling into the world of paychecks and withholding taxes, and the baby bust of the late 1960s and 1970s has dramatically cut the numbers of young people available to fill jobs well into the next century. The result: most firms face an extremely tight labor market. The work force grew 14 percent between 1975 and 1980 and 8 percent between 1980 and 1985, but will grow only 6 percent between 1990 and 1995.[32] Experts predict that by the mid-1990s there will be 23 million unfilled job slots in the American economy.[33]

If the work force is shrinking, it is also changing its face and form. Once upon a time, not very long ago, the term *work force* conjured up images of white men in ties or blue collars. And in the 1950s and 1960s few employers had to reach beyond the male Caucasian in his prime, except to fill the least-wanted jobs. All this is changing. Increasingly, employers must look to women and minorities—workers who are often either overburdened or ill prepared. Between now and the year 2000 over 40 percent of all labor-force growth will be accounted for by blacks and Hispanics. Add in the growing number of white women entering the job market, says former Secretary of Labor Ray Marshall, and "almost all of the increase in our workforce will be women and minorities for the next hundred years."[34] Indeed, over the next decade *only 12 percent of net new entrants to the labor force will be white males.*[35]

The United States has no statutory parenting leave and little public support for day care or preschools. It should therefore come as no surprise that most working mothers are heavily burdened by family responsibilities. This increases absenteeism and labor turnover and eats into productivity on the job. Blacks and Hispanics suffer other disadvantages. Underinvestment in schools and other types of social infrastructure has hit underprivileged segments of the population particularly hard. Consequently, blacks and Hispanics tend to be severely undereducated. For example, in many inner-city black neighborhoods more than 40 percent of teenagers fail to graduate high school. These youngsters are virtually unemployable in the modern workplace.

But productivity and skills problems are not confined to working mothers and minorities. As mentioned earlier, underachievement and educational failure reach deep into the white middle class. According to one survey, fewer than half of all American youngsters can determine the correct change after purchasing a hamburger and a Coke at McDonald's![36]

If a large proportion of our youth lack such basic skills as making change, they are clearly deficient in those higher-level math and language abilities demanded by an increasingly competitive labor market. A 1989 report warns that "from the top to the bottom of the American talent pool, our students' academic achievements have failed to keep pace with the competitive requirements of the international marketplace." The authors of this study are particularly concerned that "even our best mathematics students would be ranked just average in almost any Pacific rim nation." It seems that too few of our brightest students take the "arduous courses of study necessary" to prepare for the knowledge-intensive occupations of the future.[37]

Skill requirements do seem to be escalating throughout the economy. Qualifications for jobs, even low-wage jobs, are rising rapidly. "In 1965, a car mechanic needed to understand 5,000 pages of service manuals to fix any automobile on the road; today, he must be able to decipher 456,000 pages of technical text, the equivalent of 250 big city telephone books."[38] A study by the Hudson Institute shows that jobs created in the 1990s will require almost a year's more education than those generated in the mid-1980s.[39]

America's emerging human capital deficit not only undermines the profitability of Chemical Bank and IBM, it also threatens the competitive strength of our national economy. This is not the first time a powerful country has been undermined by deteriorating conditions amongst its young people.

A Cautionary Tale

Picture the scene. It is the 1851 industrial exhibition at the Crystal Palace in London. Britain, the dominant world power, is using this glittering event to show off its industrial and commercial muscle and demonstrate that it is still the workshop of the world. Of the 13,000 exhibitors, 7,400 come from Britain and the British Empire. But lurking in the wings is the United States, already No. 2 in industrial production and catching up fast.

Made-in-America McCormick reapers, Colt revolvers, Hobbs locks, and sewing machines are the wonders of the show. British industrialists are amazed at what they see, for these products are assembled from identical, interchangeable parts. They suspect that this "triumph of standardization" might be the beginnings of new and more efficient production methods.[40]

Worried delegations of British businessmen cross the Atlantic to investigate this newfangled American system of manufacturing. What do they find? American manufacturing prowess is due in large part to a highly skilled, educated work force. These upstart Yankees have an impressively high literacy rate of 90 percent among the free white population. In the industrial centers of the Northeast, 95 percent of adults are literate. By way of contrast, just two-thirds of the working population in Britain can read and write.

A surprisingly similar scene is being played out at the end of the twentieth century. The United States is the dominant world power, but Japan is No. 2 and closing in fast. American business executives marvel at the quality of Japanese products flooding their markets. They form study missions and fly off

to Tokyo in their corporate jets. What do they find? Manufacturing superiority is being forfeited to the Japanese. And yes,
once again, behind this industrial success story lies a highly
skilled, better-educated work force.

Illiteracy is just one dimension of a large educational gap
between the United States and Japan. According to sociologist
Merry I. White, "much of the success of Japan stems from the
fact that its blue-collar workers can . . . read complex engineering blueprints and perform sophisticated tasks on the factory
floor far better than blue collars in the U.S."[41] The skills of
Japanese workers do not fall out of the clear blue sky; they are
a result of a much more rigorous education system. Ninety
percent of Japanese teenagers complete high school, compared with just 73 percent in America.[42] Not only do more
Japanese youngsters graduate high school, but due to a long
school year (forty days longer than in America) and high
academic standards, these graduates seem to know much more
than their American counterparts. Some experts believe that
an average high school education in Japan can be equated with
an average college education in America.[43]

Behind these educational discrepancies lie extremely important differences on the family front. Marriages in Japan are
impressively stable, most mothers stay at home with their
children, and enormous quantities of parental time and money
are spent supporting the educational process. In his 1989 book
The End of the American Century, economist Steven Schlossstein
tells us how the average Japanese mother visits her child's
school twice a month, and every day "the child carries a note-
book back and forth to school, in which mother and teacher
alternately write notes regarding the child's health, mood and
activities both at home and at school." Contrast this with the
United States, where only a quarter of parents ever visit their
child's school. According to Schlossstein, it is the extraordi-

nary coherence and strength of the Japanese family that has permitted "the unparalleled development of human resources" in Japan, which in turn has fueled its postwar economic miracle.[44]

In a landmark study Chicago sociologist James S. Coleman has shown that family background matters far more in determining student achievement than any attributes of the formal educational system. Across a wide range of subjects in literature, science, and reading, "the total effect of home background is considerably greater than the total effect of school variables." Overall, Coleman estimates the home to be almost twice as powerful as the school in determining student achievement at age fourteen.[45] Given this kind of evidence, it seems clear that "unless we work together to strengthen the family . . . all the rest: schools and playgrounds, public assistance and private concern, will never be enough"[46] to save our children.

For the last several decades Japan has invested heavily in its human resources, acting on the belief that in the modern age it is people and not machines or raw materials that comprise the driving force behind economic growth—a notion that is supported by a considerable body of research. Economist Edward Denison, for example, in analyzing the years 1929 to 1982 in the United States has found that 47 percent of the growth in GNP can be explained by the size and educational characteristics of the labor force. A further 26 percent of the growth rate can be attributed to advances in knowledge, which is itself a function of education. Overall, Denison finds that three-quarters of the increase in GNP over this fifty-three-year period is a result of enhanced human capital—a gradual improvement in the knowledge, skills, and motivation embodied in people. He attributes a mere 17 percent of the growth rate to investments in machines or any other type of physical capital.[47]

Recent American administrations have chosen to ignore this critical link between human capital formation and economic growth and have scrimped and saved on investments in young people. To take just one example, Head Start, a preschool program that has proven effective in bolstering families and improving the educational performance of poor children, is underfunded to such an extent that today only 25 percent of eligible youngsters are able to participate (see chapter 8).

As we head toward the end of this century, the great unanswered question is, Are the looming skill and labor shortages of the 1990s sufficiently threatening to trigger a significant new commitment to families and children? There is at least some good news. In important sectors of the economy, the mounting demographic pressures, particularly the increased reliance on women and minority workers, are beginning to trigger constructive action.

Win-Win Scenarios

In the winter of 1986–87 the International Brotherhood of Teamsters invited me to Dallas to be the keynote speaker at their first-ever National Conference on Women in the Workplace. That Saturday night at dinner, as I looked out at the sea of male faces in my audience, I appreciated the irony of the situation. Here was one of the most conservative and most macho groups of men in America inviting me to tell them how to help working women and their children—despite the fact that many of them didn't want women in the workplace to begin with. But I quickly forgot the cowboy boots, the diamond tie pins, and the assorted criminal indictments when my audience started taking notes during my speech. Not only was I received with great courtesy and respect by these Teamsters, but they actually seemed prepared to put into action the policies I recommended. You see, that winter the Teamster Union needed me and my policy proposals. Three hundred thousand flight attendants had just voted to join its ranks. If they were going to keep these new members (and they desperately needed new recruits), they had to get up to speed on parenting leave, child care, and flextime, and introduce these issues into contract negotiations. For the first time it was in the self-interest of the Teamsters to develop a healthy interest in family support policies and to join the ranks of progressive unions that had already developed programs in this area. As Jackie Presser, then president of the Teamsters, put it, "We need these women, so we have to learn to look out for their children."[48]

A similar story can be told in corporate America. In the 1970s and early 1980s family support policies were limited to a short list of progressive companies that, for a variety of public-spirited reasons, developed elaborate benefits for their employees. Merck, Campbell's Soup, Polaroid, Control Data, IBM, Johnson & Johnson, and Eastman Kodak became famous for their on-site child care, flexible work options, and generous maternity and paternity leave policies. Today, companies need not be farsighted or altruistic to have such policies; all they need do is consult their bottom line. Family supports are fast becoming win-win propositions: good for the working parent, good for the child, good for the company.

The Corning Glass Works is a case in point. Corning, an old-fashioned family firm in upstate New York, is not an obvious place to look for state-of-the-art personnel policies. It is a blue-collar industrial firm that has dominated the small town of Corning for generations. Until recently its work force had been almost exclusively male. But along with most American corporations, over the last decade it has experienced a rapid expansion in the ranks of its women workers. The number of women executives at Corning tripled between 1978 and 1988, while the number of women in technical, administrative, and manufacturing jobs almost doubled. This increasing dependence on women workers brought with it one major problem: a turnover rate among female employees that was twice as high as that of males. This worried top management a good deal—it was bad for image and morale, but it was also bad for the bottom line. The Corning managers did some careful calculations and discovered that it cost $40,000 to replace each worker they lost (for search costs, on-the-job training costs, and the like). Corning ran a survey and discovered that family stress—particularly child-care problems—was the main reason so many women quit their jobs. The company acted quickly. By the end of 1988 Corning had in place a policy package that included parenting leave, on-site child care, part-time work options, job sharing, flexible spending accounts for child care, and a parent resource center. According to its chairman, James P. Houghton, Corning's efforts "go way beyond simple justice; it's a matter of good business sense in a changing world . . . it's a matter of survival."[49]

If corporations are scurrying to prop up working Moms and Dads—and over five thousand firms now have programs of family supports[50]—a smaller but significant group is reaching beyond the parents to intervene directly in the lives of children. Again, the driving force is the bottom line.

General Electric is plowing $1 million into the poor rural schools of Lowndes County, Alabama. The company has a $700 million plastics plant in that county and is experiencing difficulty recruiting skilled workers. The hope is that better-prepared schoolchildren will go on to "study chemical engineering at schools like Tuskegee and one day work in a high technology business like GE."[51]

AT&T is devoting $100,000 to a "mother and daughter" program at Arizona State University. The idea is to encourage Hispanic families to break with cultural patterns and prepare girls for college. This program brings teams of mothers and their thirteen-year-old daughters on campus to impress on them the advantages of college training and to help the teenagers meet college entrance requirements. AT&T is anticipating the day when the majority of its recruits will be minority women.[52]

In Cleveland, AmeriTrust Company has taken corporate intervention in the lives of children to its logical limit by getting into the business of prenatal care. The catalyst was a tiny baby girl, at birth no bigger than an adult's hand. Born to an AmeriTrust employee in 1986, this premature infant survived, but her medical care cost the company $1.4 million. After that pricey birth, AmeriTrust started holding free "Perfectly Pregnant" seminars at lunchtime for employees. Mothers-to-be now get advice on everything from medical care and company maternity benefits to how to cope with unenlightened supervisors. Lynn Ahlers, senior benefits administrator at AmeriTrust, says that the new program has reduced the incidence of prematurity and paid off handsomely for the company. In-house studies show that "for every week an expectant mother is kept pregnant, the company saves as much as $10,000 in health insurance costs."[53]

To the casual observer much of this new corporate activity seems unexpected, even odd. What is going on with our kids that has grabbed the attention of hard-nosed corporate leaders? Why do labor unions and companies feel impelled to get into the business of families with children? After all, we live in a culture that has often insisted on a strict separation between the world of work and the world of the family. Home is supposed to be "a haven in a heartless world," not a branch of corporate benefits policy.[54]

There is nothing strange about these new private sector policies. They are fueled by the convergence of those two powerful trends already discussed in this chapter: the massive deterioration in the life prospects of children, and the looming worker and skill shortages of the 1990s. Whatever their private opinions or political values, business leaders are finding that they cannot sit on the sidelines and watch the human resource base of this economy degenerate.

As the new policies at Corning Glass and AmeriTrust testify, the pressure is already on the private sector and will only become more urgent as we head toward the end of the century. Across economic sectors, "executives are beginning to see family-sensitive policies as giving them a competitive edge in the tight labor market of the 1990s." Firms that drag their heels on this front will "pay a price in the labor market" in that they will fail to attract or to keep qualified workers, and this will put a brake on their profits and growth.[55]

Which brings us to an important point. This book does not paint a pretty portrait—what is happening to America's children is much too grim. The life and times of Fatima Hernandez and Becky Kraus do not edify. There is, however, some light at the end of the tunnel. The economic facts of life in the 1990s will conspire to make mothers and children scarce and valuable resources, assets that businesses will be loath to neglect or squander. Women and minorities will have to be utilized more efficiently if we intend to cope with the looming labor shortages of the 1990s, and children will have to be cared for better if we expect to compete in the knowledge-intensive marketplaces of the future. A significant chunk of corporate America has come to believe that a better family support system is necessary for economic survival.

Given this backdrop, it's not surprising that one of the best statements of what we should do about families and children has come out of the business community. In 1987 the Committee for Economic Development (CED), a group of CEOs and business executives, published a study entitled *Children in Need.* This study calls for a major new commitment to families and children by the government and the private sector, and is particularly eloquent in presenting the cost-benefit case for early intervention. Improving the prospects for infants and children through better prenatal care and early childhood education, for example, is not an expense but an excellent investment, one that can be postponed only at great cost to society.

According to the CED, high school dropouts cost the nation more than $240 billion a year in lost earnings and forgone taxes, and this does not include the billions this group will undoubtedly cost the taxpayer for crime control, welfare, and other social services. To use the stirring language of the report: "The nation cannot continue to compete and prosper in the global arena when more than a fifth of our children live in poverty and a third grow up in ignorance. And if the nation cannot compete it cannot lead. If we continue to squander the talents of millions of our children, America will become a nation of limited human potential. It would be tragic if we allowed this to happen."[56]

The Limits of Private Sector Initiatives

The CED report emphasizes that any bundle of solutions involves a partnership between business and government, a point that cannot be overstressed. We must not fall into the trap of imagining that James Houghton or Jackie Presser can somehow fix our families—or our kids.

Putting all the responsibility on business's back is unrealistic. It is also a way of passing the buck. The scale and complexity of our family problems require nothing less than a new and massive commitment to children by our national government. Solving these problems also requires a wrenching adjustment in personal priorities. Elaborate family supports will do little to advance children's well-being if parents elect to spend little or no time with their kids.

The private sector is clearly capable of important initiatives. Corporations will show us how to create a family-friendly workplace; business will even help at the edges when it comes to school enrichment programs and prenatal care. But private efforts will not be enough; the dimensions of the problems affecting our children are simply too big. In 1988, 375,000 drug-exposed babies were born in our nation's hospitals, and 1 million youngsters dropped out of school.[57] Even a thousand points of light will not make much of a dent on problems of this magnitude. We need the resources of the public purse, but we also require a sense of urgency and common purpose that has to be provided by Washington. Only a massive infusion of political energy will prevent the tide of abuse and neglect rolling over yet another generation of children.

Andrew Stein, president of New York's City Council, has a favorite scenario: "Imagine the Mayor of New York calling an urgent news conference to announce that the crisis of the city's children had reached such proportions that he was mobilizing the city's talents for a massive rescue operation not unlike the one that saved us from bankruptcy 10 years ago."[58] Stein's concern is prompted by the fact that close to 40 percent of the city's children are now growing up below the poverty line[59]—an appalling fact that, on its own, should surely trigger urgent political action.

Given the cavalier way we slashed and cut into spending on families in the 1980s, however, it is very hard to imagine any

American mayor, governor, or president launching a massive operation to rescue children in distress. We need a major shift in political priorities, which will happen only if there is a concomitant shift in personal priorities. This private dimension of child neglect is especially difficult to recognize and accept.

Tilting Toward the Self

American culture has always valued independence and self-reliance, but the powerful liberation movements of the 1960s and 1970s greatly increased the weight we give to the search for self-fulfillment. Adults of both sexes have become absorbed by their inner worlds and ambitions, and this has had tremendously negative effects on children. For, like it or not, there are trade-offs between personal fulfillment and family well-being. Creating a home and raising children are supremely time-intensive activities which tend to claim large amounts of adult energy in the prime of life, energy that cannot then be spent on advancing a career, playing golf, or taking aerobics classes.

The data point to escalating divorce rates and disappearing fathers; to working mothers and fathers with considerably less time for their children; and to declining birth rates. The media glamorize yuppie DINKs (dual income, no kids), and for most men and women participation in family life has declined precipitously. While the proportion of adult life spent living with spouse and children stood at 62 percent in 1960, it is now 43 percent—the lowest in our history.[60]

Over the long haul you cannot claw your way up the corporate ladder, work sixty hours a week, *and* be a good parent, spouse, and citizen. And you clearly cannot dump spouse and kids and move on to greener pastures without risking the coherence and viability of the children you leave behind. Self-absorption is bad news for families and, in the long run, is even destructive to individuals because it can leave personal relationships in shambles and the community at war with itself. If you can't see your kids because of a hostile ex-spouse, or if you dare not go jogging because the public park is full of teenage "wolf packs," personal freedom has rather little meaning.

All of which is not a long-winded way of recommending that we reinvent the "feminine mystique," or return to the traditional world of the 1950s, when there was a neat division of labor between the sexes and women took care of all family business. Women are no longer able to take the entire responsibility for family life, to pick up the tab for our children. They now comprise 45 percent of the American labor force, and their economic contribution—to the national economy and to the family budget—is only going to increase as we head toward the end of the century.

The trick is to spread the burden around. Husbands and fathers, employers and government, all have to pull their weight. Such a sharing of effort is particularly just and fair given the fact that in the modern world the rewards of well-developed children are reaped by society at large, not by individual mothers or fathers.

Historically, this was not so. In eighteenth-century rural America, children as young as seven or eight contributed significant amounts of labor to the household, and parents were eager to raise a large number of children so that at least some of them would survive to support their parents in old age. Neither of these economic incentives for bearing children exists today. Children do not become productive until their late teens or twenties, and even then rarely contribute to the parental household. And social security has replaced children as the major source of material support in old age.

In the modern world, not only are children "worthless" to their parents, they involve major expenditures of money. Estimates of the cost of raising a child range from $171,000 to $265,000.[61] In return for such expenditures, "a child is expected to provide love, smiles and emotional satisfaction, but no money or labor." In the late twentieth century "a child is simply not expected to be useful" to his or her parents.[62]

Private Versus Collective Responsibility

Which brings us to a critical American dilemma. We expect parents to expend extraordinary amounts of money and energy on raising their children when it is society at large that reaps the material rewards. The costs are private; the benefits are increasingly public. If you are a "good" parent and put together the resources and energy to ensure that your child succeeds in school and goes on to complete an expensive college education, you will undoubtedly contribute to "human capital formation," enhance GNP, and help this nation compete with the Japanese, but in so doing, you will deplete rather than enhance your own economic reserves.

The U.S. government has been extremely reluctant to take direct responsibility for children, as is clearly demonstrated in our public policies. We are the only rich country that fails to provide new mothers with maternity benefits or job-protected leave and the only industrialized country that fails to guarantee access to higher education for qualified poor youngsters. More than any other developed country, America expects individual parents to foot the child-raising bill from childbirth all the way through college; and, more than any other rich

country, America is facing profound and systematic child neglect. These two phenomena are clearly related. In the modern age, relying on irrational parental attachment to underwrite the child-raising enterprise is a risky, foolhardy, and
cruel business. It is time we learned to share the costs and
burdens of raising our children. It is time to take some collective responsibility for the next generation.

In the following chapters I will address large policy issues in
the public arena: How can we best harness the labor force
concerns of the private sector and use them to upgrade the life
prospects of our children? How can we join the family concerns of the liberal left and the conservative right and unleash
urgent political energy? But I will also ask much more personal and uncomfortable questions: How can we put sensible
limits on unfettered individualism? And how can we limit our
infatuation with ourselves so as to build a better future? At a
gut level, we have met the enemy and he is us.

Beyond Economic Calculations

One final note. Much of the analysis in this book will be
grounded in the language of economics, and at least some of
the solutions will be driven by a cost-benefit logic. But I want
to stress that I believe that the constellation of painful problems around our children go way beyond material issues.

   We should care about Fatima and those 330,000 homeless
children going to bed scared and often hungry, because these
youngsters are in distress. We should seek to improve the life
circumstances of Becky and the millions of children of divorce
because these kids are seriously disadvantaged through no
fault of their own. We should look after those drug-addicted

boarder babies in city hospitals because these infants have been abandoned and are in pain. In my view, one of the first priorities of any civilized society is to take care of its children, to prevent needless suffering in the ranks of the vulnerable and the blameless. In a profound sense, "the ultimate test of a moral society is the kind of world it leaves to its children."[63]

But if the problems of our children resonate to higher values of decency and justice, it is a hard-headed investment logic that will call forth new resources and unleash fresh energy in government and in boardrooms around the nation.

We are living in a tight-fisted, conservative age, where social consciences are limited and almost no one is interested in funding another handout for the needy—no matter how young or how deserving. Besides which, despite a potential "peace dividend" (much of it spent on the Persian Gulf war), public policy in the last decade of the twentieth century is likely to remain a cutthroat contest for limited funds. If children are to do well in that contest, every politician and business leader needs to know that $1 spent on preschool education saves $4.75 in remedial education, welfare, and crime control.[64] He or she also needs to understand that the United States is facing a "monumental mismatch" between jobs and the ability of Americans to do them. Unless we invest in our young people on a new and massive scale, a burgeoning human resource deficit will undermine our ability to compete so thoroughly that the U.S. economy will go into a tailspin. It is the neglect of children, and not military overreach, that will bring about the decline of America's preeminence in the world. As historian Aaron Friedberg points out in his 1988 book, *The Weary Titan,* Britain dug its own imperial grave in the last century by shortchanging its children and developing a "certain distaste for education."[65] Let's learn from this historical precedent and face the fact that we can no longer afford child neglect.

In the waning years of the twentieth century, doing what is right for our kids and what is necessary to save our collective skins will finally come together. Conscience and convenience will converge. We should therefore take heart and not be afraid to apply the hard-edged power of cost-benefit analysis because, for once, this intellectual tool can be used to produce both competitive strength and a kinder, gentler nation.

Part One

The Faces of Neglect

2

Disadvantaged Kids
and the Resource Deficit

A cold wind whistled across Hart Island the other morning. It bent the leafless trees and swamp grass, and sent whitecaps dancing on Long Island Sound.

Inmates in orange jumpsuits moved briskly, spoke little and didn't smile. In armfuls of three, they unloaded 53 foot-long pine boxes from the rear of a Ford dumptruck onto the muddy ground. For 50 cents an hour, they were burying New York City's poorest infants.

"It's good they're getting buried and not thrown in a garbage pail," said an inmate who is the father of eight children.

"It takes some getting used to," said another inmate. . . .

Bruce Leggard, a correction officer who lost his daughter when she was 13 years old, groped for meaning. "Everyone dies; you're born to die," he said. "But these babies never had a shot. Whether they would have been strong or weak, they never got much of a chance to be either."

The little coffins had pink labels pasted on them. Some had

names. There was a Liz, an Eileen, a Sam. Some were F/C or M/C, for female child or male child. Each slip recorded the lifetime of these former residents of Planet Earth—two hours, newborn, five days . . .[1]

Burials of indigent infants are on the increase. In 1986, 1,128 babies were buried on Hart Island; in 1989, 1,606: a 42 percent increase in three years. In New York's burgeoning poor population, parents often can't afford a "proper" burial for a newborn infant. Instead they fill out forms to reserve a space in a mass grave. The Health and Hospitals Corporation freezes the tiny bodies, then delivers them unembalmed to the trucks that will take them to New York City's potter's field on Hart Island.

A Catholic priest sometimes comes by to bless God's little children, en masse. . . .
    The wind blew harder. Inmates moved faster. Some boxes contained twins. A few were broken. An inmate cradled one in his arms, much as if things were different.
    "This is a heavy little baby," he said.[2]

Each day in the United States, sixty-seven newborn babies die. Had they been born in Japan, only thirty-seven would have died. Over the course of a single year approximately 40,000 American babies die before their first birthday.[3] The U.S. international ranking in infant mortality worsened from sixth in the mid-1950s to twentieth in 1987.[4] Japan, on the other hand, went from seventeenth to first place over the same span of time.[5]

A fundamental problem in the United States is that more than one-third of pregnant women (1.3 million each year) receive insufficient prenatal care, mainly due to financial barriers. According to research carried out at New York's Alan Guttmacher Institute, 26 percent of pregnant women in the United States have no insurance coverage at the start of pregnancy and 15 percent are not covered at the time of delivery.[6] Women who receive late or no prenatal care are twice as likely to give birth to premature, low-birth-weight babies, and these "preemies" are forty times more likely to die in the first month of life than normal-weight infants.[7] The National Commission to Prevent Infant Mortality finds that "more than half of all infant deaths in the U.S. could be prevented" if this country emphasized low-cost prevention strategies in the manner of other nations.[8] Senator Lawton Chiles (D-Fla.) for one "is amazed at how simple and obvious so many of the strategies are that other countries use to promote the health of mothers and infants."[9] As we shall see in chapter 6, all other rich democracies provide prenatal and maternity care for those who need it; offer job protection and paid leave from work for childbearing; give cash grants to families at the time of birth; and generally pay attention to these issues at the highest level of government.

The overwhelming issue here is a moral one; even prison inmates doing time on Hart Island recognize that Liz, Eileen, and Sam deserved a better shot at life. It is shameful that so many poor babies are allowed to die at birth in this immensely rich nation. With our vast resources and egalitarian ideology, how can we rank twentieth in the world in infant mortality, after such countries as Ireland, Spain, and Costa Rica?

We often pretend that America can't afford to provide poor women with prenatal or maternity care, but the irony is that this neglect of pregnant women and babies is a very expensive business. The cost to "graduate" just one preemie infant from neonatal intensive care can be as much as $100,000.[10] Prenatal care, on the other hand, is relatively inexpensive: an effective mix of preventive, diagnostic, and therapeutic services for the nine months of pregnancy costs approximately $400.[11] One recent study by the Institute of Medicine shows that every dollar spent on prenatal care for high-risk women saves more than three dollars in medical costs during a baby's first year of life.[12] Given the strength of the moral and practical case for treasuring and cherishing our children, why do we then continue to neglect them in such a heartless, profligate fashion? This is a question that will haunt the pages of this book.

Trend Lines and International Comparisons

Children have not shared America's prosperity in recent years. The number of children growing up below the poverty line rose from 16 percent in 1979 to 20 percent in 1988. Two and a quarter million more children are poor today than in 1980, swelling the ranks of America's poor children to almost 13 million.[13]

Poor children are defined as those growing up in families with incomes below the amount the federal government says is necessary for bare survival. In 1989 the official poverty line was $9,890 for a family of three and $12,675 for a family of four. Applying these standards:

· Among all children (up to eighteen years old) in America, one out of five is poor.
· Among children younger than six, almost one in four is poor.

- Among children in families headed by young adults (younger than thirty), one in three is poor.
- Among black children, one out of two is poor.[14]

One thing seems clear: With higher-than-average poverty rates among very young children, the situation will continue to deteriorate into the 1990s.

It is particularly instructive to examine what has happened to children under six—the youngest and most defenseless group in our population. Between 1968 and 1979 the poverty rate for young children in the United States was stable, at about 17 percent. After 1979, however, the proportion of children under six living in poverty rose dramatically, peaking at 25 percent in 1983 (a year of deep recession). Since 1983, despite generally improved economic conditions in the United States, the proportion of young children in poverty has decreased only slightly. In 1988 the poverty rate for young children in the United States was 23 percent—still nearly one child in every four. The poverty rate for children under six is now higher than for any other age group in the population; it is more than double the rate for adults aged eighteen to sixty-four and nearly double the rate for the elderly.[15] Indeed, if you take into account non-cash benefits (medical care and the like), "the rate of poverty among the very young in the United States has become nearly seven times as great as among the old"[16]—an unprecedented state of affairs.

Compared to children in other advanced countries, American children are doing extremely badly. A 1990 report by the Select Committee on Children, Youth, and Families compared the status of children in the United States with that in a group of advanced industrialized countries, and found that the United States (along with Australia) had the highest percentage of children in poverty (15 percent), even after tax and transfer benefits were factored in.[17] Using a slightly different comparison group and methodology, economists John Coder, Lee Rainwater, and Timothy Smeeding found that "the United States has by far the highest fraction [of children] living in poverty, over 21%, with two other large countries [Australia and Canada] near 15%, and with all European and Scandinavian countries with less than half our child poverty rate."[18] The United States is the only country where the number of poor children has increased significantly in recent years.

Three powerful economic and political trends have contributed to this frightening increase in child poverty. The first revolves around a dramatic drop in wages, particularly male wages, which has pushed many working families into poverty. A second is tied up with escalating divorce rates, rapid increases in out-of-wedlock births to teenagers, and the abandonment of children by their fathers. Both of these structural trends are bad news for children, but the negative impact of these shifts has been compounded by government policy. Inadequate (and, in some instances, declining) public investment in day care, housing, medical care, and other social supports has made it extremely difficult for parents in low-paying jobs to get by without falling into poverty—or joining the welfare rolls.

In the 1980s poverty among working families proliferated. Increasingly, America's poor are people like Glen Whitbeck, a short-order cook whose $8,000 annual salary doesn't stretch to cover his two little girls' medical bills. Or Rose Hummel, a divorcée who struggles to support two adults and three children on a minimum-wage job at a dog kennel. These people contradict the stereotype of who is poor in American society, since poverty tends to be equated with the black urban underclass. On television and in newspapers the poor are often portrayed as shiftless black men dealing drugs on street corners, or as fourteen-year-old inner-city mothers on welfare. And we lap it up, for it is convenient to think of the poor—with all of their desperate problems—as safely over there in the ghetto.

But as Mary Jo Bane of Harvard's Center for Health and Human Resources reminds us, "the hard truth is that the poor are all around us."[19] In trailer parks in Johnstown, Pennsylvania, in garden apartments in Tacoma, Washington. Economists Erol Ricketts and Isabel Sawhill have shown that less than 10 percent of America's poor population live in inner-city underclass communities.[20] What is more, while the size of the ghetto poor has risen only modestly over the last decade, the number of working poor has mushroomed. Roughly 60 percent of all poor adults now work, if seasonal and part-time employment is included. In 1989 there were 8.4 million adults who worked but still had incomes below the poverty line. This figure has risen by a third since 1978.[21]

A father trying to support his family on a minimum-wage job, a divorced mother struggling to get back on her feet, displaced factory workers, dispossessed farmers, young families starting out—these are, increasingly, the dominant forms of American poverty.

Rose Hummel of Johnstown, Pennsylvania, is typical. She and her husband were each making $16,000 a year when she was laid off from the local steel mill in 1979. Her husband left her, and Rose, who had just given birth to their second child, went looking for work, eventually finding employment as a groomer at a dog kennel. Several years later Rose still earns the minimum wage. Last year her earnings totaled $5,850—hardly enough to support two children, a stepson, and a new husband, who was recently laid off himself by the car wash where he had worked for nineteen years. Rose says her job is hard; she must clean the dog kennels of feces and urine and work weekends without pay. She has no employee benefits and her boss has her take her two sick days at Christmas. "What we have to go through to make just a little money," she says bitterly. "I feel like a slave."[22]

A common thread that binds the working poor together is the absence of health insurance. At least two out of every three poor workers have no employer-based or union-subsidized health insurance. As Glen Whitbeck and his wife, Darlene, of Tacoma, Washington, can testify, the problem is particularly severe among poor workers who have only part-time jobs. Glen was forced to file a complaint against the owners of the restaurant he worked at because they had him work an average of twenty-six hours a week—one hour short of the amount needed for him to be eligible for medical coverage. Glen finally got that extra hour, but not before accumulating $2,500 in medical bills—mostly for emergency room treatment for himself and his five-year-old daughter. But the new health insurance doesn't cover the $60 corrective shoes the Whitbecks need but can't afford for their little girls. Without the shoes, both girls frequently fall and hurt themselves; in the last three months, Katherine, age five, has fallen twice, suffering cuts that required thirteen stitches. "Katherine," Glen Whitbeck says softly, "can't do most things others her age can do—like skip and hop."[23]

The Job Crunch

During the 1980s increased global competitive pressure triggered a wave of plant closings, and millions of American workers were laid off. According to the Bureau of Labor Statistics 11.7 million Americans lost their jobs between January 1981 and January 1990. One-third remained unemployed or left the work force, and of those who found new jobs, about half took either cuts in pay or part-time positions.[24] Many displaced blue-collar workers who had held skilled jobs in manufacturing ended up in service jobs, many of them menial and poorly paid.

These structural changes precipitated a sharp decline in earnings, particularly male earnings, reversing years of steady progress. Between 1955 and 1973 the median income of men grew substantially: from $15,056 in 1955 to $24,621 in 1973. Then, quite suddenly, the growth stopped. Earnings, adjusted for inflation, started to fall and by 1987 the male wage was back down to $19,859, *a drop of 19 percent.* [25] Wives and mothers flooded into the labor market in an attempt to shore up family income, but the bottom line is that most modern families are working much harder for approximately the same income. In 1988 average family income was only 6 percent higher than in 1973 *even though almost twice as many married women were working.* [26] In many households one well-paid smokestack job has been replaced by two marginal service jobs. Burger King simply does not pay as well as Bethlehem Steel.

Congresswoman Patricia Schroeder (D-Colo.) talks about modern families having to work twice as hard to stay even: "Like the hamster in the wheel, they run and run and run but they're still at the bottom. Health care insurance, homes, automobiles—those are the basic American dream items, and they're being priced out of the range of a lot of people we define as middle class."[27]

Prior to 1973 a male head of household could count on a steady growth in income as he moved up the job ladder and as the economy grew. Most families could rely on a rising standard of living even if the wife chose not to join the paid labor force. After 1973, there were no such guarantees. Even if a man held a full-time job, his wages often did not keep up with inflation and his job was increasingly unlikely to carry decent medical coverage. In his 1987 book *Dollars and Dreams,* economist Frank Levy calculates that young men who joined the labor market in the 1950s and 1960s saw their real earnings increase 50 to 60 percent during the first ten years on the job. In contrast, young men who entered the labor market in 1973 saw their earnings fall over the next decade.[28]

Thus, the large increase in poverty among children in run-of-the-mill working-class families is a result of what has happened in the labor market. Specifically, it is due to falling wages, structural unemployment, and the proliferation of badly paying jobs without benefits. Poverty no longer discriminates. In 1991 a child need not grow up in the ghetto to be economically disadvantaged.

It seems clear that this type of poverty is not going to go away in the near future. As the U.S. economy becomes increasingly integrated into the world economy, "the ability of the U.S. government or American unions to insulate workers without skills from competition with workers in other countries is declining." A decade ago it might have been possible "to pay unskilled janitors in automobile plants $12 per hour, because they worked in unionized plants in a wealthy economy,"[29] but by now most of these janitors have been either demoted or fired. America is no longer the dominant economic power and cannot create or sustain high-wage, low-skill jobs. For working men and women, the good jobs of the future will belong to those who have skills that enable them to be productive in a knowledge-intensive global economy. Many won't make the grade, at least not until there is massive new investment in education, health, and other types of social infrastructure.

One lesson to draw from the swelling numbers of "regular" American kids growing up below the poverty line is that we simply have to start providing benefits and services to *all* needy families with children and not just certain categories (the bulk of the assistance we currently provide targets single mothers through the Aid to Families with Dependent Children program). Health care, for example, should be a birthright; no American child should fall outside the medical safety net.

Family Breakdown

A second trend that contributes to child poverty is an accelerating rate of family breakdown. This tragedy is closely bound up with escalating divorce rates (discussed at length in chapters 3 and 4) and a rapid increase in the incidence of out-of-wedlock births. The main results of these trends have been a tremendous increase in the number of female-headed poor households, and a dramatic rise in the rate at which children are abandoned by their fathers.

The rate of divorce tripled between 1960 and 1982 and then leveled off at the 50 percent mark. Couples marrying today face an even chance of divorcing at some point during their lives together. For women (and their children) divorce often entails severe economic hardship. In the years following divorce living standards for ex-wives drop by an average of 30 percent while those for men rise 8 percent.[30] Half of all divorced fathers fail to see their children in the wake of divorce and two-thirds fail to pay child support.[31] For some children divorce means financial insecurity and intermittent fathering. For others, it means poverty and the complete loss of their father.

The other face of family breakdown is the growing number of out-of-wedlock births and the virtual absence of a male presence or male support in these new single-mother families. The statistics are appalling. Although births among teenage girls declined from 1960 through 1986, the proportion of unmarried teenagers who have children has risen sharply. There are now close to half a million live births to unwed teenagers every year.[32] In 1960, 15 percent of teenage girls who gave birth were unmarried; by 1986 this figure had reached 61 percent.[33] Teenage unwed motherhood is rising among whites but it is still much more common in the black community. One out of every three black mothers is an unwed teenager, and a third of these go on to have a second child while still in their teens. "Marriage has become an almost forgotten institution among black teens. In whole sections of the black community, children are being raised almost exclusively by very young mothers without male role models."[34]

There are all kinds of reasons why children bear children out of wedlock, but at least some of them are grounded in the realities of the modern labor market. It is difficult for a seventeen-year-old black woman to believe that she might one day hold a well-paying job, or that she might marry a man who earns enough to support a family. It is hard for her to imagine that there is an alternative to babies and welfare. And the facts would bear her out.

Chicago sociologist William Julius Wilson has related the dramatic decrease in marriages among blacks to an equally dramatic fall in the number of "marriageable" men—that is, those who hold jobs. According to Wilson, in 1960 there were seventy employed civilian black men for every hundred black women. By 1980 this figure had dropped to forty-five.[35] Black and Hispanic men have been particularly hard hit by the labor market trends described earlier in this chapter. The earnings of minority men have followed much the same downward path as those of white men, but a significant number of minority men seem unable to find work at all. The unemployment rate for black men stood at 11.5 percent in 1989, well above the national average. Many have stopped looking for work and don't even show up in the unemployment figures. In a typical month "only about half of all civilian men aged 20–24 report having any job at all."[36]

A generation ago, 60 percent of all employed black males were craftsmen, operators, fabricators, or laborers. These categories of employment have shrunk dramatically in recent years. Many jobs that used to be performed by unskilled operators are now done more efficiently by machines. And if young black men can't find jobs as laborers, they are badly positioned for well-paying jobs in the fast-growing high-tech end of the economy. This is largely due to their poor educational backgrounds. Across the nation the average black seventeen-year-old reads at the same level as the average white thirteen-year-old.[37]

Until we invest heavily in our inner cities, until disadvantaged youths are given the opportunity to join the mainstream of society, out-of-wedlock births to teen girls will continue to spiral out of control. The consequences of such pregnancies can be catastrophic. Many teenage mothers and their babies suffer from poor health. Three-fifths of teenage mothers drop out of school, and their lifetime earnings are less than half those of women who wait until age twenty before bearing their first child. To compound the problem, children born to teenagers achieve academically and economically at rates substantially below those born to adults.[38]

We often fail to recognize that adolescent childbearing is much more than a private tragedy. Teenage parenthood constitutes a heavy drain on the public purse. One national study estimates the average cost of a single birth to a teen who goes on public assistance at $16,140. Nationwide, teen births cost $19.8 billion in 1988.[39] Programs aimed at preventing adolescent pregnancies have the potential to cut these costs dramatically.

Dorothy Mason has brains. She was an honor student. She has concrete goals: she wants very much to be a fashion designer and has demonstrated talent for this work. But she now faces enormous difficulties in reaching that goal, for Dorothy Mason also has a baby. Dorothy is 17.

When she learnt that she was pregnant, she tumbled into a deep depression, crying frequently. She would often come home from Farragut High [a tough school on Chicago's South Side] and just curl up in her bed and cry. "I thought my life was going to be messed up," she says. "I couldn't think much about school." Her grades began to drop. There was friction with her stepfather and she moved in with an older sister.

When the baby, Dorquiece, arrived in November, Dorothy had to miss eight weeks of school to care for her baby and to recover from a troubled pregnancy that left her anemic and with high blood pressure. She got two F's and two D's and is still struggling—to catch up with her schoolwork and her dream, and to be a mother at the same time.

There are many students like Dorothy in the nation's inner-city schools. . . . The system hasn't adjusted to what is happening out on the streets. Few schools provide child-care for infants. Farragut does sponsor a day-care center for children over three, but a proposal to open one for infants was shelved because the cost would have been too high. So, many teenage mothers have no choice but to leave school.

Dorothy is luckier. At least for now she has a sitter, her baby's godmother. But how long will that last? And if it lasts, will she be able to endure the enormous physical and emotional burden she carries? A recent day in her life:

Up at 6 a.m., and feeling terrible. Dorothy is still battling the stomach flu that has kept her home from school for a day. She probably ought to take another day off and rest, but she doesn't think she can afford to. "I like to try to get to school every day because I missed all that time already," she says. By the time she has finished getting the baby fed and dressed, there is no time left for her to have breakfast.

Dropping the child off at her godmother's at 7:30, she gets to school by 8:15, still feeling ill. She misses her first-period class, modern world history, to meet with a social worker who wants to be assured that Dorothy has indeed found a regular babysitter. Because of her tight schedule, she doesn't have time for lunch. By 2 p.m. when she leaves for home, she's tired, hungry and nursing a headache. Then it's time for motherhood all over again.

It might be easier to quit, but Dorothy refuses to abandon her dream of becoming a fashion designer. She ordered a class ring with a pair of scissors inscribed on it, and she still tutors other design students, earning $33 every two weeks. It goes for Pampers and baby powder.

If she can hang on for a few more months she will graduate: even with the disastrous grades she got last fall, she still has a 2.5 grade point average and ranks 60th in her class of 250. . . . But school—and life—has become a gray, exhausting grind for Dorothy now. She has dropped out of student government and taken herself off the girls' softball team. She still hopes to attend college, but she doesn't think she will be able to begin before January. "It's hard," she says in a near-whisper, "trying to look after a baby and doing homework and all that stuff."[40]

Dorothy's case is far from hopeless. She has a better track record and more motivation than many youngsters in her position. She could, however, use a little help.

Dorothy would benefit enormously from a program like the one at the New Futures School in Albuquerque, New Mexico, which offers health care, parenting education, child-care services, and vocational training to adolescent parents and parents-to-be. The goal of this program is to help school-age parents have healthy babies, complete their education, and become self-sufficient—and it works! Teenage parents at the New Futures School are much more likely to graduate high school and find employment than those at schools like Farragut. They are also much less likely to have a second child while still a teenager, or to end up on the welfare rolls.[41]

As Lisbeth Schorr demonstrates in her 1988 book *Within Our Reach,* "throughout this country there are programs that have changed outcomes" for high-risk children.[42] Systematic intervention and support can significantly improve the life chances of disadvantaged youngsters.

If "family structure and labor market performance [are] the two biggest factors that influence the poverty of families,"[43] the impact of these structural trends on children has been greatly exacerbated by inadequate and underfunded public programs. We spend a small and declining proportion of the federal budget on young people. Public funds for child care, early childhood education, remedial education, maternal and child health care, Aid to Families with Dependent Children (AFDC), and low-income housing have all been squeezed in recent years. Federal expenditure on children (in constant dollars) dropped 4 percent between 1978 and 1987. Contrast this with spending on the elderly, which rose 52 percent over the same time period.[44]

Poor children are at risk in all kinds of ways. A small but growing proportion are homeless; many fall outside the medical care system and as a consequence suffer poor health; many endure poor quality, even dangerous, child care; and the majority fail to make it through our educational system.

Lack of Housing

In 1991, 600,000 to 3 million people are homeless in this nation of plenty.[45] Approximately 30 percent of the homeless are families, generally a parent with two or three children.[46] The average child is six years old, the average parent twenty-seven.[47] In New York City homeless families are warehoused in shelters and in welfare hotels. In Phoenix and Los Angeles they sleep in huge encampments on the edges of town. In Miami and San Diego most end up on the streets. The loss of a home often leads to the dissolution of a family: two older children in foster care; the wife and baby in a public shelter; the husband sleeping on a park bench or under a bridge.

Homelessness can be a devastating experience for a child, as it was for Fatima and Brian, whom I discussed in the prologue. A home is much more than four walls and a roof. It provides warmth, security, and continuity. Homeless children quickly lose their emotional anchor—and their chance at an education. In 1988 more than half of the children at the Prince George Hotel failed to attend school on a regular basis.[48]

The growing ranks of the homeless are just the most visible indicator of an acute housing shortage that stretches across the nation. In 1989 more than 10 million Americans were living near the edge of homelessness, illegally doubled up in the homes of friends or family. The arrival of a new baby, a landlord's displeasure, or simply rising tensions due to overcrowding can cost these people a place to live.[49] According to Barry Zigas, director of the National Low Income Coalition in Washington, conditions are "the worst since the Great Depression." Local officials report that there is no public housing available for hundreds of thousands of poor families who qualify for help. There are 44,000 persons on the waiting list in Chicago, 60,000 in Miami, and 200,000 in New York City.[50]

The amount of inexpensive rental housing available to low-income families declined by 19 percent in the period from 1970 to 1985.[51] The main cause of this decline was a cutback in federal housing programs that supported the construction of public housing or provided housing subsidies. Federal support for low-income housing dropped from $32.2 billion in 1978 to $9.8 billion in 1988. After adjusting for inflation, this constitutes a decline of more than 80 percent. In the late 1970s HUD made commitments to provide federal rental assistance to an average of 316,000 additional households a year. Ten years later this had dropped to 82,000. Today, fewer than one in three poor renter households receive assistance through federal, state, or local housing programs.[52]

This massive cutback in federal subsidies has been accompanied by two other trends: the gentrification of inner-city neighborhoods, which has prompted a sharp rise in the price of private housing (rents for poor people living in unsubsidized units increased by one-third during the 1980s); and a rapid increase in the number of households living at or below the poverty level (the median income of young single parents *fell* 36 percent between 1974 and 1987!).[53] By the end of the decade some 45 percent of all poor renter households were paying at least 70 percent of their income for rent and utilities.[54] These families are clearly on the brink of homelessness. A small rent increase or a medical emergency easily pushes them over the edge into the abyss inhabited by Fatima and her family.

And the situation seems to be getting worse. Most analysts see the gap between the demand for and the supply of low-income housing getting wider in the future as commitments under existing federal housing programs expire. For example, under one program—Section 8 certificates—local housing authorities (using HUD dollars) contract with private owners to make housing units available to low-income tenants for a specified time (usually five to fifteen years), with the housing authority paying the difference between 30 percent of a recipient's income and a "fair-market" rent. Over the next few years contracts covering 700,000 such units will expire.[55] If they are not renewed (and it seems clear that the Bush administration will not renew all of them), owners will raise rents and convert the units to occupancy by a high-income clientele.

Shortfalls in Health Care

If 330,000 children are homeless, 12 million are uninsured and have little or no access to health care. During the 1980s growing numbers of families with children fell through the medical safety net. The reasons are simple. Since 1980, far fewer families have been able to rely on company-sponsored insurance to take care of their health needs. The number of uninsured Americans has risen by one-fifth, from 30.9 million in 1980 to 37.1 million in 1987.[56] More parents are working at low-wage jobs that offer no benefits—like Rose Hummel and Edith Harris.

Edith, a single mother with two young sons, works as a part-time nurse's aide. She receives no health benefits and, like many parents who cannot provide health insurance for their children, is familiar with the guilt of delaying her sons' vaccinations and treating their fevers with compresses rather than antibiotics. But nothing caused as much pain as the time Edith had to use manicure scissors and tweezers to pull stitches from the face of her three-year-old son, Wayne. "He was very, very hysterical and I couldn't hold him down at all," Edith remembered, adding that Wayne's crying unleashed a flood of her own tears. "I felt terrible but I had to do it. I just couldn't afford to take him back to the doctor."[57]

Even workers who have insurance are finding that their health coverage is shrinking. During the 1980s many employers tried to cut expenses by reducing their contribution toward the cost of dependent care. When this happens and the cost of paying the premiums for dependent care is switched from employer to employee, children almost always lose coverage. For families the alternative to employer insurance is our chronically underfunded public health care system. In the 1980s it conspicuously failed to fill in the growing gaps in private insurance coverage.

Low-income families often turn to Medicaid to help cover their health costs, but they are unlikely to get help unless family income is at or below AFDC eligibility level (often considerably below the poverty line) and their children are under six years old.[58] The Medicaid system finances health care for only 40 percent of those below the poverty line, compared with 65 percent in the mid-1970s.[59] Families with children who do not qualify for Medicaid must rely on a patchwork of public health programs which fail to serve the eligible population because of a shortfall in public funds. The nation's 550 community health centers, for example, serve only 5 million patients each year, leaving 20 million eligible people, two-thirds of them mothers and children, without such services. Funding for Title V (the maternal and child health block grant program targeted at the uninsured) is now so low that fewer than half of all states are able to offer prenatal programs on a statewide basis; only a handful of them can pay for hospital delivery services for low-income, uninsured women; and none is able to offer comprehensive pediatric health services statewide.[60]

Education and nutrition programs that help prevent costly medical intervention are also increasingly underfunded. The family planning program, a key player in the effort to prevent teenage pregnancies, reduce abortions, and halt the spread of AIDS, has been slashed. In 1989 its budget was only $131 million, half the 1981 level—the year before the Reagan cutbacks.[61] Even WIC—the Supplemental Food Program for Women, Infants, and Children—which received some additional funding in the 1980s, reaches only 60 percent of those eligible.[62]

WIC is a program through which the federal government channels money to the states to provide food for 4.5 million expectant and new mothers and young children who are at risk of malnutrition. Several evaluations of WIC, including studies financed by the federal government, have shown it to be extremely effective—it improves the health of women and children, increases birth weight, and reduces infant mortality. By preventing illnesses and hospitalization, it also saves money. For example, the research shows that one dollar invested in the prenatal component of WIC saves as much as three dollars in short-term hospital costs.[63] Because of these indisputable savings, Congress spared WIC when other welfare programs were cut back during Reagan's years in office.

Despite this backdrop, WIC is now threatened with cutbacks. Food prices increased an unexpected 8 percent at the beginning of 1990, and the $2.1 billion Washington gives the states for this program is no longer enough to cover the increased cost of milk, orange juice, cereal, and infant formula, the main items in the WIC food package. The federal government is reluctant to increase the WIC budget, so most states, under severe fiscal pressures of their own, are "either cutting the food package or reducing the number of participants."[64] Some states are doing both.

For example, Texas has cut the cereal allowance for one-year-olds and two-year-olds by a third, from 36 to 24 ounces a month. It also plans to drop 27,000 women and children from the WIC program. Among those dropped are pregnant women, breast-feeding women, and infants whose diets have been diagnosed as inadequate but who show no clinical signs of malnutrition. California plans to halve the juice allowance for children three to five years old and to eliminate vouchers for cheese, the major source of calcium for poor families. Missouri is terminating benefits for 14,000 children who show no clinical signs of malnutrition. Richard Blount, director of food and nutrition services for the Missouri Health Department, says that some of these children will undoubtedly develop symptoms of anemia and malnutrition after a few months without WIC, and will again qualify for the program. But by that time, some of these youngsters may have succumbed to serious illness.[65]

Increasingly, large numbers of poor children are simply left out of our medical system, with predictable results. Progress in maternal and child health care, which moved steadily upward in the 1960s and 1970s, faltered in the 1980s. In many key areas—for example, reducing infant mortality—progress has slowed or stopped. In several others children are actually losing ground. The number of children immunized against polio declined in the 1980s, and half of all small children are now not protected against this crippling disease.[66] And measles is back. Eight years after its supposed elimination in the United States, the nation is in the midst of an epidemic: 17,850 cases of measles and 41 deaths were reported in 1989, up from 1,500 cases in 1983. The reasons behind this upsurge are simple. Federal subsidies have failed to keep pace with the price of vaccination, and our public health system increasingly lacks "the resources and know-how to immunize many of the youngest inner-city children."[67] In short, we have failed to find the money to keep measles at bay. In 1991 America does a poorer job of looking after the health needs of its children than do Poland, Singapore, or Sri Lanka. It is hard to be proud of this record.

Substandard Child Care

If we fail to keep our children healthy, we also fail to provide them with decent child care. Every day millions of youngsters—infants, preschoolers, and latchkey school-age children—are forced to cope with this nation's massive shortfall in quality child care. These children need out-of-home care because both parents (or the sole parent living with them) are in the work force. Forty years ago just 12 percent of preschool children in America had employed mothers. Today 57 percent do, and projections are that the proportion will climb to 70 percent by the turn of the century.[68] Families increasingly need two incomes to underwrite basic living expenses—to pay the rent, to buy the groceries. As we have seen, the male wage plummeted in the 1970s and 1980s, and wives and mothers have attempted to cushion the impact of this by going out to work. In addition, more and more families are headed by single mothers who need child care if they are going to work at all. For reasons of economic survival, the majority of American families are now dependent upon out-of-home child care.

It is extremely difficult to obtain an accurate picture of child care in America because there is no systematic collection of data at the national level. But experts in the field agree that hundreds of thousands of preschool children spend the working day in poor-quality, even dangerous, care, and as many as 10 million schoolchildren aged six through thirteen are without adult supervision for several hours each day.[69] The child-care deficit is most severe for infants, the most vulnerable of our children. This is because mothers of very young children have entered the labor force at a particularly rapid rate in recent years. In 1976, 11 percent of infants under one year of age had mothers in the work force; by 1988 this figure had climbed to 51 percent.[70]

Many parents would like to stay home with their newborn babies for a few months but cannot because it would imperil their jobs. Unlike all other advanced nations the United States does not have a state-mandated parenting leave policy guaranteeing new parents paid leave or job protection at the time of birth. In the absence of such a policy, large numbers of working parents must seek substitute care for their newborns. Since infant care is in short supply and the cost of quality care extremely high—$125 to $200 a week—many babies end up in third-rate situations. In many states only a tiny fraction of licensed child-care centers offer slots for infants. A recent study shows that nearly half of all mothers who resume work three to seven months after childbirth have serious problems finding affordable child care.[71]

Most low-income families give up on day-care centers—with their trained personnel, they are nearly always too expensive—and resort to family day care. It is thought that approximately a third of all young children (three months to three years) with employed mothers are in this type of care.[72] Family day care comprises informal arrangements whereby a neighborhood woman cares for several children in her own home. Only a small proportion of this kind of care is licensed—estimates are in the 10 percent range—and the standard of care is very uneven. Its cost, however, is relatively modest—$40 to $75 a week. For many parents, this is one of the few affordable options.

Another inexpensive child-care solution for low-income families is a "package" whereby parents piece together a mixture of their own time, relatives' time, neighbors' time, and paid help to get through the working day. Many parents resort to this desperate juggling act when they cannot find or cannot afford decent family day care. Approximately a third of all children under three with working parents are cared for in such a package. In her survey research in Westchester County, Sheila Kamerman found that a package composed of relatives, neighbors, and paid help was the most common child-care arrangement. In her sample "more than half of all preschool children experienced 2 or more types of care each week, and half of these were exposed to 3 or 4 types of care in a routine week."[73] All this added up to a great deal of strain and stress for parents and children.

Rita Diego* is a single mother who earns $8,500 a year working in the cafeteria at Florida State University in Tallahassee. When I interviewed her in early 1989, she had a six-month-old baby daughter named Corinne. According to Rita "child care has been a nightmare." When her daughter was born she was not entitled to any maternity leave, so she took a few weeks' accumulated sick leave and vacation time and was back at work before her baby was two months old. The first type of child care she tried was a neighborhood woman who looked after eight children in her own home. The price was right—$55 a week—but Rita quickly realized that it was impossible for one untrained woman to take care of eight babies and toddlers. When she picked up Corinne she would often find her strapped into an infant seat in front of the television set, hungry, dirty, and miserable. After an exhaustive search, the

*A pseudonym.

only "quality" situation Rita came up with was a day-care center near campus that charged $125 a week for infant care. "The center is real neat," said Rita wistfully. "It has all this equipment and the staff really seem to know what they are doing, but there's no way I can pay that kind of money. They want more than half my take-home pay." The solution Rita finally hit upon was a package arrangement.

Every morning at 6:00 A.M. she drives forty minutes to her sister's house, where her niece is able to look after Corinne until noon (her niece works the afternoon shift at a local restaurant). Rita picks up the baby on her lunch break and delivers her to a neighbor who, for $40 a week, watches Corinne until 4:30 P.M. when Rita gets home from work. According to Rita, "it's hard, all this driving, and I never have time for lunch, but at least it's a setup I can afford and the baby gets to have real good attention in the morning." A recurrent problem is that Rita's neighbor is elderly and asthmatic, and on several occasions has not been able to watch Corinne in the afternoon. Rita calls in sick four or five times a month. She is worried about losing her job.[74]

Quality care for three-to-five-year-old children is relatively easy to find, but only if you have a high enough income to pay for both nursery school and considerable additional baby-sitting. Nursery school enrollment has doubled over the last decade and 35 percent of all three- and four-year-olds now attend preschool. But most of these preschoolers are middle and upper class. Unhappily for low-income working parents, more than 90 percent of nursery schools are private and tuition charges (borne by parents) average $3,350 a year.[75] An additional problem for many working Moms and Dads is that most of these schools are in session for only three hours a day, a schedule that does not begin to cover normal working hours.

For women with jobs, nursery school is often part of a more complicated, more expensive package.

Head Start was meant to help fill this vacuum and provide early childhood education to poor children, but it has been systematically underfunded and over the years has failed to expand to accommodate the burgeoning number of children in need. Today it serves only 25 percent of those eligible.[76] The laudable premise of Head Start is that disadvantaged youngsters need extra help in the preschool years if they are to succeed in the formal education system and become productive members of society. The program encompasses a whole battery of compensatory services. In addition to a standard preschool curriculum it provides hot meals, vaccinations, medical screening, dental checkups, and parenting education. Four out of five Head Start parents volunteer in the program, where they both help the children and upgrade their own parenting skills.

The shortfall in funds for Head Start, like the cutbacks in WIC, is extremely shortsighted. Every dollar invested in enriched preschool programs saves six dollars downstream in lowered costs for special education, truant officers, welfare benefits, and prison charges.[77] As I shall discuss at greater length in chapter 8, the benefits of early childhood education last through school into adult life.

Finally, there is the problem of latchkey kids. Working parents who think they have solved their child-care problems because Johnny and Susan are finally old enough for public school are faced with a decade of trying to deal with those hours before and after school (7:30 to 8:30 A.M., 3:30 to 6:00 P.M.), those nine to twelve weeks of vacation in the summertime, and sundry holidays. No one knows for sure how working parents cope with their children over this long haul, but only a tiny fraction of schools offer after-school or before-school programs. As many as 10 million schoolchildren ages six through thirteen are latchkey kids—that is, they return home every day to empty houses because both parents are at work.[78] Sometimes they spend their time with friends or siblings, but they are still without adult supervision for several hours each working day. A recent survey in Los Angeles found nearly one-quarter of seven-to-nine-year-olds in self-care after school. In a 1987 survey more than 1,000 teachers interviewed cited isolation and lack of supervision after school as major reasons why children have difficulty in school.[79]

Many children find the experience of being a latchkey kid negative—full of fear, loneliness, and conflict. According to one study, approximately 25 percent of latchkey children experienced serious problems coping with self-care: "Fear levels were high enough to cause hiding, sleeplessness and nightmares. Isolation was intense enough to cause depression or strong feelings of rejection. The responsibility placed on them was overwhelming enough to cause bitterness, resentment and anger."[80]

Child development experts agree that under certain conditions out-of-home care need not harm children. These conditions tend to be quite rigorous. For example, newborns do not thrive in day care; infants belong with a parent for at least the first few months of life. A toddler, on the other hand, can thrive in day care providing the facilities are appropriately designed, the caregivers properly trained, and the child-staff ratio generous enough to allow individual attention. The National Association for the Education of Young Children recommends a child-staff ratio of at most 4:1 for infants and 5:1 for toddlers.[81] Staff turnover rates should be kept low so that a child can benefit from continuity in care. And finally, working or not, a parent needs to find time to be with a child for a substantial period of each day. If these conditions are met, a one- or two-year-old can flourish.

There is no way to provide any of this on the cheap. Millions of American children endure unsafe, low-quality care not because out-of-home care is intrinsically bad but because we have failed to channel significant resources into caring for our children. For example, day-care workers have one of the highest turnover rates of any occupation, 40 percent a year. This is bad news for children, but it's easy to understand why these workers leave their jobs so readily: the average annual salary of a trained day-care worker is only $9,400.[82] Until we boost salaries in this sector, until we learn to value our caregivers, children will be looked after by a revolving cast of underpaid, alienated workers.

Expecting hard-pressed parents to buy whatever child care they can afford on the private market is asking for trouble. Recently, in a small town near Chicago, forty-seven youngsters—half of them younger than two—were discovered being cared for in a basement by one adult. At $25 a week the program was a bargain—one-third the cost of alternative child care in this community—and many of the parents objected when the state closed this "center." These desperate parents (mostly single mothers) were not seeking to harm their children; an overcrowded basement was simply the only child-care arrangement they could afford.[83]

Think it through: the cost of licensed child care averages $3,000 a year, and yet the typical young single mother had an income of just $4,859 in 1987. Placing one child in quality child care eats up more than half of family income.

Despite the economic convulsions that make child care an unquestionable necessity for most parents, we still have no broad federal program that addresses the quality and affordability of out-of-home care. On the contrary, government efforts to help low-income families obtain decent child care have been scaled back in recent years. For example, federal aid for child care through Title XX of the Social Services Block Grant has dwindled. On average, states use 18 percent of Title XX funds to help low-income families pay for child care, and this money has never come close to meeting needs. In 1977 the program served 12 percent of 3.3 million poor children under six. During the Reagan era Title XX appropriations were cut in half, and the number of preschool children in poverty increased to almost 5 million. By 1989 a mere 5 percent of poor preschoolers received day-care subsidies through Title XX.[84]

The dependent care tax credit is the only type of federal support for child care that has increased significantly in recent years. This credit allows families to offset some of their tax bill by claiming a portion of their child-care expenses. Nine million middle- and upper-income families received $4 billion in credits in 1987.[85] Unfortunately, this dependent care tax credit fails to help low-income families, who have little or no income tax liability in the first place; 43 percent of this tax credit goes to families making more than $50,000 a year.[86]

Shortchanging Education

Poverty is a key roadblock in the educational system. Children who begin life in poverty are already at a disadvantage when they enter kindergarten, and a shortage of resources dogs them relentlessly through every stage of the educational process.

It starts early. The inadequate prenatal care poor mothers receive increases their babies' risk of being born early and underweight, conditions that can lead to growth deficits and learning disabilities as they grow up. Impoverished parents are often unable to provide their children with the building blocks of early development—adequate nutrition, decent medical care, a safe and secure environment—and at age five, poor children are often less alert, less curious, and less effective at interacting with their peers than are more privileged youngsters. As they start school, poor children are already way behind.

A further disadvantage is that a substantial number of poor children live with parents who are uneducated. However motivated to help their children learn, they often lack the skills to do so. And, as we have seen, the option of supplementing learning in the home with early childhood development programs is more often available to affluent than to poor children. In 1986 two-thirds of four-year-olds in families with annual incomes of $35,000 or more were enrolled in some type of preschool program, compared with only one-third of four-year-olds in families whose incomes were less than $10,000.[87]

At older ages, poor children are more likely to attend schools that are poorly staffed, overcrowded, and ill equipped—despite their clear need for an enriched educational experience to overcome early learning deficits and a lack of support at home. Poor youngsters are in special need of high-quality teachers, classroom equipment (such as computers), a low student-teacher ratio, and extracurricular programs to supplement classroom learning. These needs are rarely met.

Last spring, the rain began leaking into the rooms on the fourth floor of Public School 94, an elementary school in the North Bronx. Then, last fall, about an hour before parents' night began, huge pieces of the ceiling fell down covering the classroom floors with debris.

But a crumbling sixty-year-old building is not the worst problem at PS 94. Overcrowding is. Every day 1,300 students pour into a building designed for half that number. To make more room the school has had to give up its gymnasium and its library. There are English classes in the hallway, speech classes in a stairwell, and science classes in what is supposed to be a locker room. Pupils in several first-grade classes are somehow learning to read in the gym. Rows of filing cabinets serve as makeshift dividers, but they do not work as sound barriers. One of the teachers, Lynn Hiller, often has trouble hearing what her students are trying to tell her.

In her cramped office on the second floor Judy Markowitz, one of three guidance counselors, worries about too many children with too many problems. She thinks she knows why one boy has been fighting with his classmates—he is on the brink of homelessness. His mother, who is on public assistance, has just lost her apartment and she and her son are temporarily staying with relatives in another part of the Bronx. Mrs. Markowitz, who has a caseload of 500 children, is trying to find time to counsel the boy—and help his mother find a place to live.[88]

New York City schools desperately need more resources to upgrade dilapidated school buildings; to hire additional guidance counselors; to build gymnasiums and libraries; to buy books. In 1989, 105 of 621 elementary schools in the New York City school system had no library.[89] Libraries cost money, and the city is in the red. Schools Chancellor Joseph A. Fernandez estimates that the system needs an additional billion dollars a year just to catch up on deferred maintenance. He does not count on getting any of that money soon. Indeed, due to New York City's fiscal problems he is facing a $90 million cutback in the 1990–91 fiscal year.[90]

Given the decentralized funding typical of the American system, schools with large poor and minority populations usually have the least money to serve children well. The state of

New Jersey, for example, has attempted to make up for fiscal inequities among school districts, yet per-pupil expenditures are still $2,880 in poor districts and $4,029 in wealthy districts.[91]

Even if a disadvantaged child beats the odds and manages to do well at the primary and secondary school levels, his or her chances of going on to college are shrinking. For decades federal support for college education improved poor children's options, allowing many to attend college. But in the 1980s funding did not keep pace with the skyrocketing costs of tuition. Between 1980 and 1988, the inflation-adjusted cost of attending a four-year college increased by 28 percent and the cost of attending a private university increased by 52 percent. Yet the Pell grants (which comprise the main federal support for college-bound low-income students) increased by only 11 percent.[92] As one might expect, college enrollment among poor students has declined significantly.

The bottom line seems to be that poverty—and the absence of compensatory public resources—dramatically reduces a child's chances of entering kindergarten "on track," keeping on grade level, graduating from high school, or attending college.

During the 1980s child poverty became entrenched in the United States on a scale unprecedented in the postwar period and unmatched in the advanced world. Close to 13 million children are currently growing up in families that live below the poverty line, and this exacts a huge price whether measured in moral or economic terms. Family poverty is relentlessly correlated with high rates of infant mortality, child neglect, school failure, teenage childbearing, and violent crime.

Despite the severity of these problems, they share one hopeful characteristic. They can all be ameliorated by an infusion of funds. This seems like a simple-minded point, but it is often ignored. The polls tell us that most ordinary decent Americans believe that nothing works, that the ills of poor children are insoluble. Not true. Clearly, programs and policies have to be designed so that they work to empower families rather than increase dependency. But we know how to make a difference. Head Start, WIC, Section 8 rental vouchers—all of these programs succeed in buttressing poor, fragile families in ways that improve the life prospects of children. There are ways to halt that "fateful march from unmet needs to joblessness and crime."[93]

The problem is not that we don't know how to improve the circumstances of poor children—prenatal care is not some kind of well-kept secret, and books such as Lisbeth Schorr's *Within Our Reach* and David Ellwood's *Poor Support* have done much to provide a blueprint for policy makers. It's just that we have chosen not to allocate significant resources to these problems. Quite the reverse—as children's problems have mounted we have cut deeply into the social supports that underpin families with children. To use the words of Anthony Alvarado, former superintendent of schools in New York City: "It's strange, we know what to do, we just don't do it."[94]

The odd thing is that while our leaders spend a lot of energy convincing themselves—and the public—that America just can't afford parenting leave, Pell grants, or enough vaccine to keep measles at bay, the evidence mounts that we are paying through the nose for our moral turpitude, for our failure to look after our children. It is now abundantly clear that it's a whole lot cheaper to take care of our children than to foot the bill for the swelling tide of child neglect. There is no way to dispose of these children we have failed to provide for. They cannot be thrown away or even ignored. In the end, "we all pay to support the unproductive and incarcerate the violent,"[95] and our common stake in preventing child neglect goes way beyond the economic.

In 1988 five-year-old Jennifer Royal testified at the trial of Michael Ward, a young man who shot and killed "Peaches," her eight-year-old best friend, who just happened to be in the wrong place at the wrong time. Jennifer, who was wounded in the attack, lives in Opa-Locka, a poor community in Florida, where high dropout rates, unemployment, and single parenthood contribute to a violent drug scene and one of the highest crime rates in the United States.

> In the morning I ate breakfast and brushed my teeth. We was playing outside. Peaches and me play ring-around-the-rosy. Little boys was fighting about a dollar in front of the house, and it scared me. Then I see Michael Ward—I didn't know his name then—and he say, "Anybody move, I shoot," and he shot me. It scared me.
>
> When the bullet got me, it felt like a firecracker. My head hit against the door. I had a long scratch on my head. Peaches almost made it. Then I knew Peaches was dead. Mama froze. The police-

man held me. He was crying. It was hard for me to talk. I swallowed my throw-up. Then the doctors put me on a board to go to the hospital with my mama and my auntie. The bullet fell right out of my back. I told them, "I'm not going to die. God's not ready for me yet." But there was blood coming out of me. Michael Ward. He shouldn't have did that to me . . .

At my house the drug boys throw bottles and rocks outside. The drug boys aren't nice to me. When I come home, they say, "Hi, asshole." They will steal your stuff, they will steal your purse. Last week the police took them boys to jail. Ten of them. They put their hands up and then the police put those things on their hands. But they come back. They sit and play cards and smoke drugs. Put their noses in their hands and go sniff, sniff. I have to stay inside with my brothers and sisters . . .

I saw Peaches at the funeral. She had on a pretty ol' dress, a pink one. And some nice shoes. I cried at the funeral. We went to the graveyard and buried her in the dirt. I saw three angels there, and they took her away.[96]

At some point, Jennifer—who is an extremely intelligent five-year-old—is going to figure things out. Peaches was not taken away by three well-meaning angels; she was murdered, one of ten American children shot dead on that particular day, a victim of the many-layered neglect we heap on innocent children in this society. By the time Jennifer is old enough to know why Peaches died, she might not be cute and trusting anymore. She might well be angry, alienated, and strung out on drugs herself. And who could blame her. As Marian Edelman, president of the Children's Defense Fund, warns us, some time very soon "the rage and pain of these homeless, hopeless, abused, alienated children will . . . explode in our faces in communities all over America."[97]

3

Mainstream Kids
and the Time Deficit

On April 21, 1989, ABC-TV's newsmagazine "20/20" was devoted to examining a group of teenagers who seem to have it all and yet are hooked on drugs and alcohol. They live in Pacific Palisades, California, one of the country's wealthiest suburbs. In this lush community of big homes, fast cars, and swimming pools, youngsters seem intent on self-destruction.

The parents of these kids work hard at "making it" in a highly materialistic culture, and they're often generous with their children to the point of indulgence. What they don't give them, however, is enough time and attention.

Brandy Page's father, an orthopedic surgeon, is buying her a fancy new car for her sixteenth birthday. His philosophy is typical:

DR. JOSEPH PAGE, PARENT: I have very little time to give to my children. I work long hours, I'm not here and I think I do compensate by at least allowing them to have what they like to have. My only requirement is that I have asked them to do well in school and to stay out of drugs and alcohol.

VOICEOVER: And what has happened with his kids?

DR. PAGE: Well, they have not done well in school and they're into drugs and alcohol.

VOICEOVER: Dr. Page's kids are not alone. The students at Pali High say that an education isn't the only thing you can get on and around their pristine campus.

HOWIE SHERMAN, SEVENTEEN YEARS OLD: You can get coke on campus. You can get pot on campus. You can get, you know, acid. You can get whatever you want. It's there for the taking.

STACY NADEL, SIXTEEN YEARS OLD: I was at a friend's house one day at lunchtime. And this girl's mom and her brother walked in and we were all partying. . . . My first reaction was, "Parents," like "Hide," you know, "Hide everything." And she comes in and she's like, "Oh, can I have a hit?"

Linda Levine is the school psychologist and the organizer of Pali High's own on-campus chapter of Alcoholics Anonymous.

INTERVIEWER: Why AA on a high school campus?

Ms. LEVINE: Because we have drinkers and I want them sober.

If there is any question that Pali High needs such a program, some grim facts provide the answer. During the two years before this program aired, ten teenagers from Pali High died, all of them from drugs or alcohol. The previous October four seventeen-year-olds burned to death in a fiery car crash. Three of them, including the driver, had been drinking.

A student who witnessed the crash was still in shock as she described the scene at a packed meeting of concerned parents and fellow students: "I went back and thank God there was a friend with me. And I watched four kids burn to death. And a friend calls up and she says, 'Did you hear what happened to Lisa?' And I said, 'Oh, my God, Lisa was in that car.'"

Just weeks later, kids were partying as usual. In April, a Friday night party was advertised around the campus with a flier that promised kegs of beer and tanks of nitrous oxide, or laughing gas. Pali High officials knew about the party and contacted parents and the police to try to stop it. But in the end, police, parents, and the school administration chose to turn a blind eye.

A camera crew from "20/20" showed up at the party at 10:00 P.M. and found high school students drinking, smoking marijuana, and snorting cocaine. The kids talked about why they used drugs and alcohol.

HOWIE: I need something inside of me to make me feel like I am normal.
STACY: If I'm not loaded, then I don't feel all right with myself, and I want to, like, get out of my skin.[1]

It used to be that middle-class Americans could isolate themselves from the problem of child neglect by imagining it affected only the poor. But today, from East Harlem to Peoria to Pacific Palisades, American youngsters are in trouble, whether their parents have money or not. Our television screens are filled with images of children—black kids, white

kids, poor kids, privileged kids—brimming with pain and ano-
mie, opting out of the system, escaping into drugs and violence.

According to a 1990 National Commission, "too many of
our children have lost their way and are engaged in destructive behavior that imperils their immediate health . . . and
their prospects for a fulfilling life. . . . This is not confined to
communities that are suffering from poverty and crime.
Rather it involves millions of teenagers in every neighborhood across the nation."[2]

Faced with the rampant misery of Watts or Chicago's South
Side, it is relatively easy to wrap one's mind around the problems of disadvantaged children. It is much harder to understand the equally real problems of children who live deep
within the reaches of America's huge middle class.

Clearly, the problem goes beyond a resource deficit. Even
if we were to eliminate poverty and vastly improve the benefits and services provided to families with children, it would
still be difficult to touch the more complex problems that
routinely derail children in contemporary society. Becky
Kraus, whom I introduced in the prologue, does not like
eating rice and beans for supper, but she is not poor in any
ordinary sense. Nor can her problems be solved by the simple
application of large doses of money. Better social supports
would help at the margin—an after-school program, for example, would reduce the emotional toll of being a latchkey kid—
but in the main, Becky's enormous load of pain, her poor
performance at school, her inability to make sense of the
future are all wrapped up in her parents' divorce, her absentee
father and stressed-out mother. She feels that both her parents
missed out on her childhood, leaving her exposed and rudder-
less, coping more or less badly with the difficult business of
growing up in the 1980s.

Becky's experiences—and those of the teenagers interviewed on "20/20"—highlight a burgeoning parenting deficit that is increasingly threatening the well-being of children. The root causes range from the massive increase in the amount of time adults spend in the workplace to spiraling rates of divorce and single parenthood. Over the last twenty-five years the proportion of mothers in the paid labor force has tripled and the number of children growing up without a father has increased by a factor of two. The central consequences for youngsters have been little contact with parents and large quantities of time badly spent. By and large the vacuum left in children's lives by the retreat of the traditional mother has not been filled with attentive fathers, quality child care, expanded educational programs, or any other worthy activity. Hundreds of thousands of kids like Becky have been left to fend for themselves in a society that is increasingly inhospitable to children.

In 1991 children in the mainstream of our society are at risk in a variety of ways. Compared to a previous generation, these children are more likely to: underperform at school; commit suicide; need psychiatric help; suffer a severe eating disorder; bear a child out of wedlock; take drugs; be the victim of a violent crime. According to a recent study, even privileged youngsters are overwhelmed "by drugs, pregnancy, bad grades and bad jobs."[3]

Academic Underperformance and Failure

A central fact about contemporary middle-class children is that they are not doing well in school. No matter how you judge performance, whether you compare American students with students in other countries, or compare this generation of children with their parents, or simply ask whether these youngsters are learning enough to become viable members of society, it is hard to be complacent about educational standards among American youth.

Take the comparison with other countries. "It has become a regular international ritual—like the Olympics or the Miss Universe pageant or the morning gold fix in London. Teams of academic testers fan out into classrooms around the world to see how students stack up in various subjects. American educators brace themselves for results that show Japanese or Korean students leading the academic parade with Americans in the rear, somewhere between Togo and the Falklands."[4]

Back in the early 1960s, when the first International Mathematics Study was conducted, American educators had reason to be pleased. The upper 5 percent of our mathematics students were comparable with the upper 5 percent of students anywhere in the world. But the second international test, taken in 1981–82, showed quite different results: the upper 5 percent of American students was now in the bottom quartile of the international sample.[5]

Recent evidence from the International Assessment of Math and Science confirms this negative trend. This project, which was sponsored by the Education Department and the National Science Foundation, looked at students in the United States and eleven other advanced industrial countries. The American students came in last in mathematics and next to last in science. These findings are particularly significant because the study, in looking at thirteen-year-olds and not high school students, showed that underperformance reaches deep into the system.[6]

A dramatic measure of the failure of the U.S. educational system is our track record on the illiteracy front. Over the last thirty years the United States has dropped from eighteenth to forty-ninth place among nations in terms of the proportion of the population that is literate.[7] Today approximately 6 percent of the adult population has not attained "basic literacy" (a fourth-grade reading level), and fully 20 percent—36 million people—are functionally illiterate in that they cannot read or write at the eighth-grade level, which is thought to be the minimal educational requirement for most jobs.[8] Functional illiteracy among minority youth may run as high as 40 percent.[9] Standards in some high schools are so low that hundreds of thousands of functionally illiterate young people graduate every year. William Brock, Secretary of Labor in the Reagan administration, estimated that 700,000 high school graduates "get diplomas each year and cannot read them." He calls it an "insane national tragedy."[10]

In 1987 almost half this nation's seventeen-year-olds could not correctly determine whether 87 percent of 10 is greater than, less than, or equal to 10; nor could they determine the area of a rectangle.[11] Some 35 percent of American eleventh-graders write at or below the following level: *"I have been experience at cleaning house Ive also work at a pool for I love keeping thing neat organized and clean. Im very social Ill get to know people really fast."*[12]

Such an impressive level of educational failure has serious repercussions in the labor market. In 1987 New York Telephone had to test 57,000 people before it could find 2,100 who were well educated enough for entry-level jobs as operators or repair technicians.[13] One-third of the nation's large corporations now provide courses in reading, writing, and arithmetic for those who need it, and the army gives courses to bring recruits up to ninth-grade reading levels.[14] Xerox's chairman, David Kearns, estimates that U.S. industry spends $25 billion a year on remedial education for workers.[15]

In 1983 the National Commission on Excellence in Education told us that "for the first time in history, the education skills of one generation will not surpass, will not equal, will not even approach, those of their parents."[16] The clearest evidence of educational decline is the pronounced drop in the SAT scores of college-bound high school seniors.

Between 1963 and 1981, mean scores on the mathematical portion of the test fell 32 points, while mean scores on the verbal portion fell 51 points. There have been some modest improvement since 1981, but scores started to dip again in 1987. The total recovery has amounted to less than 13 points. Average SAT scores remain 70 points below those of 25 years ago.[17]

Attempts to explain this decline as the result of an increase in the proportion of high school students who take the SATs do not stand up to critical analysis. Average scores still show significant decline after adjustment for the composition of test takers, and the absolute number of students with high scores has declined markedly. For example, in 1966–67, more than 33,000 students had scores of 700 or above on the verbal portion of the SAT, compared with fewer than 14,000 in 1986–87—despite a jump from 1.4 million to 1.8 million in the number taking the test. Thus, the decline in scores reflects a real decrease in educational standards and not just some statistical quirk. Scores declined in all types of schools, among all socioeconomic groups and in all parts of the country.[18]

Data collected by the National Assessment of Educational Progress (NAEP), which has been testing national samples of students aged nine, thirteen, and seventeen each year since 1969, confirms a picture of overall decline in educational achievement.[19] In recent years the NAEP has found a slight improvement in basic reading, writing, and arithmetic skills, but fewer students are developing "the capacity to use the knowledge and skills they acquire in school for thoughtful or

innovative purposes."[20] The back-to-basics reform movement
of the 1980s seems to have raised minimal levels of compe-
tency, but as soon as students encounter more complex demands—reading a simple chart, or knowing that six dimes are
worth more than eleven nickels—they begin to lose ground.[21]
These higher-level skills are less well developed than they
were twenty years ago: for example, in 1989 only 5 percent
of seventeen-year-old high school students could calculate
the unit cost of electricity given a simplified utility bill; in the
early 1970s, 12 percent of seventeen-year-olds could solve
this same problem. According to the NAEP, as of 1986, only
6 percent of graduating high school seniors could solve a two-
step arithmetic problem, and only 5 percent could read and
understand a short, complex article.[22] And these disappoint-
ing statistics actually overestimate teenagers' ability, since they
apply only to those seventeen-year-olds still in school, exclud-
ing the 27 percent who have already dropped out!

We are not just talking about a deficit in math and writing
skills—American students seem to absorb very little factual
knowledge during their years in school. Geography is a particularly weak area. A 1987 study of five thousand high school
seniors in eight major cities found that "25 percent of the
students tested in Dallas could not identify the country that
borders the U.S. on the south. In Boston, 38 percent of the
students could not name the six New England states. . . . And
40 percent of those in Kansas City could not name three
countries in South America."[23]

Students are also less well informed than their parents were
when they were young. According to a series of *New York
Times* surveys, forty years ago 84 percent of college students
knew that Manila was the capital of the Philippines; today only
27 percent know the correct answer to that question.[24] Senator Bill Bradley (D-N.J.) is among those worried: "This news

Drawing by R. Chast; © 1989 The New Yorker Magazine, Inc.

is not only shocking; it is frightening. . . . When 95% of
college students cannot locate Vietnam on a world map, we
must sound the alarm. We cannot expect to be a world leader
if our populace doesn't even know where the rest of the world
is."[25]

Only 72.6 percent of American students who enter ninth
grade earn a high school diploma four years later, a figure that
has slipped five percentage points since 1968.[26] Most policy

makers see this as a national disgrace in an age when our economic competitors have near-universal secondary school education. In Japan, for example, 90 percent of seventeen-year-olds graduate high school.[27] Equally worrisome is the fact that only about 60 percent of college students graduate. A recent federal study found a sharp decline in the proportion of students completing higher education in both two- and four-year colleges. Only 18 percent of the class of 1982 had earned a degree or diploma four years after high school, compared with 45 percent ten years earlier.[28]

Emotional Problems

Not only is a large proportion of American youth growing up badly educated and ill prepared for the world of work, but a significant number of youngsters are failing to cope on psychic and emotional fronts.

Suicide among adolescents has increased dramatically over the past quarter-century (in contrast with suicide among adults, which has remained stable). The suicide rate for teen-agers ages fifteen to nineteen tripled between 1960 and 1986, going from 3.6 to 10.2 deaths per year per 100,000 persons in that age range. The rate for younger adolescents is considerably lower, but it too has been climbing, going from 1.2 to 2.3 deaths per 100,000 between 1978 and 1986. Teen suicide is a highly disturbing phenomenon. Each of these deaths has an enormously demoralizing effect on family and community. Parents, grandparents, siblings, friends, and fellow students are left coping with guilt, anxiety, and unanswered questions. It should be remembered that suicide is only the extreme expression of emotional problems present among a much larger number of young people who either attempt suicide or self-destruct slowly through substance abuse or violent behavior. In 1986, 10 percent of teenage boys and 18 percent of teenage girls attempted suicide.[29]

A wealth of less dramatic evidence indicates that the emotional well-being of children and adolescents has deteriorated over the past three decades. According to a 1990 American Medical Association report, today's youngsters "are having trouble coping with stresses in their lives and more have serious psychological problems" than a generation ago.[30] State surveys on the number of schoolchildren needing help for chronic emotional problems point to a growing problem among grade-school students. Elementary-school teachers identified twice as many needy children in 1986 as in 1970. And more teens seek psychiatric help than ever before. Since 1971 the number of adolescents admitted to private psychiatric hospitals has increased fifteenfold, a particularly striking statistic given that the teen population has shrunk over the last twenty years.[31] Experts in the field point out that these disturbing trends are not due to a national epidemic of crazed kids; rather, family turmoil—provoked by divorce, disappearing fathers, mothers at work, and lengthening work weeks—has left many parents too overburdened to set limits or impose controls on their children. For example, the pressures on newly divorced mothers are often so severe that "parenting breaks down and becomes inconsistent and erratically punitive." The children retaliate, venting their pain and frustration on the only available parent. One divorced woman said that the constant harassment felt "like being bitten to death by ducks."[32]

Obesity, which very often has emotional roots, is also on the rise and is now a major disorder among American children. Twenty-seven percent of youngsters aged six to eleven are now defined as obese, up from 18 percent just twenty-five years ago.[33] Obesity causes severe psychological and social problems and is linked to a set of physical ailments that range from hypertension, respiratory disease, and diabetes to orthopedic malfunctions.

If a quarter of American children are obese, some 10 to 15 percent of all teenage girls have some type of eating disorder, and a minority of these—approximately 2 to 5 percent—suffer from a serious form of anorexia (self-induced near-starvation) or bulimia (binge eating coupled with self-induced vomiting and purging).[34] Both disorders can have serious physical, psychological, and social consequences. Anorexia and bulimia took off in the 1970s, and since that time the incidence of these disorders has increased by a factor of three.

Laurel Mellin, director of the Center for Adolescent Obesity in San Francisco, sees these eating disorders as intimately linked to family dysfunction. "Mother's increasing presence in the work place, father's failure to pick up the residual fifty percent of parenting . . . and marital instability" all contribute to a situation where "children are not likely to receive the balance of warm nurturing support and effective limit-setting that protects them from exhibiting various forms of distress, including eating and weight problems."[35] In one study, 46 percent of adolescents with eating disorders came from "chaotic families."[36]

Maria, a twenty-one-year-old Philadelphia college student, is a case in point. In an interview, she said she became anorexic at fourteen in response to her parents' marital problems and divorce. "My mother and I got involved in a vicious cycle of taking care of each other instead of looking after our own needs," Maria said. "I would give her sympathy and she would respond by cooking lots of food—which I then rejected."[37]

Contemporary children suffer a slew of other problems.

"Theft and violence, use of illicit drugs and early sexual activity outside marriage are all more common among today's teenagers than they were among the teens of 20 to 30 years ago."[38] There was a sharp increase in the use of marijuana in the 1970s and an even more worrisome increase in the use of cocaine in the 1980s. Between 1977 and 1985 the proportion of high school seniors who reported using cocaine during the previous month tripled.[39] Alcohol is an increasingly common intoxicant among adolescents. According to a recent American Medical Association report, 39 percent of high school seniors report getting drunk within the previous two weeks.[40]

The Parental Time Deficit

The problems that plague mainstream kids seem to be different as well as much more complicated than those that beset disadvantaged kids. If a poor child comes down with measles, suffers a hearing loss, or fails to learn to read, the difficulty can often be resolved by spending more public money on health care or education. In affluent homes, problems of academic underperformance, suicide, and obesity cannot be clearly or directly linked to material deprivation. The plight of the middle-class child is often centered on a massive deficit in parental time and attention.

The huge jump in the number of mothers at work, the escalation in job-related stress, the expanding work week, the sharp increase in divorce and single parenthood, and the abandonment of children by their fathers all play a part in explaining why so many mainstream American kids are in distress. In millions of homes around the nation, these trends translate into a significant decline in the quantity and quality of time parents spend caring for their children.

Parents are devoting much more time to earning a living and much less time to their children than they did a generation ago. Stanford economist Victor Fuchs has shown that parental time available to children fell appreciably between 1960 and 1986: "On average, in white households with children there were ten hours less per week of potential parental time . . . while the decrease for black households with children was even greater, approximately twelve hours per week."[41] A prime cause of this falloff in parental time is the enormous shift of women into the paid labor force. In 1960, 30 percent of mothers worked; by 1988, 66 percent of all mothers were in the paid labor force. This dramatic increase has eaten into the amount of time mothers are able to devote to their children.[42]

University of Maryland sociologist John Robinson has shown that the more hours mothers are employed, the fewer hours they can give to "primary-care activities" such as playing with and talking to children; dressing, feeding, and chauffeuring children; and helping with homework. According to Robinson, employed mothers spend an average of six hours each week in primary child-care activities—just under half the average time logged by nonemployed mothers and roughly twice that of fathers (employed or nonemployed). In single-parent households, children typically receive two or three fewer hours per week of primary care from their mothers, and three fewer hours from their fathers, than do children in two-parent homes. Robinson points out that wage labor not only eats into primary care but also influences the amount of contact parents have with their children. The data show that the amount of "total contact time"—defined as time parents spend with children while doing other things—has dropped 40 percent during the last quarter-century.[43] This drop is significant because many of the things parents do with children, whether it's visiting Grandma or shopping for groceries, play an important role in building strong parent-child relationships and in giving families a shared identity. Studies that focus on "all-out, undisturbed, down-on-the-floor-with-the-blocks time"[44] fail to provide an accurate gauge of parent-child interaction precisely because they do not recognize the importance of just being together.

In harried dual-worker or single-parent families, even time-honored rituals such as eating family dinners or taking summer vacations are being squeezed. Over the last decade the length of the average family vacation has declined 14 percent, and the number of families that eat their evening meals together has dropped 10 percent.[45]

Many parents are uncomfortable with this loss in family time. A national survey commissioned by the Mass. Mutual Insurance Company found that nearly half the parents who responded were concerned about not having enough time to spend with their families. The majority believed that "parents having less time to spend with their families" is the single most important reason for the decline of the family in American society.[46]

It is extremely important to stress that *growing economic pressure on families with children*—particularly young families and single parents—is at the heart of the parental time famine. Male wages have fallen 19 percent since 1973 and divorce rates have doubled.[47] These are the main reasons why so many mothers have flooded into the labor force over the last two decades. Many parents are squeezed on two fronts. Not only are they dealing with falling wage rates; they are also facing sharply higher living costs. Mortgage payments now eat up 29 percent of median family income, up from 17 percent in 1970, and college tuition now consumes 40 percent of family income, up from 29 percent in 1970.[48] In the main, it's not a question of greedy yuppie mothers going out to work to pay for ski vacations and mink coats. Home ownership and access to college are basic aspirations of middle-class life that have become increasingly unaffordable on a single income. In a national housing survey conducted by Chicago Title & Trust, the proportion of families that purchased a home on a single income fell from 47 percent in 1976 to 21 percent in 1989.[49]

Stress and Strain

The parental time deficit has so far been discussed as a decline in the amount of time parents spend with their children. But the parent-child relationship depends on qualitative as well as quantitative factors, and in 1991 severe time constraints are compounded by mounting job-related stress. In contemporary society a majority of children not only have two parents who work; they have mothers as well as fathers who routinely work fifty-five-hour weeks, who come home preoccupied and stressed out, unable to give much of anything to their children. If you have been biting bullets all day at the office—meeting deadlines, rushing orders, humoring the boss—it is extremely difficult to produce quality time for the kids in the evening.

A body of new evidence shows extremely high levels of stress among women who both hold demanding jobs and deal with home and family in their "spare" time. Contrary to conventional wisdom, the most stress-filled occupations are not in the executive ranks; rather, they are the less glamorous jobs in the pink-collar ghetto, held mostly by mothers.

On October 19, 1987 (Black Monday), a forty-eight-year-old New York stockbroker named Gianni Fidanza went to work as usual. The only thing out of the ordinary was that as part of a "stress in the workplace" experiment, he had wired to a cuff on his arm a little metal box that measured his blood pressure and pulse.[50]

In the first hour of trading, the Dow plunged 93 points, and Fidanza's pulse and blood pressure rose rapidly. As he watched prices tumble on his Quotron screen, angry telephone calls rained in from panicked clients demanding that he do something to stem their losses. Over the course of this one crazy hour, Fidanza's pulse rose from 64 to 83, while his blood pressure surged from 132/87 to 181/105.

This is a classic situation in the stress literature: a male executive reacting to a crisis by pumping adrenaline and flooding arteries. But while coping with the biggest one-day drop in the history of Wall Street is clearly strenuous, recent studies show that male managers may actually be less stressed-out than "support" workers. It seems that it's the underlings— word processors, assembly-line workers, waitresses—who need to worry about dangerous levels of stress. This is especially true of working mothers, who often deal with children and housework after a full day on the job. John Tierney describes a day in the life of Cathy Collins, a black mother of two who works as an administrative aide at New York Hospital:[51]

On the morning she wore her stress monitor, Cathy woke as usual at 5:30 A.M. She then fixed breakfast for her family, left her split-level home in Teaneck, New Jersey, and took two buses to work. Almost two hours later she arrived at her office, a tiny, windowless cubicle at New York Hospital's cardiology unit. Cathy had hardly taken off her coat when telephone, patients, and surgeons started clamoring for her attention. She reached a point of peak load at 10:26 A.M. Standing up, the phone cradled on her shoulders, Cathy was simultaneously dealing with:

- A patient waiting to talk with her.
- A colleague with a question about another patient's chart.
- A buzzing intercom.

- Two lighted buttons on her telephone, indicating incoming calls.
- Her boss, who had just emerged from his office with a sheet of paper saying, "Cathy, I need this Xeroxed right away, please."

At this point her pulse peaked at 82 and her blood pressure at 116/72. Her diastolic pressure had risen a full 26 percent, an even greater percentage change than Fidanza had registered that first hour of Black Monday.

The experts categorize work-related stress according to the demands of the job and the amount of control exercised by workers. The lowest stress situation exists for a person who works in a calm, orderly environment and enjoys a considerable measure of control in deciding how and when tasks get done. A tenured professor at an Ivy League college might well fall into this category.

Harried, fast-track professionals—surgeons, litigators, stockbrokers—fall into an intermediate category of stress. Although these workers often face extremely heavy work loads, they also exert a high degree of control. Fidanza may have felt his financial world spinning out of control on Black Monday, but at least he was in charge of deciding how to respond in terms of advising clients and allocating staff energies. According to stress expert Robert Karasek, "When you have freedom to decide how to act, you can perceive the job's demands as . . . challenges . . . opportunities to learn new strategies."[52]

The trouble with Cathy Collins's job is that it is replete with high-demand, low-control tasks, a combination that triggers the highest level of tension. "The really stressful jobs," says Karasek, "are some of the pink-collar specialties."[53] Women, particularly women with children, hold a disproportionate number of these jobs.

Which brings us to a critical difference between a male stockbroker and a female administrative aide. After Fidanza walked home on Black Monday (he earned enough to be able to live in Manhattan, near his job), he sat down to watch television with his wife. He had no pressing responsibilities that evening, and his blood pressure gradually dropped 20 points. But when Cathy Collins left the office at five o'clock to take two buses back home to New Jersey, there were new stresses awaiting her arteries.

She picked up her ten-year-old daughter, Candra, at ballet school, sorted out a missed appointment, arranged a car pool for the weekend, helped her husband pack for a business trip, tested her sixteen-year-old son, André, for a quiz the next day, and prepared supper. By the time the family sat down to eat, Cathy's blood pressure was higher than at any point during the "work" day.

It is hardly surprising that there were angry explosions at the dinner table. Candra got into an argument with her father. Cathy tried to intervene but made matters worse. By the end of the meal Candra was sobbing in her mother's arms. But there was little time to comfort a child: there were dishes to wash and a bed to be made up. At 9:34 P.M. Cathy's blood pressure was still higher than it had ever been at the office.

It is still true that men get home from the office and relax. Women may face a madhouse in the office but the biggest challenge of the day seems to be that "second shift" in the evening.

Not all the strain in Cathy Collins's life is generated by her job, and at least some of it could be avoided. If her husband had picked Candra up from ballet or cooked supper, the evening would have been less stress-filled for Cathy and she would have had more time and patience for her needy younger child. But Cathy Collins, like most working mothers, seems to do most of the shopping, cooking, housework, and parenting, in addition to her job.

Despite the fact that wives and mothers have entered the paid labor force at a very rapid rate in recent years, men have picked up relatively little on the home front. In a classic study Alexander Szalai found that working women average three hours a day doing housework, while working men average seventeen minutes; working mothers spend fifty minutes a day exclusively with their children, while working fathers spend twelve minutes. On the other hand, husbands watch television an hour longer a day than their working wives and sleep a half-hour longer each night.[54]

In her 1989 book *The Second Shift,* Arlie Hochschild studied fifty working couples over the course of ten years, visiting them in their homes, observing them, trying to become as unobtrusive as the family dog. Her goal was to find out who really did what in the home. She found that nearly all the women in her sample were caught in the powerful and difficult bind of the second shift. They worked one shift at the office or factory and a second shift at home, a double burden that was straining them to their limit. These women are not unusual. Hochschild estimates that if you add together paid work, housework, and child care, American women work roughly fifteen hours longer each week than men. Over a year this adds up to an extra month of twenty-four-hour days.[55]

No wonder the women in *The Second Shift* talked intently about being overtired and emotionally drained. In Hochschild's words: "Many women I could not tear away from the topic of sleep. They talked about how much they could 'get by on.' . . . They talked about who they knew who needed more or less. Some apologized for how much sleep they needed. . . . They talked about how to avoid fully waking up when a child called them at night, and how to get back to sleep. These were women who talked about sleep the way a hungry person would talk about food."[56]

Lengthening Work Weeks

If children tend to be squeezed out when their moms are dealing with pink-collar stress and second shifts, their problems are exacerbated by changes in the economy that have increased the number of hours both mothers and fathers need to spend on the job.

Ironically, just twenty years ago we assumed that modern technology—computers, satellites, robotics—would make the American worker so much more efficient that income and GNP would rise while the work week withered away. In 1967, in testimony before a Senate subcommittee, a prominent economist predicted that by 1985 people would be working just twenty-two hours a week, or, alternatively, that they would retire at thirty-eight.[57]

In fact, due to global competitive pressures, Americans are working harder than ever. According to a recent study, the average work week jumped from under 41 hours in 1973 to nearly 47 hours in 1989.[58] In better-paying, more prestigious jobs, time demands have become even more onerous. Entrepreneurs in small businesses are now working 57.3 hours a week; professionals, 52.2 hours a week; and those with incomes over $50,000 a year 52.4 hours a week.[59] A 1988 survey by the *Wall Street Journal* found that 88 percent of senior executives work ten or more hours a day, and 18 percent work twelve hours or more. On average, top executives are working three hours a week more than they did ten years ago and are taking two fewer vacation days each year.[60] Interestingly enough, female executives now work longer hours than their male colleagues, averaging fifty-six hours a week compared with the men's fifty-four hours.[61]

Other, more impressionistic evidence also points to a lengthening of the workday. In August 1989 the *New York Times* reported a stunning 28 percent increase in ridership on the Metro-North Commuter Railroad between the hours of 6:00 and 7:00 in the morning, mainly due to the fact that "people seem to be putting in longer hours at the office."[62]

These long hours are not the result of some collective pathology—our offices and factories are not full of neurotics propelled by inner demons. Rather, there are some new and highly rational reasons why people are working this hard. Harvard sociologist Rosabeth Moss Kanter links the longer work week with "the nature of the workplace itself and how it has changed" in the deregulated, newly competitive environment of the 1980s.[63]

The most obvious pressure emanates from a new level of employment insecurity. The U.S. labor market has been in turmoil during much of the last decade. In an effort to become more competitive, hundreds of corporations have rushed to restructure—merging operations, purging employees, buying this company, selling off that division. In the space of four years, 1983–87, well over 2 million people saw their jobs disappear or deteriorate due to mergers and acquisitions. No industry is immune. The semiconductor industry, for example, a star performer in the early 1980s, laid off nearly 25,000 employees after losses of $2 billion in the mid-1980s. Overall, almost 12 million Americans lost their jobs in the 1980s.[64]

Clearly the threat of unemployment and the knowledge that

any new job is likely to involve a wage cut have led many employees to work longer hours in order to show how indispensable they are. In the words of one middle-level manager, "when you see people being laid off all around you, you'd have to be irrational not to put your nose to the grindstone."[65]

Another clear-cut consequence of restructuring is the loss of organizational "fat." As companies get leaner and meaner, a smaller number of people are expected to do the same amount of work. Tasks don't just go away when jobs are cut; the remaining workers just put in longer hours, something they are willing to do because they are afraid of being laid off themselves.

But employment insecurities and productivity speedup are only part of the story. The newly competitive environment has fundamentally altered the nature of work itself. According to Kanter, there has been a significant increase in the "lure of work."[66] In many corporations competitive pressures have produced a weakening of hierarchy and a broadening of participation in problem solving and decision making. The trend has been to empower workers at ever-lower levels of management so that they take initiative and try out new ideas. Middle-level managers now have the chance to collaborate in teams and help start up new ventures. And these new, more entrepreneurial ways of working are encouraged by compensation structures that emphasize performance bonuses and profit shares. The net result is a more challenging and more time-consuming workplace. Predetermined responsibilities and predictable hours seem to be things of the past.

A heavier work load and a longer work week are not, of course, burdens that companies simply impose on employees; at least at the management level, executives often want to invest themselves in more challenging work, especially given performance-based pay scales. For this new breed of corporate entrepreneurs, work is not grudging toil—many work hard because they love it, using the words *creative* and *exhilarating* to describe what they do during the day.[67]

But whether employees are eager or reluctant to work a fifty-five-hour week, the escalating time demands of the modern workplace can detract from the quality of family life. Life on the job not only takes huge chunks of time; it can use up enormous quantities of psychic and emotional energy. At least some of this time and attention used to be spent on spouse and children.

Charlie Heald* is a middle-level manager at the Irving Trust Company. According to Charlie, "ten years ago things were pretty cut-and-dried around here. You made loans to established clients, stuck to the rules, and went home at six o'clock." Since then Irving has been through a bruising takeover battle. Middle management has been cut in half and, in Charlie's words, "I've had to work my tail off to avoid getting the push." Charlie survived and is now part of a team that puts together deals in the corporate finance division. He earns much more than he used to and finds his work much more exciting than before. "Structuring and closing deals is a lot of fun, and it's great to get a piece of the upside . . . sure beats following a rule book." The only problem is that Charlie now works much longer hours and travels a great deal. He hasn't been home in time to eat dinner with his wife and daughters on a weekday evening in five months. The arrangement he has worked out with his family is the following: "I try to hold from ten P.M. Friday to five A.M. Monday to be home. I mean I can work in the den for a few hours Saturday morning but not be *gone* gone."[68]

*A pseudonym.

* * *

When Kanter asked successful executives what their accomplishments cost, their answers always included "gaining weight, getting a divorce, getting in trouble with the family."[69]

Increased challenge and increased time on the job is not just a managerial phenomenon. Many support workers face overload problems because of doing-more-with-less strategies. Cathy Collins works for a hospital that is attempting to shave costs by cutting back on administrative staff, which is one reason why her job now encompasses so many disparate functions.

Throughout the economy in so-called high-commitment workplaces, productivity-improvement efforts have offered factory and office workers the chance to contribute ideas and initiate change—characteristics that often go along with enhanced responsibility and longer hours. Again the idea is to empower workers by giving them greater independence and opportunity. Kanter looked at several thousand corporations with productivity-improvement programs and found that the most common strategies involved such approaches as eliminating layers of management, encouraging teamwork, and setting up performance-based pay scales.[70] Under these conditions blue- and pink-collar workers also experience greater work absorption and longer hours.

One of the best examples of a new high-productivity workplace is NUMMI (New United Motors Manufacturing, Inc.) in California, a joint venture of Toyota and General Motors. With the cooperation of the United Auto Workers Union, NUMMI has attempted to improve productivity by combining three strategies: forming partnerships between management and workers, restructuring to get leaner, and actively encouraging ideas from employees. Assembly work at

NUMMI is now done in teams, job classifications have been reduced to a minimum, and compensation is linked to performance.

The NUMMI workplace is imbued with excitement, enthusiasm, and a high level of voluntary after-hours participation. People arrive early at the plant to maintain their equipment or do calisthenics, and groups hold problem-solving meetings on their own time. Team members do not let their peers slack off or duck involvement. Longer hours spent at work or thinking about work are an inevitable consequence of these changes.[71]

This newly competitive and time-consuming job market can be seen in benign terms. When Kanter describes "the celebrated new breed of corporate entrepreneurs—in hot pursuit of new opportunities, dynamic, fast-moving and constantly innovating,"[72] it is obvious that modern-day managers lead exciting if overloaded lives. Or when she conjures up images of blue-collar workers doing aerobics in their high-commitment factories or offices, it seems clear that wage labor can be less alienating than it was a generation ago. For many people work has become attractive, even sexy. Is there anything wrong with more hours on the job if that is what people prefer to do with their time?

The rub comes with the children. The truly bad thing about fifty-hour work weeks is that when both mothers and fathers work these long hours, family life gets short shrift. Back in 1956 when William H. Whyte, Jr., wrote *The Organization Man*,[73] a celebrated study of the generation of managers then rising to power, Father was immersed in work but Mother was home devoting prime time to the children. She was available for the nurturing and catering tasks—making lunches and pediatrician appointments, taking children to Little League games and choir practice—but she also had time and energy

for those more difficult tasks of parenting that involve imposing limits, setting standards, and teaching values. It is strenuous, this business of being a responsible parent. The tasks
range from enforcing curfews and insisting that homework be
completed before bedtime to explaining why it is wrong to
pull the legs off a frog or laugh at a stuttering child.

Paul Leinberger recently interviewed the children of *The
Organization Man* and found some interesting differences between the generations.[74] In the 1980s both the sons and the
daughters of the original organization men were scrambling
up the corporate ladder, and these young managers worked
"much, much longer hours" than their fathers did. Think of
what this means for the grandchildren of *The Organization
Man*—the current generation of children. Compared to their
parents' generation, they face a huge parenting deficit: most
of them see much less of their fathers and mothers than children did in the 1950s.

Fallout on Children

Research in the field has uncovered ominous links between
these absentee working parents and a whole range of emotional and behavioral problems among children.

One obvious consequence of both parents at work is the
latchkey kid syndrome—children in the house alone during
those long, lonely after-school hours. A 1989 study that surveyed five thousand eighth-grade students in the San Diego
and Los Angeles areas found that the more hours children
took care of themselves after school, the greater the risk of
substance abuse. In fact, latchkey children as a group were
twice as likely to drink alcohol and take drugs as children who
were under the supervision of adults after school. The study

found that the increased risk of substance abuse held true regardless of the child's sex, race, family income, academic performance, or number of resident parents.[75]

One surprising finding of this Southern California study is that it is white children from affluent homes who spend the largest number of hours on their own each week. Kids from upper-income families seem more likely to have fathers and mothers who invest long hours in their careers, coming home at seven or eight o'clock, tired and preoccupied. Brandy Page and her friends at Pali High fit right into this category of privileged youngsters who have very little contact with their parents.

Sometime in the 1970s American parents discovered a "magic bullet" that helped them feel better about the mounting time pressures in their lives: it was called "quality time." In their 1987 book *Quality Parenting,* Linda Albert and Michael Popkin assured Moms and Dads that by working hard at the content and caliber of their interaction with their children, parents could transform ordinary moments into encounters that, like "a healthy diet high in natural foods and vitamins . . . sustains the kids throughout the day"[76] when they had to be busy elsewhere. An appealing idea—the only problem is that most parents find it almost impossible to conjure up these sustaining encounters at the end of a stress-filled working day.

Cathy Collins did not work that late, but when she got home to her split-level house in Teaneck we know that she was exhausted and tension-filled from a job that was particularly high on the stress scale. Cathy's parenting energies were further compromised by the fact that her evenings were filled with household chores, which made it especially difficult to produce good time for her children. In her research Arlie Hochschild found that working mothers are often driven to do several things at once as they juggle housework and children in the crowded evening hours of the second shift. She describes women writing checks while returning phone calls, doing a load of laundry while keeping an eye on the three-year-old, peeling potatoes while going over a spelling test with the nine-year-old. If you have ever tried to combine these tasks (and most working moms have), you will know how frustrated a three- or nine-year-old can become dealing with, and depending on, half the attention of a weary, irritable mother. The three-year-old is screamed at for taking the top off the bleach container; the nine-year-old is scolded for allowing water to spill on her spelling sheet; and both children retreat behind slammed bedroom doors.

There is no need to belabor the point. It seems clear that overload, exhaustion, and strain do not make for good parenting, and yet these qualities are part and parcel of mainstream American family life now that there are so many dual-worker and single-parent households. An even more intractable set of problems center on the psychological contradictions posed by high-achieving, professional parents.

The Good Professional Versus the Good Parent

The hard-edged personality traits cultivated by many successful professionals—control, decisiveness, aggression, efficiency—can be directly at odds with the passive, patient, selfless elements of good nurturing. The last thing a three-year-old or a thirteen-year-old needs at eight o'clock in the evening is a mother or father who marches into the house in his or her power suit, barking orders, looking and sounding like a Prussian general.

Consider the contrasts in the following list:

A. QUALITIES NEEDED TO SUCCEED IN CHOSEN CAREER	B. QUALITIES NEEDED TO MEET NEEDS OF CHILD
1. Long hours and one's best energy.	1. Time to be together as a family and energy for the hard tasks of parenting.
2. Mobility.	2. Stability.
3. A prime commitment to oneself.	3. Selflessness and a commitment to others.
4. Efficiency.	4. A tolerance for chaos.
5. A controlling attitude.	5. An ability to let go.
6. A drive for high performance.	6. An acceptance of difference and failure.
7. Orientation toward the future.	7. Appreciation of the moment.
8. A goal-oriented, time-pressured approach to the task at hand.	8. An ability to tie the same pair of shoelaces twenty-nine times with patience and humor.[77]

Not all high achievers display all of the traits in column A and not all good parents possess all of the traits in column B, but most professionals and most parents will recognize themselves in a handful of categories. It seems that the aptitudes, skills, and talents people hone to be successful professionals may well backfire when they assume the role of parent. As *Fortune* magazine warned in a January 1990 issue, "don't think that your brains, money or success will pave the way to parenting glory . . . the intensity and single-mindedness that make for corporate achievement are often the opposite of the qualities needed to be an effective parent."[78]

The struggle to stretch across the family/work divide can be painful and fraught with failure for both parent and child. It is one thing to pound home at seven o'clock in the evening and somehow find the time to help a child with a math assignment; it is something else entirely to put together the energy and the attitudes that enable one to be a constructive presence at this point in the day. High-powered parents often find it difficult to switch gears, to abandon the take-charge, critical sensibility that has been the driving force all day at the office and replace it with patience or humor. According to Susan Davies Bloom, a Connecticut family therapist, "professionals are so accustomed to functioning at a high level of control at the office that when they get home, they try to exert the same kind of control."[79]

In the old days, when the organization man was alive and well, the father, who had the most highly developed marketplace skills, was buffered by the mother, who had the time and the motivation to develop child-raising skills. Not so anymore. Both sexes now need to develop their marketability. Families increasingly need a second income, and society increasingly values paid work above homemaking and child-raising. A woman's training and current job responsibilities may do little to prepare her for parenthood; indeed, her career skills and those of her husband might be antagonistic to the needs of their children. It becomes tempting for high-achieving parents to avoid the challenges of parenting by ignoring or appeasing a child. Some use junk food and television; others, like Dr. Joseph Page, use fancy cars.

Psychologist Lynne McClure argues that at least some of a modern executive's immersion in work represents an attempt to escape problems at home: "If your marriage is breaking up, if you're not quite sure what's expected of you as a parent . . .

"Pleasant dreams, Billy, and here's Daddy with one
of your favorite bedtime stories."

Drawing by Bernard Schoenbaum; © 1989 The New Yorker Magazine, Inc.

where do you turn for a measure of stability and support?
To your job of course." One of her clients, Larry Iwan, an
executive at the Easton Corp., concedes that "my wife says that
I put in so much time at work because that's where I get
stroked."[80]

If the newly competitive job market requires a business
manager to put in fifty hours a week, ineptitude or failure on
the family front might well cause that manager to volunteer
another eight or ten. This process obviously feeds on itself:
once a parent is working fifty-five to sixty hours a week, it

becomes even harder to make a good connection with a child—or a spouse, for that matter.

Workaholism *à deux* has become an increasingly common pattern in the professional echelons of society: "Life at the office comes first for both partners, life at home is uniformly second best and relegated to paid help." These parents muddle through. Small children are enrolled in day care and after-school programs, teenagers are left in self-care, housecleaners are hired, laundry is sent out, pizza is ordered in. "What we're doing is contracting out for family care," says Peter Morrison, a demographer at the Rand Corporation, "but there's a limit. If you contract out everything, you have an enterprise, not a family."[81] Children tend not to thrive in enterprise households.

Hallmark now markets greeting cards for overcommitted professional parents who find it difficult to actually see their children. "Have a super day at school," chirps one card, meant to be left under the Cheerios in the morning. "I wish I were there to tuck you in," says another, designed to peek out from behind the pillow at night.

Divorce and Father Absence

While the well-being of middle-class children is being compromised by a new and more rigorous set of work pressures, it is also jeopardized by escalating divorce rates and a sharp increase in father-absent households. Fifteen million American children—one-quarter of all children under eighteen—are now growing up with little or no contact with their fathers. Father absence is twice as common as it was a generation ago, and there is no relief on the horizon. In 1970, 12 percent of children lived with their mothers alone; by 1988 this figure had reached 24 percent.[82]

Of the 15 million children without fathers, some 10 million are the product of marital separation and divorce and close to 5 million are the product of out-of-wedlock births.[83] As we saw in chapter 2, out-of-wedlock births are still primarily concentrated in the poor, black population. Divorce, on the other hand, crosses class lines with impunity and now wreaks havoc in children's lives throughout society. In 1950 one out of every six marriages ended in divorce; in 1987 the figure was one out of two.

Despite our new familiarity with marital breakdown, it remains a major trauma for the divorcing couple and, especially, for their children. Over the last decade research by Lenore Weitzman, Judith Wallerstein, Frank Furstenberg, and others has shown that the effects of divorce on children are unexpectedly profound and long-lasting. Not only does divorce place children at a considerable economic disadvantage, but marital disruption—and the near-disappearance of the father—triggers severe emotional and educational problems. Divorce seems capable of derailing a child's progress in school and is often the "single most important cause of enduring pain in a child's life."[84]

All the evidence shows the financial repercussions of divorce on children to be extremely serious. The economic harm to children from parental divorce revolves around the fact that fathers generally earn a good deal more than mothers, but in 90 percent of divorce cases children remain with their mothers. Noncustodial fathers are, of course, expected to contribute their share to the costs of raising a child by paying child support to the mother, but a substantial number of divorcing men (41 percent) walk away without a child support agreement. Even when there is an agreement in place, child support payments tend to be low and unreliable. Despite increasingly tough child support enforcement laws, a recent Bureau of the Census survey found that only 51 percent of mothers who were entitled to child support received the full amount, 25 percent received partial payment, and 23 percent received nothing at all.[85]

A poignant example of the low priority the legal system and divorced men attach to children is contained in a survey of child-support practices in Denver. This study found that two-thirds of the fathers were ordered by the courts to pay less for child support than they reported paying on monthly car payments. While most were current on their car payments, more than half were delinquent in their child-support payments.[86] Nationwide, $4.6 billion dollars is owed by fathers to the children of divorce.[87]

Compounding the problems of collection is the low level of child support awards. In 1987 the average amount of child support paid to a divorced woman and her children was $2,710 a year.[88] Even if this sum were paid regularly, it covers less than a quarter of the average costs of raising one child.

Inadequate child support combines with low female earnings (mothers with dependent children earn, on average, 46 percent of the male wage)[89] to produce a situation in which the income of ex-wives and their dependent children plummets after divorce. Women's standard of living drops, on average, 30 percent in the five years after divorce, while men's rises 8 percent.[90] The drop is sharpest for women and children in families that were relatively well off before divorce.

A dramatic expression of the heavy financial burdens borne by divorced mothers is the rapid jump in the incidence of moonlighting. The number of women holding two or more jobs quintupled between 1970 and 1989. Most of these women are divorced or never-married mothers who are driven to "take two jobs because it is the only way to eke out a working-class life and stay above the poverty line." Patricia Keammerer is typical. A recently divorced mother of a ten-year-old girl, she gets by by holding three jobs. Her main job is working as an administrative assistant in the Harrisburg, Pennsylvania, school system, but she also works two nights a week and every other weekend at a fabric store. In addition, she manages forty-one investment properties from her home in her spare time. She moonlights, she says, so that her daughter, Sara, can live in the same neighborhood and attend the same school as she did before the divorce.[91]

While the economic fallout of divorce on children has received widespread public attention, the emotional and educational consequences are less well known. There is, however, a great deal of new evidence showing that the breakup of a marriage can trigger severe emotional and intellectual problems for children, many of which center on the fact that the children of divorce see very little of their fathers. For all the talk about the new nurturing American father, the reality for many youngsters is quite the opposite: the disappearing father who abandons his children financially—and emotionally.

The data show minimal contact between noncustodial fathers and their offspring in the wake of divorce. University of Pennsylvania sociologists Frank Furstenberg and Kathleen Mullan Harris followed a representative national sample of one thousand children from disrupted families between 1976 and 1987 and found that 42 percent had not seen their fathers at all during the previous year. Only 20 percent had slept over at the father's house in the previous month, and only 1 in 6 saw their fathers once a week or more.[92] According to Furstenberg, "men regard marriage as a package deal. . . . they cannot separate their relations with their children from their relations to their former spouse. When that relationship ends the paternal bond usually withers."[93]

For most children the partial or complete loss of a father

produces long-lasting feelings of betrayal, rejection, rage, guilt, and pain. Wallerstein shows how children yearn for their fathers in the years after divorce, and how this longing is infused with new intensity at adolescence. For girls the peak years are early adolescence, twelve to fifteen; for boys the need for a father crests somewhat later, at ages sixteen to eighteen.[94] According to psychiatrist Alfred Messer, "father hunger" among boys can be traumatic and often produces "sleep disturbances, such as trouble falling asleep, nightmares and night terrors."[95] Even frequent contact between noncustodial father and child doesn't fill the emotional void. In her upper-middle-class sample, Wallerstein finds many children who have considerable contact with their fathers; nevertheless, three out of four of these children still "feel rejected by their fathers."[96]

Of course, there are success stories: examples of children who make healthy adjustments and cases where divorce is better for children than a severely troubled marriage. But the scholarly evidence increasingly confirms that divorce—and father absence—can lead to serious emotional damage.

Divorce seems to be an important factor in teenage suicide, which has tripled over the last twenty-five years and is now the second leading cause of death in the fifteen-to-twenty-four-year-old age group. A study of 752 families by researchers at the New York Psychiatric Institute found that youngsters who attempted suicide differed little from those who didn't in terms of age, income, race, and religion, but were much more likely "to live in non-intact family settings" and to have minimal contact with the father.[97] Divorce and father absence play a role in the entire range of psychological troubles. A 1989 survey of teenagers discharged from psychiatric hospitals found that fully 84 percent were living in disrupted families when they were admitted.[98] Indeed, the research shows that in nations as diverse as Finland and South Africa, anywhere from 50 to 80 percent of psychiatric patients come from broken homes.[99]

Fathers play a particularly important role in preventing drug use. According to a 1988 UCLA study, although "mothers are more active than fathers in helping youngsters with personal problems . . . with regard to youthful drug use, father's involvement is more important." Among homes with strict fathers, only 18 percent of children used alcohol or drugs. In contrast, among single-mother homes, 35 percent of children used drugs frequently.[100]

But a child doesn't have to end up in a psychiatric hospital, or strung out on drugs to suffer the emotional fallout of divorce. Some of the psychic consequences are much more subtle. Wallerstein talks about the "sleeper" effects of marital disruption, problems of commitment and attachment that may surface many years after parental divorce. According to Wallerstein, when it comes to forming relationships in adult life, "it helps enormously to have imprinted on one's emotional circuitry the patterning of a successful, enduring relationship between a man and a woman."[101] This is precisely what most children of divorce lack.

Becky Kraus is a case in point. "It's just very hard to think you can deal with having children of your own if you come from divorced parents," Becky told me one memorable evening in the fall of 1988. "There's, like, so much pain—for the children and for the parents too. I totally understand how hard single motherhood can be because I have seen my mother struggle."

"But Becky," I protested, "you needn't repeat your mother's history. Why do you think you have to have children on your own?"

Becky looked at me, amused and indulgent. "It would be

great to get married and lived happily ever after and all that," she said. "But, don't you see, I have never seen a relationship up close that lasted, so why should it be different for me? Nearly all the adults I know are divorced, most of them more than once."

Becky was in an expansive mood and wanted to share some of her hopes and fears: "You know, every so often I think that maybe there is a way for me to have kids. If I can manipulate the pain I have felt and use all the bad experiences I had growing up to create a truly beautiful family. You see I should know what to avoid.

"I sometimes dream of marrying an architect, moving to New Mexico, and building a beautiful home together in the desert. We would have four children and cherish them together." Becky's voice lingered on the word *cherish.* She giggled. "But then I would wake up and realize that my husband would most probably leave me, and I would be stuck in some desert with four kids!"

I wanted to know more about Becky's dream. "What are the critical ingredients in your beautiful family?" I asked.

"Two parents together," said Becky without hesitation. "That is the most important thing. . . . I guess I would like my children to take some basic things for granted: parents they can trust and depend on; a home they can be safe in; three meals a day; maybe even a backyard." Becky sounded wistful. "I never had this kind of normal stuff."[102]

In addition to weighty emotional consequences, there is mounting evidence that marital disruption and father absence contribute to educational underperformance and failure.

Two-parent families seem to make for better students than do one-parent families. To cite a report by the National Association of Elementary School Principals: "One-parent children, on the whole, show lower achievement in school than their two-parent peers. Among all two-parent children 30% were ranked as high achievers, compared to only 17% of one-parent children. At the other end of the scale the situation is reversed. 23% of two-parent children were low achievers— while fully 38% of the one-parent children fell into this category."[103]

The scholarly literature supports these findings. A survey carried out by Columbia University and Bowling Green State University comparing the SAT scores of 295 students from father-absent homes with those of 760 students from father-present homes found that father absence had a "dramatic" negative effect on scores, a result that could not be explained away by differences in income.[104] And in a study of 2,500 young men and women, Sheila Fitzgerald Krein and Andrea Beller found that "even after taking into account the lower income of single-parent families, the absence of a father has a significant negative effect on the educational attainment of boys."[105] These effects persist regardless of race. Psychologist Norma Radin has shown that, among blacks, children in father-present homes show a clear tendency to outperform children in father-absent homes by the late elementary years.[106]

Father absence reduces both math and verbal skills, but math skills suffer the most. Lyn Carlsmith of Yale University believes that this strong link between absentee fathers and lower math scores in children is due to the fact that men tend to excel at quantitative skills and are often able to help children develop the thinking skills that lead to success in mathematics.[107]

We are left with the conviction that *a father's contribution to family life goes way beyond his paycheck.* All of this research linking father absence to psychological stress, drug use, cognitive deficits, and poor performance in school serves to underscore a basic theme of this book: America's shortfall in human resources is intimately linked to its overburdened and fragile families. Specifically, the decline in American educational performance over the past generation—which is most pronounced in science and mathematics—seems to be directly related to the rapid increase in the number of father-absent households. School failure may well have as much to do with the disintegration of families as with the quality of schools.

Consider the connection between absentee or preoccupied parents and TV viewing, homework, and academic performance. The Nielsen surveys show that contemporary children watch twice as much television as their parents did. The average child now spends more time watching television than attending class, and a third of all school-age children are still watching TV at eleven o'clock in the evening.[108] At the same time there has been a dramatic decrease in the amount of homework done by children, a falloff that is linked to declining test scores. Fifteen years ago high school students did ten hours of homework a week; by the late 1980s that figure had fallen to five hours a week. At least 20 percent of all high school students now flatly refuse to do any homework at all![109]

What is behind this decline in homework? Most analysts lay the blame on overburdened single or working parents who are too busy to monitor television viewing or supervise homework.

The Scapegoat of Maternal Employment

In the scholarly literature much of the discussion of the problems of middle-class children has focused on maternal employment, and experts have tended to line up in opposing camps, either blaming or exonerating women. Conservatives have marshaled evidence that purports to show the harmful effects of maternal employment on the development of children,[110] and liberals have assembled data that attempt to demonstrate that the "employment status" of mothers has no effect on the life chances of children.[111] There are, of course, hidden agendas on both sides of the ideological divide. Traditionalists on the right would like to re-create an era where "Father Knows Best" and mother is at home taking care of the family. Progressives on the left are committed to equal treatment and have not wanted to fan the flames of maternal guilt by suggesting that full-blooded careers for women are anything but a societal blessing. How can we be critical of women's quest for economic opportunity? How can we encourage women to accept second-class status in the labor market for the sake of the children?

So much emotional and ideological baggage has been brought to this debate that scholars who cross the Rubicon into enemy territory (as Jay Belsky did when he published his findings on negative outcomes for infants when both parents work) find themselves viciously attacked by colleagues.[112] So far, the controversy has served mostly to obscure the fact that the plight of our children is not solely or even mainly a woman's issue. Global competitive pressures, falling wages, deteriorating social supports, and absentee fathers all contribute to the deepening parenting deficit in our society. In particular, these ideological skirmishes have tended to camouflage the fact that men are at least as much to blame for the parental time famine as are women.

In our preoccupation with maternal employment and the retreat of the traditional homemaker, we tend to forget that over the last thirty years there has been a truly dramatic decline in men's involvement in the lives of their children. Demographers Peter Uhlenberg and David Eggebeen calculate that the average number of years men (aged twenty to forty-nine) spend in families where children live has dropped 40 percent, falling from 12.3 years in 1960 to just 7 years in 1980.[113] This reduction in time spent living with children owes something to later marriage and lower fertility rates, but is mostly a result of the sharp increase in divorce rates. The grim truth is that in the wake of divorce most men cease to have much to do with their children.

There is no one recipe for raising children. The feelings that parents themselves bring to the role—their pleasure in parenting, their respect for the child—are clearly important. Jerome Kagan says that precisely how a parent feeds an infant, hugs a toddler, or interacts with a teenager is less important than "the melody those actions comprise."[114] Even more critical is ensuring adequate time. If a divorced father hasn't seen his son in six weeks, or if a mother holds down two jobs, it's hard to be a constructive presence in a child's life. Melodies cannot work their magic unless they are given time and space. Child raising is not a mysterious process. A child simply does better with loving, sustained, systematic attention from both Mom and Dad.

It is time to shift the focus away from maternal employment, to abandon the increasingly useless debate over whether or not women should work. The economic data presented in chapter 2 make it abundantly clear that most wives and mothers have no choice but to join the paid labor force. In 1991 what matters are the terms and conditions of employment for both men and women.

The good news is that there are ways of relieving the time pressure on working parents—of reducing pink-collar stress and combating lengthening work weeks—without returning to a 1950s homemaker/breadwinner model. In chapter 8 I will discuss "sequencing" and show how parents can seek to "do it all" over the course of a lifetime instead of all at once. I will also describe flexible ways of organizing work loads and work schedules so as to give working parents a significant degree of discretion over how, when, and where their work is performed. Such family-friendly work options are increasingly acceptable to the private sector.

Reducing the degree to which men abandon children in the wake of divorce is a much more complicated issue. The economic dimension of this problem is the easiest to tackle. As I shall demonstrate in chapter 8, it is possible to design a more stringent child-support system that better protects the interests of the child. Much harder is increasing the amount of time a divorced father spends with his children, an issue that cannot be glossed over since "fathers play difficult to replace roles in the emotional, moral and intellectual development of their children."[115] As we now understand, time and attention are at least as important as money in the child-raising enterprise.

Joint custody might help, as might more generous visitation rights for noncustodial parents, but, as Wallerstein shows in her work, there is no real substitute for the rhythms and rituals of daily life. All the visitation in the world doesn't seem to stop the children of divorce from yearning for their fathers—which brings us to a difficult question. Are we ready to reduce the number of fatherless children by constraining rights to divorce and discouraging out-of-wedlock births? Such a move would undoubtedly encroach upon those individual rights and private freedoms Americans have come to hold so dear.

So we come to the crux of the matter. We can and should design family-friendly workplaces, make career trajectories less hostile to child-raising, and reform our divorce laws to better protect children and the institution of marriage; but *there is a price to pay.* The fact is parenthood involves a great deal of adult self-sacrifice. Children are no longer the economic assets they once were on the family farm. In the modern world raising a family is an extremely expensive proposition. But beyond these economic costs, responsible parenthood involves the expenditure of a great deal of energy and effort. Done properly it is a noisy, exhausting, joyous business that uses up a chunk of one's best energy and taps into prime time. Well-developing children dramatically limit personal freedom and seriously interfere with the pursuit of an ambitious career. When psychiatrist David Guttmann talks about the "routine, unexamined heroism of parenting," he is describing the manifold ways dedicated parents "surrender their own claims to personal omnipotentiality" in the wake of childbirth, conceding these instead to the new child.[116] At bottom, there are real trade-offs between adult fulfillment and the welfare of children.

It is extremely hard to face up to these truths. In progressive circles it has been particularly tempting to imagine that we can "fix" our kids by supporting a child-care bill or hitting absconding fathers with more onerous child-support obligations. And spending more money on children is extremely important. As we saw in chapter 2, enhanced public resources are clearly central to resolving the problems of poor children. Fatima and Brian cannot begin to build coherent lives until they and their families have access to a home, to medical care, and to education. Benefits and services are also relevant to a middle-class child. If Becky had had access to an after-school program, she would not have had to deal with the loneliness of being a latchkey kid. More and better social supports may not be as critical to a middle-class family as to a poor family, but they matter.

For the majority of youngsters, however, it's not just a question of allocating more dollars. In a 1989 survey when

1,500 schoolchildren were asked, "What do you think makes a happy family?" the youngsters "did not list money, cars, fine homes or televisions"; instead they answered, "doing things together."[117] If we really want to do something about this monster of neglect and failure among our children, we need to address directly the parental time famine. This clearly involves underwriting parenting leave, enforcing child-support obligations, and designing clever strategies that alter the rules of the game—both in the workplace and in our divorce laws. But it is equally clear that none of these policies or programs will get to first base unless we move children up the scale of adult priorities.

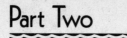
Part Two

Devaluing Our Children

4

Private Choices:
Looking Out for
Number One

Nancy smiled at both [the children] and set down her fork. "Ron and I have something we want to share with you," she said softly.

"It's taken us a long time to face up to this, but you two are just not the right children for us. It's not your fault, any more than it is ours. Please try to understand. You're a constant source of aggravation—the mess, the endless clutter and noise and confusion and hostility. It makes for a stifling atmosphere for mine and Ron's relationship. We're all the time being parents, we don't have time to grow. I choose not to accept that."

Ron took Nancy's hand. "I don't know if our marriage can survive your adolescence," he said. "We've come to a decision. We have to do what's best for us. We're going to sell you."

Ron and Nancy decided to work out this change in the family through *The Family Place,* a private agency upstairs from Wings 'n' Things. "Our society still attaches some guilt to the idea of selling kids, but not so much as in the past," said Bart, the counselor at TFP. "There's been this gradual demystification of blood

relationships, which is allowing people to admit openly what was
known all along, that some work and some don't.''

"That's interesting. How does it affect the kids?'' Ron asked.

"We're finding more and more that an outright cash sale actually boosts a child's self-esteem. I mean, for a lot of kids, this is
exactly what they need—we handled a fat boy last week who went
for almost $300,000. Eight years old. That really changed that
kid's whole . . . ''

"Three hundred? For one little fatty?'' Nancy was stunned.

TFP placed the children with a younger couple named Scott
and Lainie for $185,000 (Randy and Sue were a little older than
what the market wanted, and Randy had bad skin). Scott was the
heir to an insect-repellent fortune, and he and Lainie owned a big
ranch, La Bamba, in the Crisco Mountains a hundred miles from
the city, where the kids would have horses, a Porsche, their own
bunkhouse.

Saying goodbye wasn't easy. Sue asked, "Can we come and
visit on weekends?'' as the cab honked, and Ron and Nancy cried
and promised to feed Gipper the guppy, and Randy said, "Take
care of yourselves, you two. Have a good life.'' Ron and Nancy
both felt an incredible emptiness for days afterward.

But slowly Ron and Nancy rediscovered some basic values
from earlier in their marriage, such as self-expression and having
fun. . . . One spring they went to a little resort in Biafra which
nobody had ever been to or heard of, a gorgeous deserted penin-
sula where they spent three weeks in pure silence eating only bok
choy and something like rutabagas, and they came back deeply
emerged in selfhood in ways they couldn't explain.[1]

I s Garrison Keillor attempting here to conjure up the Rea-
gans by calling his protagonists Ron and Nancy? Whatever the
political connections, we all recognize the message behind this

not-so-charming, tongue-in-cheek story: adult rights to self-fulfillment may well have gotten out of hand in contemporary America. We might not quite be ready to sell our children, but we are almost there. In San Antonio, Texas, a father obtains a unilateral divorce and blithely deserts his two small children; in Baton Rouge, Louisiana, a middle-class couple parks a troublesome fourteen-year-old in a psychiatric facility; in East Harlem, a pregnant teenager chooses to give birth to a pain-racked crack baby; and in communities around the nation, eight-year-old latchkey children come home from school and tune in to "Geraldo." The topic up for discussion might be "Teens Trade Sex for Dope" or "Children Who Kill Their Children," but, what the heck, this is a free society and neither parents nor government cares what children watch on television anymore.

These are not random or isolated events; rather, they reflect a profound shift in private and public morality. In recent years the balance in our society has tilted dramatically toward free choice and self-realization—for adults. Children have pretty much been left to fend for themselves.

Government has gotten out of the business of telling us how to live. Our legal system has given up on the idea that marriage should be a binding, lifelong commitment and that parents should take enduring responsibility for their children. Adults can now live with whomever they want for as long as they want; they can also abort or abandon babies and bear children in or out of wedlock. Indeed, individual Americans can pretty much do anything that tickles their fancy without fear that the state will step in and constrain their freedom "for the sake of the children."

If government no longer uses the touchstone of child welfare to adjudicate personal relationships, it is increasingly reluctant to intervene in the marketplace on behalf of children.

In the early 1980s Ronald Reagan decided that the American public would best be served by deregulating the television industry, so he went ahead and dismantled controls on programming. This is why hot-and-heavy talk shows like "Geraldo" and "Oprah Winfrey" are available to schoolchildren in the afternoon. Ten years ago these programs would not have been allowed on the air in the late afternoon hours because in 1981 the Federal Communications Commission (FCC) still controlled the degree to which the networks expose young children to sex and violence. In a similar spirit George Bush has refused to regulate day-care centers. In his opinion this type of regulation inhibits supply and interferes unnecessarily with the proper workings of the market. When pitted against the needs of consumers or producers, children increasingly lose out.

But we are not just talking about the rules and regulations of our society—how we weigh the welfare of children in our divorce laws and at the FCC; we are also talking about the allocation of public resources. As I shall discuss in chapter 5, children are being shortchanged on at least two fronts. In recent years we have cut taxes and reduced the amount of money we spend on children—to a paltry 1.1 percent of GNP.[2] At the same time we have increased the national debt by a factor of three. In other words we have pumped up adult living standards while dumping onto the backs of our children an enormous mountain of IOUs—a profound act of fiscal irresponsibility which fits right in with the self-indulgent mood of the day.

Which brings us to a key issue. The American government did not wake up one morning and decide to shaft children. Government is not some disembodied, alien force. In a democracy, it is comprised of elected representatives whose job it is to carry out the will of the people. If we are revamping the rules of the legal game and reordering our fiscal priorities so as to tilt the balance away from children and toward adults, we can rest assured that these new policies reflect a shift in what ordinary Americans deem important. We can't, in any simple-minded fashion, blame the plight of our children on George Bush or Congress. If the government is abdicating its role as protector of children, we all have to take at least a little personal responsibility. The fact is a new and frightening level of self-absorption is loose in the land.

The Search for Self-Fulfillment

In the late 1960s Americans began their modern quest for personal growth and self-realization. Some were fleeing the cloying domesticity of the "feminine mystique"; others were retreating from the political turmoil of the civil rights struggle and the antiwar movement. Whatever the motive force, millions of adult Americans turned inward and started focusing on their own needs and desires. Psychic self-improvement became chic, and books with titles such as *Looking Out for Number One, Pulling Your Own Strings,* and *How to Be Your Own Best Friend* sold like hotcakes. A whole generation became newly determined to consume every dish on the smorgasbord of human experience.

In *Habits of the Heart* sociologist Robert Bellah and his co-authors describe how the values and goals of psychotherapy became central in this modern quest for personal fulfillment.[3] According to Bellah, starting around 1965 a new "therapeutic mentality" took root in our culture. It shows itself most clearly in the relationship between psychotherapists and their patients, but the language and attitudes of therapy now resonate throughout the American middle class.

The therapeutic mentality focuses on the self, rather than on a set of external obligations. It encourages an individual to find and assert his or her true self, and to define this as the only source of genuine relationships to other people. External obligations, whether to parents, children, or religion, are to be severely limited because they interfere with a person's capacity for self-love and relatedness. In its purest form, the therapeutic mentality denies all forms of duty or commitment in relationships, replacing these values with the ideal of full, open, honest communication among self-actualized individuals. Like the classic obligation of client to therapist, the only requirement for the therapeutically liberated lover or spouse is to share feelings fully with his or her partner.

There are some obvious problems with the therapeutic mentality. It may liberate individuals by helping them get in touch with their own needs and wants "freed from artificial constraints and guilt-inducing demands,"[4] but it does not bode well for children who need the sustained support of their parents. Perhaps in some utopian adult world, love should mean the full exchange of feelings between authentic selves, not enduring commitments resting on binding obligations. But in the real world of 2:00 A.M. feedings, homework, and mortgage payments, no marriage can last and no child can flourish without adults living up to at least some of these guilt-inducing demands.

Christopher Lasch believes that in late-twentieth-century America, therapy has replaced religion in providing the core values in adult lives. As he puts it, "even when therapists speak of the need for 'meaning' and 'love,' they define love and meaning simply as the fulfillment of the patient's emotional requirements. It hardly occurs to them . . . to encourage the subject to subordinate his needs and interests to those of others, to someone or some cause or tradition outside himself."

In Lasch's bitter words, mental health has come to mean "the overthrow of inhibitions and the immediate gratification of every impulse." He quotes Woody Allen in the movie *Sleeper*: "I believe in sex and death."[5]

Not so very long ago love meant submission to a higher loyalty. Men and women toiled for their family, fought for their country, or fasted for their God. This kind of love was intermingled with selflessness, even self-sacrifice. But these old-fashioned notions strike the therapeutic sensibility as oppressive nonsense, guaranteed to get in the way of personal goals and private pleasures. Indeed, many post-Freudian therapists deliberately set out to "liberate" their patients from such outmoded ideas and obligations.

What is extraordinary about this therapeutic mentality, this cultivation of self in contemporary America, is that it is not confined to a few bold spirits or an elite class. Several studies show that the search for self-fulfillment is a grass-roots phenomenon involving the majority of all adults. Surveys by Yankelovich, Skelly, and White show that by the late 1970s, 63 percent of Americans were spending a great deal of time thinking about themselves and their inner lives,[6] and in the mid-1980s Bellah and his colleagues found therapeutic language "extremely prevalent" in mainstream, middle-class America.[7]

Obviously, not everyone has become a true believer. At least some of those self-actualized people contemplating their innermost desires have enough residual religious sense, or old-fashioned family loyalty, to be caught between the ideals of duty and freedom. But while adult commitment to the therapeutic mentality is less than complete, priorities have undoubtedly shifted so as to give greater weight to the self.

Which brings us to the critical matter of what newly self-absorbed adults do (or don't do) for children. To use a concept developed by Daniel Yankelovich in his 1981 book *New Rules,* in recent years the "giving-getting compact" in our society has changed radically.[8] As a result of the therapeutic mentality, Americans are struggling in novel ways with the issue of what they should give to and what they can hope to get out of their marriages, their children, their jobs, their lives. As recently as the 1950s the giving-getting compact would have been summarized this way: I give the fruits of my labors to my family. I give loyalty and steadfastness. I swallow my frustrations and suppress any impulse to do what I would enjoy; instead, I do what is expected of me. In return, I get the respect of my family because I bring home the bacon or keep up the house. The respect of the community because I strive to live up to the ideal of breadwinner husband or home-maker wife.

As Yankelovich points out, respectability can be a relentless taskmaster. It has never been easy to be a *mensch*—to drag one's frail body to some boring job every day of the year, to mop the same floors or make the same beds endlessly. Willy Loman's son Biff in *Death of a Salesman* (1949) gives vent to a typically male complaint: "It's a measly manner of existence. To get on that subway on the hot mornings in summer. To devote your whole life to keeping stock or making phone calls, or selling or buying. To suffer fifty weeks of the year for the sake of a two-week vacation, when all you really desire is to be outdoors with your shirt off."[9] Women had their own problems. Many of the bright, smiling housewives of the 1950s were up to their eyeballs in frustration and wanted nothing more than to break free of their doll's houses and get on with their own lives. In her 1963 book *The Feminine Mystique* Betty Friedan told us that "the very condition of being a housewife can create a sense of emptiness, non-existence, nothingness, in women." In her view, most housework "can be capably handled by a eight-year-old child."[10]

Times have clearly changed for both men and women. Our new therapeutic sensibilities have dramatically diminished our enthusiasm for self-denial, delayed gratification, and other *mensch*-like behavior patterns. Sacrifice is out of style, and future orientation is for the birds. The current getting-giving compact reads as follows: I give time, energy, resources to a relationship as long as my needs are fulfilled, as long as I am stroked. If I become unhappy (or just plain bored), I have every right to move on to seek what I need elsewhere.

This modern version of the getting-giving compact has dire implications for children. In this brave new world it has become much more acceptable for a parent to off-load, or abandon, a child. As I explained in chapter 3, almost half of all divorced fathers fail to see their children, and two-thirds fail to support them. This new level of negligence is tied up with changes in our divorce laws and the advent of easy "no-fault" divorce.

No-Fault, No-Responsibility Divorce

Over the last twenty years there have been profound changes in the laws that govern divorce in practically every Western country. It is now widely accepted that men and women have the right to expect a happy marriage, and that if a marriage does not work out, no one has to stay trapped. Divorce is increasingly seen as "morally neutral, just another option—a life choice no better or worse than staying married."[11] In most advanced democracies, governments have gotten out of the business of enforcing marriage as a lifelong contractual commitment. According to a report by a British Law Commission, "society has no special interest in permanently maintaining the legal shell of a marriage that has failed, and the role of the law in such cases is to manage the dissolution process with the minimum human cost."[12] Throughout the Western world, divorce has become much less laden with societal disapproval and legal fault, but in the States these changes have been particularly radical. In the words of Harvard law professor Mary Ann Glendon, it has gone further than any other country in turning "no-fault" divorce into "no-responsibility" divorce—with disastrous effects on the welfare of children.[13]

In the past our divorce laws were based on the assumption that marriage was a partnership that lasted in almost all cases "until death do us part." Prior to 1970, divorce was a legal option, but only upon proof of such serious, fault-based conduct as adultery, cruelty, or desertion. By the 1960s large numbers of adults were failing to live up to these traditional standards, and the reality of divorce practice had become increasingly at odds with the expectations of the law. Indeed, the frustrations of lawyers and legislators with the hypocrisy of the laws was itself a major impetus for change.

The divorce reform movement of the late 1960s and 1970s had two main goals: to shift the focus of a family court's enquiry away from evidence of fault toward evidence of actual and irretrievable marital breakdown; and to produce greater equality between men and women at the time of divorce.

Neither of these goals were realized. Busy judges with crowded dockets could give little attention to the circumstances under which a marriage had allegedly broken down and routinely granted no-fault divorce decrees. (*No-fault* was a term borrowed from the automobile insurance industry.) They simply accepted a spouse's claim that there were "irreconcilable differences." Under this new practice, if both spouses wished to terminate a marriage, regardless of the reasons or of the potential of their relationship, they were allowed to do so.

In 1969 California became the first state to initiate no-fault divorce, and since that time many states have followed suit. Eighteen states and the District of Columbia have adopted "pure" no-fault divorce laws. Other states have put in place a compromise system: for example, fault grounds combined with a marital breakdown or incompatibility provision that allows divorcing couples to avoid allocating blame. None of the mixed-grounds statutes are particularly restrictive. The bottom line seems to be that "in forty-one American jurisdictions one spouse can terminate a marriage without the other's fault or consent and without delay beyond that normally attendant on civil litigation."[14] According to Glendon, in practice the new laws promote the idea that "a marriage is irretrievable if one spouse says it is."[15] Marriage in America has become a relationship terminable at will.

As far as the equity goal is concerned, the shift to gender-neutral rules seems to have increased inequality, at least on the economic front. The emphasis is now on equal treatment for men and women. Alimony or spousal support is awarded in only a minority of cases. In the mid-1980s fewer than 14 percent of divorcing women nationwide were awarded spousal support, and even in those cases it was short-term (two to three years).[16] In place of alimony women are now entitled to a more equal share of marital property (through the new equitable distribution laws), and are expected to earn their living in the labor market in much the same way as men. These new policies do not add up to much financial security for divorced women and their children.

For starters, a division of property rarely solves the economic problem. The vast majority of divorcing couples, particularly young couples with small children, own few assets. Even if the property is divided up in an equitable manner, it does not mean as much to an ex-wife as old-fashioned alimony. A New Jersey study found that the average value of marital property at the time of divorce was only $4,650.[17] Even if this sum were split evenly, it would simply not be large enough to make much of a difference to the long-run security of a family.

Increasingly, judges are instructing divorcing women to seek their economic salvation in the labor market. The new litany tends to read: Any woman who wants to can get a job and be self-supporting; she therefore doesn't need alimony or any other long-term supplement to her income. In a Florida legal decision, an appellate court denied a forty-eight-year-old housewife's request for continued alimony (she had been divorced for two years) with the following statement: "In this era of women's liberation movements and enlightened thinking . . . the woman is as fully equipped as the man to earn a living and provide for her essential needs."[18]

This Florida judge could not have been more wrong. Not only is the typical divorcée faced with the lower wage rates typical of women's jobs (and year-round, full-time women workers still earn only 71 percent of the male wage)[19] but often she is returning to the labor force after years of being a full-time homemaker. It is extremely hard to get a well-paid job if you are older or inexperienced. Add to this the fact that 52 percent of divorced women have custody of minor children.[20] Inadequate and expensive child care provides a further constraint on the kind of employment a divorcée can get or accept.

Contemporary divorce laws may have been inspired by the ideal of greater equality between the sexes, but given their emphasis on equal treatment they often backfire, seriously compromising the economic position of ex-wives—and their children. As Lenore Weitzman and Ruth Dixon have pointed out, "most judges appear to view the law's goal of equality as a mandate for placing an *equal burden* of support on men and women whose position and capacity for support are, by virtue of their experience in marriage, typically *unequal.*"[21] Many divorcées are simply not equipped to bear an equal burden and do not flourish when they are accorded equal treatment. If they are older "displaced homemakers," or if they have young children, they are severely handicapped in a job market that already discriminates against women.

Looking back, the pre-1970 system had its advantages when it came to producing economic justice for women and children. Under the old law a spouse's financial position after divorce typically depended on marital "fault." Negotiation was the principal mechanism for settling disputes about property division, alimony, and child support, and the system gave considerable bargaining advantage to a legally "innocent" spouse (often the wife) whose partner was impatient to get a divorce. Frances Leonard, an attorney in Oakland, California, describes the fault system: "In the old days women had a marriage contract unless it was broken through adultery, abandonment, or cruelty. If her husband wanted out of the marriage she could strike an economic bargain with him—you support me and I'll give you a divorce. The impolite word is blackmail. Nobody feels that it was a good system, but it helped place a value on the marriage contract."[22]

The economic repercussions of marital breakdown can be brutal. Divorce cuts a mother's income by 30 percent or more, and her children suffer accordingly.[23] As I showed in chapter 3, shockingly few divorced men contribute anything at all to the financial support of their children. The research evidence is overwhelming: divorce sentences a significant proportion of this generation of American children to periods of real economic hardship. What is more, financial insecurity follows the children of divorce into adult life, derailing college and compromising careers.

*   *   *

Elizabeth Kearns* is one of those tanned, leggy, knock-your-socks-off blondes more often seen in TV commercials than in real life. I met with her on the campus of the University of Southern California in the spring of 1989. We sat on a carpet of pink petals under a cherry tree. The sky was a brilliant blue and as we talked Elizabeth swung her sheets of long golden hair. It was a glorious technicolor scene, with one discordant note. Elizabeth's fingernails were bitten and bloody.

When she was a little girl, Elizabeth thought she had a perfect family and a perfect life. Her father was a successful businessman who had built up his own financial services firm; her mother was a model homemaker—beautiful, capable, loving, and supportive. She had a younger brother and lived in a large luxurious house in Belleview, a suburb of Seattle.

This world came crashing down when Elizabeth was nine. Her father moved out of the house and went to live with his new girlfriend. A year later her parents were divorced (a no-fault divorce on grounds of irreconcilable differences), and her father remarried. After that, according to Elizabeth, her life "kinda got tough."

At least some of the problems have been financial. "He's been paying $1,100 a month, $550 for each of us kids until age eighteen, so it stopped for me this last fall," explained Elizabeth. "Now he just pays $550 for my brother. My Mom barely makes it.

"She was an elementary-school teacher but quit when she had kids. After the divorce she couldn't find a teaching job, so for the last eight years she has been working at a child-care center making just over $10,000 a year."

"Who is paying for college?" I asked.

*A pseudonym.

"My Dad isn't, that's for sure." Elizabeth's pretty mouth had twisted into a harsh, thin line. Her voice had risen and now had a hard, ugly edge to it. "I'm really scrambling around, piecing together the tuition myself with loans, financial aid, and money I make working part-time. He is *supposed* to pay my living expenses but it's a total hand-to-mouth business. Last year he left me down here with my bank account negative $2,000 for three months. And he has the nerve to drive around in a Maserati and spend $150 on dinner . . ." Flushed and angry, Elizabeth busied herself picking at the flesh around her fingernails.

"I will probably transfer to a state college in Washington next year. I'll live at home, get a job, and not have to deal with hassling my Dad."

Elizabeth knew that her dad could afford to pay for college. Just this last summer she had worked in his office and helped put together his expense accounts. It was clear from the records that he had earned $155,000 in 1987.[24]

The fact that estranged fathers do not contribute significantly to the costs of college is a critical problem for many youngsters. In a recent study Judith Wallerstein followed a group of upper-middle-class youngsters for ten to fifteen years and found that children who grow up in divorced families are not climbing the economic ladder as high as their parents did. Only half of the youngsters she interviewed managed to complete college, and 40 percent of the young men are drifting— out of school, unemployed. A full 60 percent of the youngsters in her sample are on a downward educational course compared with their fathers, and 45 percent are on a similar downward course compared with their mothers. At least some of the difficulties experienced by these youngsters are financial. Two-thirds of divorced fathers in the Wallerstein study offered no help whatsoever for college, despite the fact that they are a well-heeled group. In the words of one successful engineer, "I don't care whether my son goes to college. I couldn't care less. My responsibility is to get my life together."[25]

The reason why Elizabeth's dad and the fathers in Wallerstein's study get away with not paying for college is that contemporary divorce laws make few claims on parents after a child reaches eighteen. In many states the age of majority has been lowered from twenty-one to eighteen, and youngsters over the age of eighteen are no longer considered minors in need of support unless otherwise specified, a demand rarely made in divorce settlements. In California, fewer than 5 percent of divorces require a father to pay for a child's college education.[26]

Mothers are often willing to contribute voluntarily to the cost of college, but since they typically have few resources, their generosity rarely amounts to much. Given the dramatic rise in the price tag attached to a college education (costs now range from $8,000 to $22,000 a year), few students are able to work their way through college. Without at least some parental backing many are forced to drop out or, like Elizabeth, transfer to a less prestigious local school.

The adverse consequences of divorce for children seem to be particularly severe in America. This is because, more so than in other countries, reformist energies have been directed toward maximizing adult rights to freedom and equality, rather than toward providing a safety net for children. As Glendon notes, the United States is unique among Western nations in the degree to which it has accepted no-fault, no-responsibility divorce, and in "its relative carelessness about assuring either public or private responsibility" for children.[27]

The divorce reform movement produced two models in

Western Europe: a "traditional" model (found in France and Italy), which emphasizes private responsibility and the financial obligations of the former provider; and a "Nordic" model (found in Sweden and Norway), which relies on elaborate programs of public supports for single parents with children.

France liberalized its divorce laws in 1975 but was careful to continue to protect the economic interests of women and children. All assets acquired during marriage are now divided equally, and the spouse with the higher income (nearly always the husband) is required to make payments to the other "to compensate . . . for the disparity which the disruption of the marriage creates in the conditions of their respective lives."[28] In addition, child-support awards are generous, and if the noncustodial parent fails to pay, the state rather than the custodial parent absorbs the risk. In practical terms, if there is a default in child-support payments, all the custodial parent need do is apply to a state agency. This agency then tries to collect from the noncustodial parent, but in the meantime it advances the amount of child support owed, up to a limit set by law.

Cases of unilateral no-fault divorce are governed by a particularly strict set of rules in France. A male plaintiff must not only wait six years for a divorce but "remains completely bound to the duty" of supporting wife and children in their current life-style.[29] All of these safeguards help ensure a reasonable standard of living for children in the wake of divorce.

Sweden protects its children in other ways. Like France, child support is guaranteed by the state, but instead of relying on alimony or spousal support to maintain the standard of living of ex-wives, child support is backed up with "the most comprehensive and generous package of benefits for one-parent families in the world."[30] As one divorcée explains, "everyone knows that divorced parents need more money and

more social support because of the additional pressures involved in raising children as a single parent. . . . So, as soon
as I got divorced *my income went up:* both the local and national
government increased my mother's allowance, my tax rate
dropped drastically. . . . It also helped to have the possibility
of 24-hour day care."[31]

The United States, on the other hand, has failed to develop
adequate private or public supports for the children of divorce. A divorced mother in America faces a double jeopardy:
she cannot rely on her ex-husband because our legal system
does not ensure that a former breadwinner will continue to
shoulder substantial economic responsibility for children (in
the manner of France); nor can she rely on significant help
from the state (in the manner of Sweden). Rather, she is
expected to pay for child care, housing, health care, and college education on the private market. Combined with low
female earning power, this lack of social support virtually
guarantees economic hardship for mothers and children in the
wake of divorce.

A word on the messages communicated by our new divorce
laws. According to Lenore Weitzman, "the rules governing
divorce in any society provide an opportunity to reinforce the
marital behavior it approves and punish that which violates its
norms."[32] By rewarding "good" behavior and penalizing
"bad" behavior, our divorce laws send a clear signal to citizens
about what kind of behavior is valued and what is not, as well
as nudging people in the "right" direction by creating an
appropriate set of carrots and sticks.

If a divorce court awards a significant amount of spousal and
child support to a thirty-year-old homemaker with two preschool children, it is in effect rewarding the woman's devotion
to her children and giving her permission to continue to stay
home with them. It is also reinforcing heavy ongoing responsi-

bilities on the part of an ex-husband and creating a deterrent effect (severe financial burdens may cause other husbands to think twice before divorcing). But if a divorce court denies the housewife spousal support, awards minimal child support, and tells her she must get a job to support herself and her children, then the legal system is sending out a very different signal. It is opting for day care for the children of divorce and releasing the ex-husband from most of the responsibility for the continued support of his family, thus making divorce a less onerous alternative for many husbands and fathers.

As Glendon emphasizes in her writings, when we change the rules for divorce we implicitly create and institutionalize new norms for marriage.[33] It seems that in moving toward no-fault, no-responsibility divorce, we have both weakened the institution of marriage and thwarted parents in their efforts to do a good job by their children. For example, as contemporary mothers face a high probability of divorce, and will most likely be required to pick up the tab for the children of divorce, it has become irrational for them to invest much energy in nurturing or homemaking. Rather, contemporary divorce laws encourage women to hone marketplace skills so that they can earn a decent living if and when the need arises.

Thus our new rules for divorce and our new norms for marriage not only harm children in a direct way—by depressing standards of living and dramatically reducing contact with father; they also devalue domestic roles and this further compromises the life chances of children.

In my discussion of divorce reform I have described a government in retreat, a legal and political system that has yielded to popular pressure and relaxed the rules of the game so as to free up a great deal of discretionary space for adult freedoms. Specifically, there has been a weakening and a lightening of the rules governing marriage and parenthood. It has become an extremely simple business to walk out on a spouse: you no longer even need to reach an agreement; you can do it unilaterally after a wait of only six months. Deserting a child is a little—just a little—more difficult. In some states you might run the risk of having your paycheck garnished if you are delinquent in child-support payments, but no one hassles you for failing to *see* a child. Fathers do it all the time; we don't even have a system of enforcing visitation. There are no sanctions.

If government has abandoned its role as watchdog of private morality, it is increasingly unwilling to intervene in the marketplace to safeguard the interests of the child. This reluctance to interfere in markets is nothing new; it is just more exaggerated than in the past.[34]

Capitalism in general, and American capitalism in particular, has always operated on the belief that freely operating markets produce the most efficient solution to problems of production and distribution. The assumption is that the "invisible hand" of classical economic theory will maximize output if markets are left to their own devices. Government does, of course, intervene in the marketplace, but whenever it does policy makers are expected to make a vigorous case for why a specific social objective should override and constrain the free enterprise system. In recent decades we have meddled in the marketplace to protect the family farm, to conserve the environment, to prevent industrial accidents, and to safeguard the consumer. The United States, like most modern democracies, has sought to edit and inhibit capitalism so as to reduce societal damage.

But America seems to have a blind spot when it comes to children. We are much more willing to protect tobacco farmers or to restrict the use of the wetlands than to regulate day-care centers or monitor television programming at four o'clock in the afternoon. The fact is, we intervene in the market reluctantly and are extremely selective in the causes we deem worthy. Toddlers and teenagers simply don't make the cut. Their welfare is just not a high priority.

Unlicensed Day Care

Ashley Snead's room in this elegant two-story town house stands unchanged from the day she died more than a year ago. Her dresses hang in the closet, her toy train is on the shelf, and the Victorian ruffled curtains her mother special-ordered from North Carolina frame the windows.

Her parents, Jane and Ronald Snead . . . eagerly show Ashley's baby pictures. Jane Snead cries softly as she talks. Ronald Snead, a 43-year-old Lieutenant Colonel in the Army, sits subdued. "We loved that little girl," he says.

On July 28, 1987, 10-month-old Ashley was rushed, not breathing, from her babysitter's house to Fairfax Hospital. Efforts to revive her failed. Shortly thereafter, her devastated parents were stunned again. An autopsy showed that Ashley had been poisoned by the prescription antidepressant drug imipramine.

Ashley, the Sneads' only child, had been in the care of a kindly, grandmotherly babysitter who, a neighbor later testified, "liked babies that like to take naps."

Today, the sitter, Martha Guba, is in prison, sentenced to ten years for child neglect. . . . Ashley's parents are serving a life sentence of anger and bewilderment at a system that they see as failing to ensure a fundamental goal, the safety of children.[35]

Like most other states, the Sneads' home state of Virginia requires no training for child-care providers. Nor does it check their medical backgrounds or the FBI computer files for criminal histories. Investigations after Ashley's death "turned up evidence that Mrs. Guba had been convicted in Virginia in 1968 of neglecting her own children. She had also been hospitalized in the past for mental problems and was a heavy user of prescription drugs.[36]

Despite the fact that 51 percent of all babies now have mothers in the work force, and millions of infants are in out-of-home care, the United States has no ability to regulate the thousands of child-care facilities springing up around the nation. There are no national standards, no way of enforcing minimal levels of cleanliness, competence, or safety. In late 1989 and early 1990 Congress passed two bills to expand state support for child care, and included in these proposals were quality-control measures. The Bush administration, however, was strongly opposed to the regulatory component in the House and Senate bills. The White House argued that government should not get involved in licensing day care since this "improperly interjects the state into families' affairs."[37] In the end, the child-care bill adopted in October 1990 as part of the budget reconciliation bill included some weak regulatory measures (see discussion in chapter 8).

As Jane and Ronald Snead will attest, the trouble with unlicensed child care is that it is often substandard and sometimes dangerous. Remember Jessica McClure? In October 1987 she fell down an abandoned well in the playground of an unlicensed day-care center in Midland, Texas.[38] The nation was transfixed by Jessica's tragic plight and thousands of people sent money and gifts to Jessica's family, but no one thought to tighten up state regulation of day-care facilities.

We have no trouble licensing dog kennels or mandating minimal health and safety standards for zoos, so why this difficulty in regulating child care? It seems that when push comes to shove, the welfare of children is not a pressing enough concern to warrant interfering with parental rights or the private market.

Deregulated Television

The growing reluctance of government to intervene in the market on behalf of children shows up extremely clearly in the issue of public control of the television industry. Once upon a time television played a relatively benign role in the lives of children. In the 1950s the networks broadcast twenty-seven hours a week of squeaky-clean family entertainment. In the daytime hours children had their choice of "Kukla, Fran and Ollie," "The Mickey Mouse Club," "Mr. Wizard," or "Captain Kangaroo," and evening prime-time television was dominated by the likes of "Father Knows Best" and "Ozzie and Harriet." These family shows portrayed "hard-working parents raising their children, helping them solve problems, protecting them from experiences for which they were not prepared."[39]

During the 1960s there was a gradual increase in the amount of violence, crime, and sex shown on television screens. Programs such as "The Untouchables," "Mission Impossible," and "The Man from U.N.C.L.E." were far more violent than any TV fare in the 1950s. This trend prompted much public discussion and in 1964 the Senate set up a Subcommittee on Juvenile Delinquency to explore the link between crime and violence on television and disruptive societal behavior. This was followed in 1968 by the establishment of a National Commission on the Causes and Prevention of Violence. Studies and surveys were commissioned, and the accumulated research pointed to a "pattern of positive association between the viewing of television violence and aggressive attitudes and behavior" in children.[40] Field studies of young children and adolescent boys demonstrated a deterioration in self-control and an increase in interpersonal aggression after youngsters were exposed to television violence.

In the wake of these findings the FCC warned the television industry that offerings to children would be strictly monitored. The networks responded by agreeing to a measure of self-regulation. Specifically, they promised to reduce the amount of violence in programming. But self-regulation did not work—by the end of the 1960s approximately 80 percent of network dramatic productions included scenes of violence[41]—and the FCC was forced into a more aggressive mode. By 1974 each broadcaster was required to make a "meaningful effort" to provide special programs for preschool and school-age children in the late afternoon hours. In addition, restrictions were placed on the amount of advertising allowed during children's programs, and host selling (using program characters to promote products) was prohibited. In the late 1970s, when it was clear that, despite these guidelines, the amount of "quality" children's programming had not increased, the FCC issued a "Notice of Proposed Rulemaking" that alerted broadcasters to the fact that in the future they would be expected to provide a minimum of 7½ hours a week of age-appropriate children's programs.

Before the networks had time to respond, however, Ronald Reagan was elected president and a new administration came to power that was committed to deregulation and a greater reliance on free enterprise. Mark Fowler, the new chairman of the FCC, believed that "consumer sovereignty" should be the guiding principle in television programming, and that American families would be best served by allowing the networks to show whatever attracted the largest audiences. According to Fowler, if 5 million schoolchildren wanted to watch

Oprah Winfrey instead of doing their homework, they had an absolute right to do so: "The marketplace will take care of children."[42]

By 1984 the FCC had removed virtually all guidelines on general program content and had abolished the limits on advertising in programs targeted at young people. As a result of these decisions, children's programming has become much more commercialized. The networks now air entire programs whose sole purpose is to market commodities. "Gummi Bears" features characters whose likenesses are sold as jellied candies, while "G.I. Joe," "Thundercats," and "Maxie's World" are cartoon programs about toys with the same names. Educators call these shows program-length commercials.[43]

One recent and particularly worrisome development is the blossoming of TV talk shows in the after-school hours. The three major networks now air "Oprah Winfrey," "Donahue," and "Geraldo" between 3:00 and 5:00 in the afternoon. These talk shows have a combined viewing audience of 40 million, a third of whom are thought to be under eighteen.[44] While these shows ostensibly deal with "real-world" issues,

the most frequent topics are crime, violence, and sex. To give the flavor: In November 1989 "Geraldo" ran programs on serial rapists, pregnant prison inmates, teenage prostitution, nymphomaniacs, and rape on college campuses.[45] The message communicated by "Geraldo" (or "Oprah Winfrey," for that matter) is that we live in a dangerous, sex-crazed world. The teenage culture is portrayed as deviant, uncontrolled, and irresponsible, and youngsters are shown experimenting with sex and drugs. As psychologist Nan Signorelli points out, the models and values being transmitted to adolescents through these shows are those of unimportance, devaluation, and self-destruction.[46] And yet millions of youngsters have easy access to these programs. Given the new laissez-faire regime at the FCC, the networks are allowed to air these shows in after-school hours, and, since the majority of mothers are now in the work force, there is often no adult at home to turn off the TV set.

Particularly telling is that in most other countries the 4:00 to 6:00 P.M. slot is considered prime time for specially tailored children's programs. In Britain a children's news program called "Newsround" is shown at 5:00 P.M., and a quarter of all British schoolchildren tune in to it. In Australia, all commercially licensed stations are required to broadcast an hour of children's programming each weekday from 4:00 to 5:00 P.M. And Japan has two public channels that provide programs each day in the late afternoon hours.

Catching up with the rest of the civilized world would involve two types of intervention by the U.S. government. Allocating more money to children's programming would help. Currently, our government spends a mere 57 cents per person on all types of public broadcasting. Spending in other countries is of a different order of magnitude. Britain spends $18 per capita, Canada $22, and Japan $10.[47] Much of this money goes for developing educational and informational programs for children.

But even more critical than increasing the level of public funding is imposing reasonable controls over what children are able to watch on television. The Reagan and now the Bush administrations seem not to understand that television is as powerful as school in terms of impact on the minds of our children. In the average American household the TV set is on for six to seven hours a day. Preschool children watch TV more than four hours a day, and grade-school children spend more time watching television than attending classes. The Nielsen data on when children are watching TV are astounding: the majority of American children are watching TV during the prime-time hour of 8:00 to 9:00 at night, and a fifth of all preschoolers and a third of grade-school children are still watching TV at 11:00 at night![48]

Values can clearly be changed and distorted by such large doses of unregulated commercial television. Afternoon talk shows teach children about a world where brutal killings and deviant sex are normal, and prime-time evening shows such as "Dallas," "Miami Vice," and "Wiseguy" reinforce and glamorize these messages. Rates of sexual contact in the popular soaps have increased 103 percent since 1980. Not only has sex become more explicit on television but it is often treated irresponsibly in that precautions against pregnancy or disease are almost never discussed. In unnerving ways the real world mimics television, with adolescents initiating sexual intercourse earlier than ever before and with many of them failing to use contraception. In 1971 only one of every seven fifteen-year-old girls had had intercourse; by 1986 the proportion had risen to one in four.[49]

Apart from glamorizing sex and violence, American television also produces a barrage of commercials. By the time the average American youngster has finished high school, he or she has been the target of more than 1,500 hours of TV ads. In other words, the average young person has spent the equivalent of a work-year listening to commercial messages.[50] This does more than influence brand preferences; this onslaught of advertisements colors a child's world view. It becomes easy to believe that life revolves around the buying and selling of commodities. Once again reality mimics television in that the values and goals of young people have become increasingly centered on money and what money can buy.

According to sociologist Richard Easterlin, the aspirations of high school seniors have become much more materialistic over the last fifteen years. Among their life goals the one that has increased in importance most is "having lots of money," and the one that has decreased most is "finding meaning and purpose in life." Seventeen-year-olds have also changed their notions of what makes a job attractive. The three occupational characteristics that have risen most in importance are "a chance to earn a good deal of money," a job with "high status and prestige," and a job "where the chances for advancement and promotion are good." In contrast, occupations that "give you an opportunity to be directly helpful to others" have undergone a dramatic decline in popularity. Not surprisingly, today's seniors value "big-ticket" consumer goods much more highly than their predecessors did a decade ago. Major labor-saving appliances, a high-quality stereo, and "clothes in the latest style" have all risen sharply in importance.[51]

Children from low-income families watch more television than children from more affluent homes and are dependent upon it for information as well as entertainment. For these youngsters, unregulated programming with its mix of violence, sex, and materialism can be particularly destructive. Heavy-duty advertising creates powerful desires that cannot possibly be satisfied by minimum-wage jobs in the ghetto. How can a high school dropout afford the most recent Audi, or even a pair of Calvin Klein jeans? This contradiction is often resolved through crime. Sex or drugs can be relied upon for quick money, and both areas of activity have been glamorized, even legitimized, by television.

In a recent interview, novelist and social critic Tom Wolfe tells a story that illustrates how thoroughly materialistic values have taken root in city ghettos:

> I'll never forget walking through the South Bronx, doing research [for his 1987 novel *Bonfire of the Vanities*] and seeing boys, thirteen or fourteen years old, wearing these necklaces with silvery rings hanging from them. In the rings were upside-down Y's. I thought these were peace symbols. And I said, "Isn't it interesting that these boys here in the poorest part of New York are so civic-minded that they are concerned about the threat of nuclear destruction." Of course, when I looked more closely, I saw that they were Mercedes-Benz hood ornaments. These boys knew what a Mercedes-Benz was, and they knew how much it cost because they knew that all the hotshots drive them. The drug dealers drive them. They wanted theirs. And they were taking the only part that they could get now, which was the hood ornament. This was the money fever spreading right down to the bottom rungs of the social ladder.[52]

It would be much too simple to blame the values of the 1980s on the deregulation of TV programming. But clearly, the fact that government has gotten out of the business of adjudicating what is appropriate for children to watch on television has contributed to the violence and materialism of our age.

It is important to appreciate the enormous potential of television for good and evil. Many children (particularly disadvan-

taged ones) spend the bulk of their waking hours in front of
a television screen. Indeed, the voices that millions of children
hear most often come not from living people but from boxes
that emit TV signals. In other countries governments ensure
that the immense power of television to influence the young
is used to educate and edify as well as to titillate and entertain.
But in the United States, government has abdicated responsibility for the content and timing of television programs, leaving children to the tender mercies of the private market.

Psychiatric Hospitals for Juveniles?

It's time for a commercial break on a local TV station in
Louisiana, and the face of a distraught, weeping father fills the
screen. He is talking about how he never listened to his son,
how he never paid enough attention to him, and now it is too
late. The man pauses, swallows hard, and then tells us that his
son has just committed suicide. A violin starts to play, a heart-
tugging backdrop to the pathetic sounds of a father crying
over his son's suicide. At this point the sales pitch comes on:
viewers are urged to consider seeking professional help if they
are having difficulty with their children. The not-so-subtle
message is: Let your friendly, neighborhood, for-profit, psychiatric hospital fix your kid—before anything really bad happens.[53]

The images conjure up every parent's nightmare. They certainly make for a powerful brand of advertising that's attracting thousands of new patients to psychiatric hospitals around
the nation. In 1971, 6,500 children and teenagers were hospitalized in private psychiatric facilities in the United States. By
1989 this figure had reached approximately 200,000.[54] At
least some of these youngsters are in dire need of inpatient

hospital treatment, but it seems that anxious, preoccupied parents are increasingly using psychiatric admission as a method of "parking" troublesome but otherwise normal teenagers. Psychiatrist Marvin Schwarz, who runs three juvenile psychiatric programs in the Chicago area, blames the swelling tide of hospital admissions on parents "who are too wrapped up in seeking self-satisfaction through careers to set limits for their children."[55] But it's not just a question of absorbing careers. Divorce and single parenthood seem to trigger a large proportion of these psychiatric admissions. A startling percentage of children in residential treatment—over 80 percent—are from families in which the biological parents no longer live together.

Whatever the factors that precipitate psychiatric admission, most of these teens do not suffer from serious mental disorders. A recent study at the University of Michigan found that 70 percent of adolescent psychiatric admissions are "inappropriate and potentially harmful" to the children concerned.[56] A 1988 review by Blue Cross of Minnesota came up with the following examples of teenagers who had been hospitalized unnecessarily:

• A fifteen-year-old boy was hospitalized for 102 days after discharge from a chemical-dependency unit. His mother dropped him off at the psychiatric hospital before going on vacation. He had a history of drug use, fighting with his parents, and running away. When hospitalized he complained of hallucinating and a fear of death, but later admitted that this was a ploy to stay in treatment because he did not want to go home.

• A fourteen-year-old girl was admitted for evaluation because her mother said she had trouble setting limits for her daughter. The girl apparently had left home twice without permission to stay with her father and stepmother. It was determined that the girl did not suffer from depression, but nevertheless she was kept in the hospital for eighty-five days.[57]

As one might expect, the experience of being locked up in a psychiatric hospital for two or three months has "substantial negative effects" on most normal adolescents. These run the gamut from feelings of powerlessness, helplessness, and rage to the trauma of exposure to children who are seriously emotionally disturbed.

And then there is the question of expense. Adolescent psychiatric patients stay in the hospital for 30 to 100 days, at a cost of $500 to $1,000 a day.[58] These costs can quickly mount. In 1988 it cost the Defense Department a whopping $270 million to provide inpatient psychiatric care for the troubled children of military personnel.[59] For many U.S. corporations juvenile psychiatric care is now the fastest-growing medical expense.[60]

For middle-class parents these huge costs are often hidden because most up-front expenses associated with psychiatric hospital care are picked up by an insurance carrier. In the end, of course, we all pay the bill. Medical insurance costs go through the roof and are passed on to employers and workers in the form of higher insurance rates, diminished medical coverage, and lower profits and earnings.

It's hard to understand how all this came about. Why are we spending billions of dollars to incarcerate a few hundred thousand middle-class children in psychiatric hospitals when most of them don't belong there and are actually harmed by this treatment? This bizarre development has something to do with our eagerness to promote free markets—whatever the human cost—but an even more powerful causal factor is our growing reluctance to pass laws that protect children.

According to psychologist/lawyer Lois Weithorn, the "doors to psychiatric hospitals [for adolescents] were swung wide open by the United States Supreme Court." In *Parnham* v. *J. R.* (1979), the court declined to require states to take special steps to regulate the use of psychiatric facilities by juveniles, holding that "parental discretion, reinforced by the judgment of admitting staff that inpatient treatment was medically necessary, was adequate to protect minors' constitutional interests."[61] Formal due process protections and strict standards (of the type required for the psychiatric commitment of adults) were deemed unnecessary on the grounds that the bonds of affection between parents and children would lead parents to act in their child's best interest.

As Justice William J. Brennan, Jr., noted in his dissenting opinion, however, the decision of a parent to institutionalize a child is usually a function of family turmoil, and can be quite unrelated to the problems of the child. When a confused, stressed-out parent reaches out for help in dealing with a recalcitrant child, he or she may well grab on to whatever treatment option is the least expensive or most convenient—especially if it involves getting rid of a hostile, demanding teenager for a while. In Weithorn's view *Parnham* boiled down to an endorsement of "unbridled discretion for parents."[62]

In addition to giving a great deal of committal power to parents, *Parnham* assumed that hospital personnel were "neutral fact finders," able to step in and make independent judgments that would serve to protect the interests of the child. This flies in the face of evidence that shows doctors and administrators in for-profit psychiatric hospitals to have a vested interest in admitting patients: they are paid bonuses if they drum up additional business. The *Chicago Tribune* describes one company, the Charter Medical Corp., staging an in-house competition based on the number of admissions and referrals generated by employees. First prize was an eight-day cruise for two in the Caribbean! So much for independence and neutrality. Proof of the degree to which the profit motive drives professional practices in these private psychiatric hospitals is the fact that most patients experience a remarkable and full recovery from their disorder just at the time when their health insurance benefits run out.[63]

The explosive growth of juvenile psychiatric care in the 1970s and 1980s is a distressing story. The chaos of family life and the pain of neglected adolescents have been cleverly exploited by private entrepreneurs who seduce and entrap desperate parents and their luckless children. "We entice parents, and I can't stand that," says Karen Brugler, director of adolescent programs at the Lutheran General Hospital in Chicago. "We're on television all the time, giving parents the idea that if they take their kids into a hospital, they'll come out scrubbed and fresh and beautiful again. That's not how it works."[64] But if the system is not working for kids it's certainly working for the private sector. Hospital chains like National Medical Enterprises and Community Psychiatric Corp. are growing at 20 percent a year and raking in large profits.[65] The emotional problems of young people are now big business.

These extraordinary developments in hospital psychiatric care are powerful examples of how the integrity of children can be violated by the market. They also illustrate the potentially disastrous consequences of government inaction. In an age where neglect, chaos, and rage litter the adolescent landscape, we need something more substantial than a permissive, minimalist state if we are to save our children. "Parental discretion," no matter how unbridled, fails to cut the mustard.

Drug-Exposed Babies

A needle-thin intravenous tube is lodged in an arm barely thicker than a pencil. This is how Jason eats. A respirator is threaded into a tiny, transparent nostril, its plastic tube taped in place against fragile, papery skin. This is how Jason breathes. But this particular two-pound baby is dealing with more than the usual horrors of prematurity. His diminutive rib cage flutters and shudders as painful spasms pass through his upper body. His sticklike limbs twitch and twist to the crazy rhythms of drug withdrawal. Jason is a crack baby.

He is part of a swelling stream of human misery, one of 375,000 infants born in 1988 after exposure to crack cocaine in the womb. Once a rarity in hospital nurseries, drug-exposed babies now account for 11 percent of all births in America.[66] As is true of many crack babies, Jason was abandoned at birth by his mother. She left the hospital without seeing or naming her son. Jason's name was given to him by the medical team in his neonatal unit.

As I watched this tiny child struggle with his private agony, I found myself appalled and angry. How can we allow an innocent child to be born into such a hell? In April 1989 Representative Charles Rangel (D-N.Y.) told a congressional committee that in three decades of public life nothing had made him feel more helpless than "infants being born addicted to drugs, screaming in pain and agony . . . their tiny bodies squirming and shaking. . . . this is one of the saddest indictments of a civilization."[67] I could not agree more.

The rate of increase of drug-exposed babies is frightening. Hospitals in Oakland, California, and Washington, D.C., saw the proportion of drug-exposed newborns increase from 6 percent in 1985 to 18 percent in 1988.[68] And these figures may be the tip of an iceberg. According to Neal Halfon of Oakland's Children's Hospital, "urine toxicological screens and/or self-reports vastly underestimate the problem. . . . I bet we're missing about half of those actually exposed some time during pregnancy."[69] A large proportion of these drug-exposed babies are born in city ghettos, but as the crack epidemic spreads, these damaged children can be found in increasing numbers in communities all over America.

Joanique Suggs lives in Minneapolis and is cute and cuddly "like most any three-month-old." But in her case appearances are deceptive: Joanique has many problems, all stemming from the fact she was exposed to crack in her mother's womb. In her short life she has stopped breathing six times and spent more than a month in the hospital. She is unable to sleep for more than a few minutes at a time, "throws up like a faucet," and has trouble bending her arms. Like other drug-exposed babies, Joanique has a much higher risk of sudden infant death syndrome than would a normal baby, and must be attached to a monitor when she sleeps.

While pregnant, Laverne Suggs, Joanique's mother, smoked crack "from the time I got up until I went to sleep. One hit trembled the baby so much it was like it was looking for someplace to hide." But there is no hiding. Crack reaches the fetus through the placental wall and wreaks havoc on the developing child.

Two of Suggs's four other children also show signs of crack exposure in the womb. Donald Lee, age two, is "pretty hyper. He can't sit down. He swears, hits, spits," says Laverne. "His attention span is like that," she says, snapping her fingers. Monique was a jittery and irritable newborn, and at fifteen months can't speak at all.

Laverne Suggs, now in a rehabilitation program at Turning

Point, a Minneapolis drug-treatment center, reflects on her situation: "It's one thing to screw up your own life. But I had no right to mess up theirs."[70]

Although many other drugs have plagued our society, crack, a derivative of cocaine, poses a much bigger threat to young children because mothers use it. Dr. David Bateman, director of perinatology at New York's Harlem Hospital, describes the problem: "Heroin was a man's drug and we just didn't see as much of it in pregnant women. Many more women are on crack than ever were on heroin. . . . These mothers don't care about their babies and they don't care about themselves."[71]

Cocaine is very harmful to the fetus. When pregnant women smoke crack, the drug enters the bloodstream and constricts the blood vessels in the placenta, cutting off the flow of oxygen and nutrients. The most common problems of drug-exposed babies are prematurity, irritability, inability to sleep, muscle rigidity, high-pitched crying, convulsions, a short attention span, and developmental lags. Joanique exhibits a range of these symptoms but she is one of the luckier crack babies. Other, less fortunate infants suffer severe deformities (of the heart, lung, or digestive tract), or experience a disabling stroke while still in the womb. A distressing number of crack babies—approximately 20,000—test positive for HIV, the precursor of AIDS.[72] Fatally damaged these children will stumble through short tormented lives stalked by debilitation, disfigurement, and death.

All of which could so easily be avoided.

It seems that no matter how dreadful the tragedy or innocent the victim, our government is paralyzed, unable to do what is necessary to protect vulnerable lives. For starters, pregnant addicts face a massive shortage of drug-treatment programs. Due to a dearth of public funds there is only one treatment slot for every twenty-six people whose drug use seriously impairs their health, and the situation is even worse for pregnant women. According to a 1989 survey undertaken by Wendy Chavkin of Columbia University's School of Public Health, 54 percent of the drug-treatment programs in New York City categorically refuse to treat pregnant women, and 87 percent refuse to treat pregnant women on Medicaid addicted to crack—the group that is most at risk.[73]

Not only are pregnant addicts denied access to treatment; they are also discouraged from seeking abortions. Over the last ten years many states have severely limited public funding of abortion, making it difficult for poor women (including addicted poor women) to terminate a pregnancy. This public folly has led to some spine-chilling scenarios.

In 1989 the *Los Angeles Times* ran a piece on Barbara Colbert, a twenty-three-year-old addict and prostitute who lived on the streets of Los Angeles. Colbert had a problem: she was pregnant and she didn't want to be, but it was hard to figure out how to get rid of the baby:

> Abortion was out. That costs money, and money was better spent for drugs. People suggested that she sit in scalding water or drink turpentine. But why suffer so much just to kill a child?
>
> Instead, Barbara Colbert smoked even more. If she used enough crack, she'd be high and the baby would be dead. To an addict of two years, that kind of happily-ever-after scheme made pretty good sense.
>
> "Give me a dime rock," she would tell the dealers, trading $10 for each hit, then smoking it all up and never chipping it into pieces, so that a big dose could get way down to the baby.[74]

It's hard to feel much empathy for Barbara Colbert. Only one thing seems clear: Some higher authority has to intercede, either to prevent this unwanted baby being born, or to prevent further injury to the fetus. I personally feel that a pregnant addict should have the choice between abortion or in-house drug treatment. If these options are made freely available to a woman—and in Los Angeles as in most American cities neither option is—and she still refuses to abort or protect her unborn child, then the state should step in and incarcerate the woman for the remainder of her pregnancy so that the child has a chance of being born whole.

There are profound reasons why government should intervene on behalf of crack babies. First and foremost are the compelling moral reasons. What baby deserves to enter this world screaming in agony, with a future hopelessly compromised by damage sustained in the womb?

But there are also significant economic reasons. Keeping Jason in the hospital is an enormously expensive enterprise. Estimates in New York City show that per capita hospitalization costs for crack babies are now in the $60,000 to $300,000 range,[75] and this figure does not include long-term health-care costs, special education expenditures, or foster care. The Senate Finance Committee calculated that in 1988 the nation spent $2.5 billion on intensive care for drug-exposed babies.[76] This sum of money would buy a great deal of drug treatment for pregnant women and, in the process, ensure that Jason and Joanique are given a decent shot at this life.

State Intervention

The question of how and when the state should interfere with the rights of individuals or the workings of the market has preoccupied political philosophers for centuries. It was a particular concern of the school of classical political economy.

Adam Smith firmly believed that superior economic results flowed from a system of liberty. As he explained in *Wealth of Nations* (1776), when they are free, individuals, keen in their own interest, direct their labor and their capital into channels that enrich them and their community. "He intends only his own gain [but] is led by an invisible hand to promote an end which has no part in his intention."[77] In Smith's view the state should confine itself to the defense of the realm, the administration of justice, and the construction of public works.

In the mid-nineteenth century, John Stuart Mill refined and popularized libertarian ideas. In his famous essay "On Liberty" he argued that "the protection of freedom was the one great object of wise law and sound policy."[78] In Mill's schema a laissez-faire state was the golden standard and should be the general rule. He was convinced that "every departure from it, unless required by some great good, is a certain evil."[79]

But even such a staunch libertarian as John Stuart Mill thought there was one supremely important limit to personal freedom: "The only purpose for which power can be rightfully exercised over any member of a civilized community, against his will, is to prevent harm to others."[80] Mill took a particularly strict stance on the responsibilities of parents: "to bring a child into existence without a fair prospect of being able, not only to provide food for its body, but instruction and training for its mind, is a moral crime, both against the unfortunate offspring and against society; and if the parent does not fulfil this obligation, the State ought to see it fulfilled."[81]

Modern American governments are a long way from promoting this kind of accountability for children. Indeed, our values have tipped so far in the direction of adult rights that we allow a pregnant HIV-positive woman to carry a child to term without intervening on behalf of this child. The official position of the American Civil Liberties Union (ACLU) is that we cannot "ask a women to sacrifice her right to privacy and open herself to policing during pregnancy"[82] even if this action prevents damage to a baby. The giving-getting compact in our society has most certainly tilted away from the child.

Somewhere along the line the stellar American virtues of self-reliance, individual freedom, and tolerance lapsed into self-absorption and self-indulgence. In a brave new world of rampant individualism, values are treated as a matter of taste, feelings of guilt are seen as unhealthy, and an individual's primary responsibility is assumed to be to himself. Contemporary adults have taken "self to the max"[83]—to the great detriment of children. In the words of political theorist Jean Elshtain, rights to self-fulfillment have become so exaggerated that we "no longer distinguish between the moral weightiness of, say, polishing one's Porsche and sitting up all night with a sick child."[84]

Cumulative Causation

Throughout this chapter I have been describing a twisting spiral of cumulative causation.[85] Parents have become much more involved in looking out for Number One, and many of them have relinquished at least some responsibility for their children. The state has permitted this to happen by weakening the rules that govern personal relationships and sectors of the economy. This abdication of authority has opened a window of opportunity for free enterprise.[86] Where government now "fears to tread," the market has kicked in, filling the void left by parental neglect with a whole range of goodies that run the gamut from "Geraldo" to inpatient psychiatric care. Many of these goods and services are extremely convenient for parents—which is why they are so popular—but, by and large, they are destructive to children. Preoccupied parents, permissive laws, and unregulated markets exacerbate one another and together create an environment that is remarkably antagonistic to young people.

In 1991 there is a desperate need for government to break into this cumulative momentum and force us to consider the moral and economic costs of shafting our children. As we shall see in chapter 8, policy makers have considerable leverage: divorced fathers can be required to pay for college tuition; drug-addicted pregnant women can be constrained to seek treatment; broadcasters can be held responsible for the content of children's programs; day-care centers can be compelled to adopt high standards; and psychiatric hospitals can be prohibited from admitting juveniles unless they have severe emotional problems. These new rules and regulations would constrain both individuals and markets. Unbridled parents and aggressive entrepreneurs would be reined in by a government acting as guardian of America's children.

Interestingly enough, in budgetary terms an activist state that extended a measure of protection to children would not have a higher profile than the one we have today. We would, overall, spend less rather than more money. (Inpatient psychiatric care should win some kind of prize as the least cost-effective way of treating troubled teenagers.) Clearly, very few of the issues raised in this chapter are *primarily* economic issues. If we are to reorder adult priorities so as to give greater weight to children, there is an overwhelming need to change the laws of the land.

Government should take the initiative and use the power of our legal and regulatory systems to step in to protect rather than to mend; to create conditions that allow children to flourish rather than to be sucked in after youngsters have been injured and deal in the miserable currency of damage control.

The Rules of the Game

It is important to stress that changing the rules of the game can make a difference. Government has indeed responded to the self-absorbed mood of the day by relaxing the laws concerning marriage and parenthood. But this need not be the end of the story. Any democratic government listens and responds, but it is not required to blindly follow; it can mold opinion and stake out goals. Research in the field has demonstrated a complex link between changes in values and changes in law. Andrew Cherlin has shown that attitudes about divorce changed very little in the twenty years following World War II. In both 1945 and 1966 the most common response to the question of whether divorce laws were too strict was "not strict enough." As late as 1968, 60 percent of people interviewed thought that divorce should be more difficult to obtain. But by 1978 only 42 percent thought so.[87] By that time most states had relaxed their divorce laws, a more permissive attitude had been given the official seal of approval, and millions of adult Americans had simply changed their minds. It seems that elite avant-garde groups often press for social change, but once laws are rewritten, attitudes and behavior patterns change across social boundaries. New rules beget new ways of living. In the contemporary world of no-fault divorce, adults certainly feel "much less constrained by others' welfare to remain in what they consider to be a marginal marriage."[88] According to one series of opinion polls, the percentage of respondents disagreeing with the statement "when there are children in the family, parents should stay together even if they don't get along" rose from 51 percent in 1962 to 82 percent in 1980.[89]

Cherlin's research turns into a cautionary tale. We need to

be very careful when we mess with our laws because they communicate authority and are capable of shifting values across the board. By the same token, we should take heart. Even in a noisy democracy new legislation has a chance of turning the tide, of tipping the balance in society so as to better protect the interests of the child. Presidents can still lead as well as follow.

One final point: Politicians and policy makers need to be courageous to move on this front. There are powerful reasons why legislative bodies fear to intrude on the untrammeled self—it's a surefire vote loser. Modern Americans have become extremely attached to their expanded freedoms and do not like being told that they may need to rein in their private pleasures. Nothing shows this more clearly than the reception of Sue Miller's 1986 novel *The Good Mother*. [90] This book's publication triggered a clamorous debate because it has the audacity to suggest that there are real trade-offs between self-fulfillment—specifically, sexual fulfillment—and motherhood. It implied that modern women cannot "have it all," but may have to sacrifice at least some forms of personal growth for the sake of a child.

Trade-offs on an Intimate Frontier

The book opens with Anna Dunlap and her attorney-husband, Brian, in the throes of divorce. By agreement their three-year-old daughter, Molly, goes to live with Anna, who moves into a small apartment in Cambridge and slowly builds a self-sufficient existence. Anna gives piano lessons, works part-time in a university lab, puts Molly in day care, and falls in love with Leo, a talented and unconventional artist. Despite her passionate involvement Anna is careful to integrate Leo slowly into her household. Leo and Anna sleep together at night, but he would get up each morning and be "out of the house before [Molly] emerged from her room."[91]

Things seem to be going along swimmingly. Anna is sexually fulfilled for the first time in her life, and Molly is adjusting well to the divorce. The adults become a little too relaxed, however. One day, while Leo is drying off after a shower, Molly asks whether she can touch his penis; in the interests of sexual openness he allows her to, unfortunately getting an erection in the process. Molly mentions this incident to her father, who hits the ceiling in rage, refuses to return Molly to Anna, and sues for custody.

At the trial Anna's sexual conduct is taken as the yardstick of her ability to mother Molly, and she is judged as having made two serious mistakes. In the first place she is held accountable for the circumstances that led up to the highly charged shower encounter between Leo and Molly. Anna handles this accusation well in court. She does not attempt to justify what happened; she simply admits that she did not judge the situation well and takes personal responsibility for having let it happen.

Anna's second mistake is more damaging, and she deals with it less well. During the trial Anna admits to another sexual episode. One night Molly, half asleep, climbs into bed with Anna and Leo, who have just finished having intercourse and are not yet physically separated. In court Anna makes the mistake of defending her action by describing the happiness she felt in holding her lover and her child: "I can remember feeling a sense of completeness, as though I had finally found a way to have everything. We seemed fused, the three of us, all the boundaries between us dissolved."[92] This episode and Anna's defense of her action convinces the judge that this mother could not be trusted to protect her child.

In the end, despite Anna's promise never to see Leo again, the judge awards custody to her ex-husband, Brian, and his new wife. Anna's life is destroyed. She gives up Leo, her job, and her apartment, and moves to Washington (where the ex-husband lives) so that she can see as much of Molly as the visitation arrangements allow.

These are the bones of Sue Miller's story. At the heart of this book is a gut-wrenching clash between the erotic and the maternal, between the desire to feed one's own desires and responsibility to others—in this case, a vulnerable child.

In embarking on a newly single life, Anna makes decisions in keeping with an emerging and urgent sense of self. To use her words: "I had a sense, a drunken, irresponsible sense, of being about to begin my life, of moving beyond the claims of my own family, of Brian."[93] Unfortunately, Anna's blow for freedom runs full-tilt into the needs and claims of her small daughter, whom she loves more than any being in the world (including Leo). At the end of the book the reader is convinced that Anna failed to act wisely. Although we ache for her pain and think she was made to pay too heavy a price for her errors of judgment, we do not absolve her. Grown-ups cannot allow their pleasures, no matter how urgent, to simply override their responsibilities as parents. Along that road lies chaos.

The themes developed so powerfully in *The Good Mother* are a haunting reminder that the pursuit of freedom can back-fire. Rampant individualism clearly diminishes the collective good, but it also gets in the way of individual happiness in anything like the long run. Molly was probably harmed by the trial and by the change in custody arrangements, but the damage done to Anna was on a different scale. When Molly goes to live with her father, Anna loses the cornerstone of her existence. In essential ways her life is permanently diminished.

Completely unfettered freedom is often not as rewarding as it is cracked up to be. When Janis Joplin sang the bittersweet line, "Freedom's just another word for nothing left to lose," she hit upon a central truth of all of our lives.

5

Public Choices: Shortchanging the Future

In July 1989 a piece appeared on the op-ed page of the *New York Times* entitled "Medicare Paid $65 to Do Mom's Toenails."

Mary Augusta Rodgers told the story of her mother, aged 91, who lives in a supportive care residence called Golden Valley, a home for people in their twilight years. Mary's mom needs help in many areas of her life including paying her medical bills. Mary finds this an exasperating chore, she particularly dislikes it when people say, soothingly, as they often do: "Don't worry; Medicare will pay most of it." As Mary points out indignantly, "Who do they think pays for Medicare? Santa Claus?"

The latest annoyance came in the form of a bill from a medical clinic that provides a variety of services at Golden Valley. Mary called to ask for a clearer explanation of the charges. To start with, there were two charges for "debr.

Mycotic nails" on the same day. What was that?

The person in the clinic's billing office was pleasant. That was a podiatrist service, she explained. In plain English, Mary's mother had had her toenails clipped. The charge was $38 for the right foot and $35 for the left. Medicare had paid $65, leaving a balance of $8.

Mary had one more question. How often was her mother scheduled for this service? Every two months.

That adds up to $390 a year.

Mary pondered the larger issues. How much does Medicare pay a year, nationally, for toenail clipping for the elderly? Does anybody know? Or care?[1]

For $390 you can immunize fifteen children against measles . . .

The dirty secret of contemporary social policy is that we are spending our collective resources on the wrong generation. During the 1980s the government spent five times as much money on the old as on the young, and a significant proportion of these public funds went to the affluent elderly. To a distressing degree, public policy is being used to transfer money from the needy young to the comfortable old. The results are dramatic. As Senator Moynihan has pointed out, "the United States has become the first society in history in which the poorest group in the population are the children."[2] Today, an American citizen six years or younger is twice as likely to be poor as a citizen sixty-five or older.

What has caused this redistribution of resources from the young to the old? The two obvious culprits are burgeoning Social Security benefits and the massive increase in house prices.

In recent years the cost of Social Security has grown enormously as the proportion of people eligible for benefits has increased and as the benefits themselves have increased in value. In the late 1940s, thirteen workers supported each Social Security recipient. Today there are three, and early in the next century there will be only two.

Social Security payments have also become more generous. The biggest hikes in benefit levels came after 1973, when Social Security was indexed against inflation. Average Social Security benefits—measured in 1982 dollars—were $2,575 in 1967, $4,520 in 1979, and $6,948 in 1989.[3] To pay for these hikes, Social Security payroll taxes have risen astronomically— 400 percent since 1955.[4] There was a particularly large increase in 1983, when Congress decided to increase the reserves of the Social Security Trust Fund to prepare for the day when the baby boomers retire. By 1990 the maximum payroll tax was a whopping $6,360 a year.[5] For three-quarters of American workers, Social Security taxes are now a bigger burden than federal income tax and are pushing many young working families into poverty.[6] *Forbes* magazine posed the critical question in a November 1988 issue: Is this "crown jewel" of the welfare state really serving progressive ends when at least much of the time, it's making poor young people poorer and rich old people richer?[7]

Social Security: Fact and Fiction

Because Social Security was labeled an entitlement, with people paying into a trust fund during their working lives and drawing from it after retirement, retirees have come to believe it is just their own money they are getting back. They think that Social Security is a benefit they have earned through labor, through paying taxes during a lifetime of work. This simply is not true. Depending on income level, today's retirees will collect between two and four times as much as they contributed, after adjusting for the interest they would have earned had they invested the money themselves.[8]

What makes matters particularly unfair is that by any reasonable measure, a significant number of Social Security recipients do not need handouts from the government. Ten percent of all Social Security benefits (approximately $25 billion) go to households that receive other retirement income of $30,000 a year or more. Indeed, well over a million Social Security recipients have other retirement income in excess of $50,000.[9] Forty percent of all financial assets held by Americans are accounted for by those over sixty-five and almost 80 percent of retired persons own their own homes.[10] The elderly as a group now have a higher standard of living than working-age people.

None of this is to argue against the need to subsidize older people in need. We should be proud of the fact that old age is no longer synonymous with deprivation in our society. As recently as 1959 nearly a third of the population over sixty-five was living below the poverty line. Due largely to Social Security benefits, this number has now dropped to 12 percent.[11] Indeed, when you include the market value of noncash benefits—Medicare, Medicaid, food stamps, and subsidized housing—the poverty rate among the elderly falls to 4 percent.[12] Social Security keeps many older citizens just above the poverty line. While 44 percent of retired people have financial assets in excess of $50,000, 25 percent have assets of less than $3,000.[13] It seems that while "old age benefits have been successful in eliminating systematic economic deprivation"[14] among the elderly as a class, pockets of deep poverty continue to exist, particularly among the "oldest old" (those eighty-five and over) and minority elders.[15] For example, elderly black women had a median income of only $4,500 in 1988 and could use additional help.[16] A strong case can be made for *more and better benefits for the elderly poor.*

At the moment impoverished seniors are helped by dint of enormous indiscriminate spending on the elderly, not because they are targeted for help in any rational fashion. Far from it: Social Security cash benefits are actually regressive, in the sense that those with the highest lifetime incomes receive the highest monthly payments. In the opinion of Charles Peters, editor in chief of the *Washington Monthly,* "we should give more to that lonely old lady who is solely dependent on Social Security and lives a threadbare existence. But it is shocking for my Aunt Alice to be able to use her Social Security to go to Europe, which she does."[17] Market research surveys show that 37 percent of the elderly population regularly take foreign vacations.[18]

The crux of the problem lies in the way we have bought into the principles of entitlement and universality for the elderly— but for no one else! Over the last twenty-five years we have grown to believe that all elderly people deserve generous Social Security and Medicare benefits whether they need them or not. This is a luxury the nation can ill afford. There are more urgent priorities than subsidizing the life-style of an elderly person who already has a substantial income. A case in point are those millions of American toddlers shut out of Head Start due to a shortfall in public funds. Is it fair to spend 22.9 percent of the federal budget on those over sixty-five (with a poverty rate of 4 to 12 percent) but only 4.8 percent on those under eighteen (with a poverty rate of 17 to 20 percent)?[19]

Housing: Another Windfall?

Rising Social Security taxes and benefits directly transfer resources from the young to the old. Rising real estate prices
have done the same thing. The cost of housing rose dramatically in the 1970s and 1980s for a variety of reasons. Inflation
played a role but so did strong baby-boomer demand, a drop-
off in government subsidies for low-income housing, and spec-
ulation. Today the median cost of a home is $120,000, com-
pared with $18,000 in 1963. Even adjusted for inflation, this
represents an increase of 72 percent.[20] Joseph J. Minarik of the
congressional Joint Economic Committee estimates that the
typical thirty-year-old man buying a median-priced home in
1973 would have incurred carrying costs equal to 21 percent
of his income; by 1987 this figure had risen to 40 percent.[21]

Who benefits from this massive rise in the price of houses?
The sellers, of course: typically, older people who bought
these homes years ago at a fraction of their current market
value, often benefiting from the low-cost mortgages of the
G.I. Bill. In the period immediately after World War II, 5
million returning veterans were provided with thirty-year
loans at 3 to 4 percent interest in order to buy houses.[22] There
are no such subsidies available to families today. Home prices
and interest rates are sky-high, which is why house payments
consume 40 percent of the male wage. The burden borne by
a young family buying a home puts money directly into the
pockets of older empty-nesters.

One sobering result of the transfer of resources from the
young to the old through Social Security taxes and house
prices is that *mother has gone to work to support grandpa and
grandma,* leaving no one at home to look after the children.

In an effort to shore up living standards, more and more wives and mothers have entered the paid labor force. In 1960, 30 percent of mothers worked; by 1988, 66 percent did.[23] This dramatic shift has allowed many young families to keep their heads above water despite falling wages, rapid increases in payroll taxes, and escalating housing costs. Couples also marry later and have fewer children, which has helped to maintain living standards. In the 1950s and 1960s the typical family had one earner and three children. Contemporary families have two earners and fewer than two children.[24]

It's strange to think that a by-product of responding so generously to the demands of the elderly has been the buildup of enormous pressure on mothers to work outside the home. This, in turn, has created a great deal of additional risk for children and has depressed the birth rate. Indeed, the massive income transfer from working families to senior citizens has had a powerful constraining effect on the life choices of an entire generation.

Social Security benefits and house prices are the most direct methods of transferring resources from the young to the old, but they are not the only ways in which we subsidize the elderly while squeezing the young. Medicare, Medicaid, and civil service and military pensions, paid for in the main by general taxation revenue, also channel large sums of money to the older generation.

Medicare

Medicare has been called the budgetary equivalent of crab-grass and has grown extremely rapidly in recent years. Medicare cost $96 billion in 1990, up from $12 billion in 1975.[25] It now consumes 8 percent of the entire federal budget.

Despite attempts at cost-saving reforms in 1983 (such as the introduction of a prospective pricing system now used by hospital insurance), Medicare benefits continue to rise sharply every year, propelled by the greater number and greater sophistication of services offered each elderly patient; a rapid climb in labor costs per treatment; and perverse, cost-plus reimbursement systems that insulate both health-care professionals and patients from the cost of treatment. In addition to Medicare funds, older people consume a growing proportion of the $49 billion-a-year budget for Medicaid (which is supposed to help the poor of all ages), primarily in the form of nursing-home subsidies.[26]

Analysts are beginning to question the wisdom of devoting such huge sums of public money to health care for the elderly. *Fortune* magazine devoted a large part of its March 1989 issue to these problems. In a key article, a group of distinguished doctors, medical ethicists, demographers, theologians, and philosophers came to the conclusion that the United States should move toward lightening the medical burden the elderly place on the taxpaying public.[27]

As *Fortune* correctly points out, there are complicated, wrenching dilemmas wrapped up in how we trade off compassion for the old against concern for the young. But no matter how you interpret the data, we are a long way from striking the right balance. For example, in 1988, 28 percent of Medicare's budget was spent on patients in the last year of life, and, in the opinion of doctors, in many cases large sums of money were spent "merely to extend life without making it more worth living."[28] Former Secretary of Commerce Peter G. Peterson asks a central question: "Why do we continue to devote so many resources to comforting us at the end of life . . . while we pay a Head Start teacher less than $10,000 to prepare us at the beginning of life?"[29]

Twenty-eight percent of Medicare's budget is approximately $30 billion—more than the government spends on the health care of *all* American children. During the 1980s health-care programs for families and children were starved of money. As I explained in chapter 2, due to cutbacks in public funds, hundreds of thousands of preschool children are inadequately protected against measles, and the supplemental Food Program for Women, Infants, and Children (WIC) now reaches just over half of those eligible. The sums involved in maintaining these programs are often quite small; an additional $150 million a year would enable WIC to reach all women and children poor enough to be eligible for this program.[30] Nonetheless, the pattern in Washington has been to slash inexpensive health programs for children while underwriting a massive expansion in Medicare. For example, between 1980 and 1986, real per capita Medicaid expenditures for children declined 4 percent while Medicare spending rose by 14 percent in real per capita dollars.[31]

Toenail clipping at $65 a session is the least of our problems. Thousands of people in their seventies now have coronary bypass surgery (price tag: $25,000), and surgeons routinely sew hearts into people in their sixties and seventies (price tag: $75,000 to $140,000). Medicare pays for these procedures when the patient is over sixty-five. No other country goes to anywhere near such lengths to prolong the lives of elderly people. Japanese surgeons perform no organ transplants on senior citizens. And in Britain kidney dialysis isn't generally available to anyone over fifty-five through the National Health Service. In sharp contrast, Medicare subsidizes dialysis for more than 100,000 American citizens, half of them over sixty, at a cost of more than $2 billion a year.[32]

Many specialists in the field of medical ethics now think that there should be some rationing, that maybe the United States should limit subsidized health care and deny it—at least in its more heroic forms—to certain categories of elderly people. For example, Daniel Callahan, director of the Hastings Center, a research institute devoted to issues of science and ethics, feels that Medicare shouldn't pay for big-ticket items after age eighty or for expensive procedures when the patient is terminally ill and faces a pain-filled future.[33] Callahan would allow unlimited treatment for a patient who foots his or her own bill.

We clearly have had no problem rationing the amount of health care we provide to young Americans. Because of budget constraints community health-care centers now serve only 5 million of the 25 million poor who are eligible, and migrant health-care centers serve only 500,000 of the 3 million eligible.[34] But the greatest scandal is the large number of families who struggle to get by without health insurance. In 1987, 37 million adults and children—nearly 18 percent of the nonelderly population—had no health insurance, a 20 percent increase since 1980.[35] At best, uninsured families live with constant anxiety. At worst, they are forced to make impossible choices, day by day, dollar by dollar.

David Seeger would be 6 years old if he were alive today. His mother, Diana Seeger, thinks he would be if she had had health insurance while pregnant.

"I'm still angry about it," said Mrs. Seeger, a forty-year-old resident of Grand Rapids, Minn.

Neither Mrs. Seeger, nor her husband, Melvin, had health insurance when she was pregnant with David in 1982. He worked as a logger bringing home $9,000 that year. But the value of their assets, 40 acres of land, exceeded the qualifying threshold for state medical assistance. And they could not afford private insurance.

"We're hard workers," said Mrs. Seeger. "We weren't on welfare. We built our house. But food and clothing came first."

As a result, the couple regularly drove 70 miles west to an Indian hospital in Cass Lake, Minnesota. There, prenatal care was free for Mrs. Seeger, a member of the Chippewa tribe.

"It's no big deal to have a baby," she recalled thinking. "You never think your child is going to die. That happens to other people."

Grand Rapids, a rural city of 8,000 about 80 miles northwest of Duluth, has two private hospitals. But when Mrs. Seeger went into labor, she avoided both of them because of their cost. Instead, she tried to reach a hospital 84 miles away that she hoped would not demand payment.

She did not make it in time, and ended up stopping at an Indian health clinic not equipped for births. It was a difficult delivery, and her baby was deprived of oxygen for 8 to 10 minutes. The boy, David, was born severely brain-damaged, blind and deaf.

David survived for three and a half difficult years, spending most of the first nine months of his life in hospitals in Duluth and Minneapolis.

Because of the baby's handicaps, Government paid for thousands of dollars of medical care, but as Mrs. Seeger noted bitterly, a far smaller amount of money might have prevented the family's tragedy.[36]

Civil Service Pensions

Another publicly sponsored windfall for the older generation comes in the form of civil service and military retirement benefits. In 1987, $47 billion was spent on these two impressively generous pension systems. Need is not an issue here, since poverty is practically unknown among the beneficiaries of these programs. In fact, most are not "retired" at all but working at another job and earning a second pension.

As with Social Security, the argument is that these federal pensions "belong" to the recipients. We are told that the civil service has a genuine pension system, under which federal workers and federal agencies each pay 7 percent of salary into a retirement and disability trust fund. Yet the pension level is so high (averaging 56 percent of pre-retirement pay), the retirement age so young (age fifty-five after thirty-five years of service), and the disability criteria so permissive (one-quarter of all civil service pensioners seem to be disabled) that recipients actually get between two and three extra dollars for every dollar they contribute. What is more, unlike any private pension, civil service pensions are 100 percent indexed to the Consumer Price Index—with the strange result that federal pensioners often outearn their successors in office. Such expensive entitlements are hard to justify in an age of huge federal deficits.[37] In October 1990 New York's *Daily News* ran a particularly scathing editorial on the subject:

If you would like to know why the federal budget is out of control, consider the $1,000-a-year raise that Saddam Hussein has just required you to give to Tip O'Neill.

This is how it works: In August, the Iraqi leader invaded Kuwait. The immediate increase in oil prices raised U.S. inflation by nearly 1 percentage point, which was, last Friday, added into the 5.4% automatic federal cost-of-living adjustment (COLA) for Social Security recipients and federal retirees. For O'Neill, that extra 1% is about $1,000.

This is a classic example of an entitlement program. . . . An unexpected outlay of money must go from the Treasury, which doesn't have it, to O'Neill, who doesn't need it. . . . Saddam must be laughing his head off. . . . Your only involvement is to pay. It totals about $3 billion extra.

I need not have picked on former House Speaker O'Neill. The example is true for Alexander Haig, Jim Wright, former Ambassador to Japan Mike Mansfield and scores of others. All have federal pensions of about $100,000 a year, all get the federal COLA, and none needs the extra 1%.[38]

Military Pensions: The Ultimate Bonanza

From many points of view, military pensions comprise the most generous of our entitlement programs. The serviceman or woman contributes nothing to a trust fund, but upon reaching a median age of forty-one (and completing at least twenty years of service) he or she is entitled to 50 to 75 percent of pre-retirement pay, indexed yearly, for life. Typically, military personnel spend more years collecting benefits than they spent in the service. All service men and women are eligible for Social Security and most pursue second careers to achieve a "triple-dip" pension.

Feathering the nests of military personnel adds up to a surprisingly significant amount. The lifetime pension cost of a single army colonel or navy captain now averages $590,000. Indeed, in 1990 we spent $22 billion on military pensions, *which is almost twice as much as we spent that year on Aid to Families with Dependent Children* (AFDC), our main program of income support for poor families with children.[39]

It is hard to find any redeeming features in these enormously expensive military pensions. They do not seem to help much with recruitment, and on the retention front they actively "encourage our most skilled officers to retire just when they are reaching the peak of their careers." With such generous benefits available after twenty years of service, and with no penalty attached to retiring early, "skilled persons are almost always financially better off quitting the military" than sticking around.[40] Only 7 percent of military personnel stay in their jobs until the age of fifty. So ineffective and wasteful are these pensions that the Grace Commission—appointed by Reagan to trim fat in government—proposed a major reduction in military retirement benefits, but Congress, under pressure from the Pentagon, managed to bury this particular recommendation.

The Impact of Government Spending on Old and Young

Benefits for the elderly now comprise an item larger than national defense. Federal dollars for the older generation (primarily Social Security plus Medicare) rose, in constant dollars, from $151 billion in 1978 to $230.4 billion in 1987[41]—a sum that translates into $9,500 a year in federal benefits for each older American.[42] In sharp contrast, federal expenditure on all child-oriented programs—AFDC, Head Start, food stamps, child nutrition, child health, and federal aid to education—totaled $48.3 billion in 1987, down from $51 billion in 1978.[43] During the 1980s federal expenditure on health care, education, and housing for children shrank in real terms. By 1989 Americans under age eighteen received "only $1 per capita in federal benefits for every $11 going to each American over age 65."[44]

Politicians and the population at large seem increasingly comfortable spending public money on the elderly rather than on somebody else's children. But why do we prefer to underwrite toenail clipping for Mary Rodgers's mom than maternity care for Diana Seeger and her baby? Why do we find it easy to ration measles vaccine for eight-month-olds but impossible to ration triple bypass surgery for eighty-year-olds?

The core reasons center on self-interest. While we cannot recapture our own childhoods, all of us anticipate being old someday. At some level we all perceive programs and benefits for the elderly as *mechanisms through which we transfer resources to ourselves in the future.* The logic is as follows: If we create these programs and give them our uncluttered political support, the odds are they will be there to feather our own retirement nests.[45]

There are, in fact, three types of self-interest behind our generosity to the elderly: the swelling ranks of the elderly themselves; working-age people who "vote" to subsidize older people rather than assume direct responsibility for their own elderly parents; and working-age people who "vote" on behalf of themselves in the future.[46]

The number of people aged sixty-five and over increased 50 percent between 1965 and 1985, mainly due to a very rapid decline in old-age mortality. Rising numerical strength has been combined with a high degree of political participation. Sixty-five percent of persons aged sixty-five to seventy-four vote, more than double the percentage at ages twenty through twenty-nine, and significantly more than in the prime child-rearing years of thirty-five to forty-nine. The elderly also appear to be better informed: 56 percent can name their congressional representative, compared with 30 percent of those under thirty.[47]

Political and Economic Clout

The organization that has built on these demographic trends and turned the elderly into a potent political force is the American Association of Retired Persons (AARP). The AARP has tripled in size since 1978 and now has 29 million members. To put this in perspective, it is now twice the size of the AFL-CIO and represents more than one-fifth of the country's voters. This Washington-based organization has ten regional offices, a $235 million budget, and a staff of 1,200—including eighteen registered lobbyists. The magazine of AARP, *Modern Maturity,* reaches 17.9 million households.[48]

This kind of visibility inhibits Congress. There may be a budget deficit, but virtually no congressional representative will even discuss cutting Social Security or Medicare, the two programs that together consume a third of all federal spending. Anyone mentioning cutbacks quickly earns the label "granny basher" and, more often than not, is kicked out of office.

The AARP finds it relatively easy to swing votes. For example, in the 1988 presidential election campaign, it mailed pre-election guides to its members outlining candidates' positions on a variety of issues that concern the elderly. When the AARP surveyed members before and after the New Hampshire primary it found that 12 percent had switched candidates after reading the guide. That kind of power intimidates politicians.

The AARP got off the ground in the mid-1950s when a retired high school principal, Ethel Percy Andrus, was turned down by dozens of companies in her efforts to obtain health insurance for the members of her association of retired teachers. In 1958 she finally formed the AARP as a nonprofit organization "to enhance the quality of life for older persons."[49] Its primary function was to offer health insurance and home and automobile insurance to anyone over fifty-five (later reduced to fifty).

Andrus was firmly convinced that "most older persons are able to live in independence," and she often stated that the "AARP does not welcome the welfare state as the way of life for all older persons." She was determined that the AARP would "hold no meetings to bewail the hardships of old age . . . nor urge governmental subsidy."[50] Her view on government aid was that it should target the minority of elderly people who need it.

The AARP seems to have strayed from the intentions of its founder. In recent years the organization has lobbied long and hard for middle-class entitlements. According to Charles Peters of the *Washington Monthly,* the AARP has turned into "the most dangerous lobby in Washington."[51] It certainly seems to talk out of both sides of its mouth. Through its legislative office it lobbies aggressively for more across-the-board benefits, arguing the case with Congress that most older Americans have pressing unmet needs. At the same time the business staff of *Modern Maturity* asserts precisely the opposite to the advertising community.

For example, media kits for the magazine emphasize the prosperity of the elderly, describing them as "Affluent . . . Aware . . . Active buyers with over $800 billion to spend." These well-heeled consumers are most definitely "spending on self-fulfillment now, rather than leaving large sums behind."[52]

A Conference Board report aimed at advertisers paints a glowing picture of the elderly market. It tells us that older people control half of all discretionary spending power in the nation, "while the young control a feeble fifth." The financial assets of the older segment of the population are characterized as "surprisingly sturdy," and the report points out that the average net worth of American households reaches a peak level of $125,000 in the decade between sixty-five and seventy-five.[53] The elderly are described as traveling a good deal and owning homes that are "larger and more expensive than the property which today's young can afford to buy."[54]

The conclusion is that the elderly population "offers considerable promise for marketers." While necessary expenses are low (the elderly are happily free from most of the financial obligations that confront the young), the flow of income remains "robust" well into retirement. The report ends on a rousing note: "What we have here then, is potentially a highly receptive market for a wide range of luxury goods, for frills and services and top of the price line merchandise."[55]

One may well wonder why the AARP feels that young working families with their "feeble" buying power and unimpressive homes should subsidize "frills" for the affluent elderly to the tune of $9,500 per person per year!

Advertisers have bought the message of AARP's business staff. They now advertise heavily in *Modern Maturity,* and advertising revenue is now an important element in AARP's overall budget. By the mid-1980s *Modern Maturity* had made it onto *Adweek*'s annual list of the country's ten hottest magazines.

In the last decade advertisers have redefined the way they see older people. Until very recently, consumers sixty and older were ignored in advertising strategies for luxury items. People in that age group were thought to be unhealthy and impoverished—and many of them were. It was assumed that they would be reluctant to spend what little discretionary income they might have. Times have certainly changed: with an $800 billion market at stake, advertisers are beginning to pay a great deal of attention to elderly Americans.

Rena Bartos, an executive with the advertising firm of J. Walter Thompson, specializes in what she calls the "active affluents"—that new, large class of older prosperous people. According to Bartos, seniors are "caught up in the same desire for self-realization that affected the younger generation during the sixties and seventies. . . . They don't want to just sit on the shelf. They want to travel, purchase luxury items. . . . They don't want to spend the rest of their days just building up an estate."[56]

In sharp contrast to *Modern Maturity*'s active affluents, basking in the Florida sun, children are in bad shape. As I described in chapter 2, their situation has deteriorated rapidly over the last decade. Not only have falling wages and a dramatic increase in single-mother households undermined the standard of living of families with children, but the negative impact of these structural shifts has been exacerbated by sharp cutbacks in benefits for children. In recent years public programs directed toward children have been rolled back while programs for the elderly have been expanded massively. One area in which children and the elderly compete head-on is the medical sphere. Children's share of Medicaid funds dropped from 18 percent in 1972 to 12 percent in 1988, while the elderly received 35 percent in 1988, up from 30 percent in 1972.[57]

A central problem is that very little political energy is available to children. Children don't vote; and since adults are not able to vote to improve their own childhoods, many are less than enthusiastic about spending more money on children. As one analyst put it, "I daresay that if we passed through life backwards, adults would insist that conditions in childhood be made far more appealing."[58] The parents of dependent children do support programs that target youngsters, but this constituency has declined in both numbers and impact in recent years.

We have fewer children these days. Fertility rates have hovered around 1.9 children per woman since the mid-1970s, down from 3.7 per woman in 1957.[59] It is also true that with high rates of divorce and out-of-wedlock births, men are less inclined to live with the children they father. By the late 1980s a quarter of all children under eighteen lived with a single parent.[60] One result of these trends is that only 35 percent of American households now include a child under eighteen, down from 49 percent in 1960.[61]

If parents-in-residence are declining in numbers, they are also less likely to vote than is the average child-free citizen. Approximately 60 percent of adults in households with no children vote, compared with only 38 percent of adults in households with children.[62] Parents, particularly poor parents, seem to find it hard to make the time for political participation.

Age and family circumstances undoubtedly influence how people vote. A recent Gallup poll of public attitudes toward public schools asked whether people would vote to raise taxes for schools if requested to do so by their local school board. Below age fifty the vote was evenly split: 45 percent would favor the request and 46 percent would oppose it. At age fifty and above opponents of the new taxes outnumbered the supporters 62 percent to 28 percent.[63]

Future Trends

When we look into the future, one thing seems sure: our current levels of spending on the elderly population are unsustainable. Just leaving the budget on automatic pilot will lead to fiscal disaster. The forces guaranteeing this result are the aging of America and the constraining properties of benefit indexing.

Almost a third of all federal spending now goes to that 12 percent of the population over sixty-five.[64] Even if benefits per elderly person grow no faster than our economy, we can be certain that the total cost burden will expand dramatically. This is because over the next fifty years our elderly population will grow by 139 to 165 percent while our work-age population will grow by only 2 to 18 percent. By the year 2040 there will be more Americans over age eighty than there are Americans today over age sixty-five. These divergent trend lines mean that over a fifty-year period Social Security taxes could rise to 36 percent of workers' salaries, up from 15 percent today.[65] This is clearly both unacceptable and unsustainable.

The history of indexing benefits for the elderly is one of knee-jerk response to a powerful political lobby. For example, in 1972, in its rush to protect the elderly against inflation, Congress actually "double-indexed" Social Security cash benefits, which pushed up the benefits for new retirees by two CPI indexes at once.[66] This colossal error caused the average benefit to grow faster than either prices or wages in the mid-1970s.

Indexing constrains policy in that it makes it impossible for elected officials to reorder their spending priorities by gradually allowing real benefit levels in some programs to fall behind inflation while committing new resources to new programs. This constraining mechanism now affects a large area of the budget. In the late 1960s only 6 percent of all benefits for the elderly were indexed; today 78 percent are.[67]

Indexing also poses large problems for intergenerational equity. Over the next decade most economists predict stagnant wages and moderate rates of inflation. This could mean that prices (and indexed benefits) will rise considerably faster than after-tax wages. Is this fair? Should middle-class seniors be exempt from the downward jolts in standards of living that will affect all other Americans?

Any projection of current trend lines shows that today's policies will be untenable in the near future. The relevant question becomes: When and how are benefits for the elderly going to be scaled back? In a political crisis, or gradually? Before or after we have sacrificed a generation?

Timing is critical because we will soon face a major shift in the ratio of workers to dependents. The baby boom generation is now in the prime of life and at work in record numbers, and the worker-dependent ratio is likely to remain favorable for the next twenty years. However, in 2011, when the boomers start to retire, the worker-dependent ratio will worsen considerably. Between 2010 and 2025 the number of work-age Americans is expected to decline by as much as 12 million, while the elderly population is expected to grow by 23 million.[68] If universal retirement and health-care benefits for the elderly seem unaffordable today, when a boom generation is working and a bust generation is retiring, imagine how unaffordable they will be early next century when this situation is reversed!

There is only one route to a comfortable future. If over the next twenty years the government channels significant new resources into maternal and child health, day care, and education, and if, at the same time, parents are supported in ways that enable them to give more time and attention to their children, then we can trigger a quantum leap in the productivity of the next generation of workers and create the conditions for a prosperous and contented old age. If this does not happen, if this generation continues to consume all its own product and part of the next generation's as well, then "we can count on a meager and strife-torn future."[69] Zero-sum games do not make for social harmony.

The Fiasco over Catastrophic Health Care

In 1989 we caught a glimpse of these ugly tensions in the ruckus over the financing of catastrophic health care.

When sixty-nine-year-old Leona Kozien showed up for a meeting of the Senior Polka Association in August 1989, mastering the half step was the last thing on her mind. Together with some 200 senior citizens from the Chicago area, Kozien was lying in wait for Representative Dan Rostenkowski (D-Ill.), a key sponsor of the Medicare Catastrophic Coverage Act of 1988 and the group's invited guest. Rostenkowski ducked their angry questions, so Kozien and about fifty others followed the congressman outside. They surrounded his car, beat on it with picket signs, and pounded on the windows hollering "chicken," "liar," "Rottenkowski." As the congressman tried to drive away, Kozien planted herself in front of the moving car and forced him to stop while she gave him another piece of her mind.[70]

Lawmakers privately called them the "greedy geezers" and in the months following passage of the Act they deluged Capitol Hill with angry letters and phone calls objecting to the extra taxes imposed on them by the catastrophic health care legislation. One congressman's mother was so exercised that she could no longer have a civil conversation with her son. He turned her calls over to an aide, who observed bitterly, "This is government by who yells loudest."[71]

But these riled-up seniors prevailed. They pounded and hollered and Congress heard them loud and clear. In October 1989, the House voted 360 to 66 to repeal the Medicare Catastrophic Coverage Act. It had been in place for just over a year. The winners were the well-to-do elderly, the losers were—everyone else.

The short-lived Catastrophic Coverage Act provided a smorgasbord of benefits. The program capped yearly out-of-pocket expenses for Medicare recipients at $560 for hospitals and $1,370 for doctors' bills. It covered 80 percent of the cost of prescription drugs after a $600 deductible and underwrote 150 days of skilled nursing care. It provided thirty-eight days of home health care and eighty hours of specialized care to ease the burden on family members who care for aged relatives.[72] In short, it helped elderly people across the board deal

with the enormous expenses that accompany prolonged illness. It was particularly valuable to older, less affluent elderly
people, the group most likely to face chronic illness and least
likely to carry private medigap insurance.

There was a great deal of enthusiasm for these new medical
benefits. The problem was, in an era of budget deficits, who
was going to foot the bill? After countless hearings, Congress
came up with a plan that imposed a surcharge of 15 percent
on the income taxes of elderly people who had yearly tax
liabilities of more than $150 a year. In practice some 40
percent of the elderly qualified to pay a portion of this surtax,
and 5 percent of the elderly—those with incomes over
$35,000 a year—were hit with the maximum contribution of
$800 a year.[73]

It was this funding arrangement—not the new benefits—
that sparked anger and activism. The National Committee to
Preserve Social Security and Medicare blanketed the country
with literature denouncing the measure as a "seniors-only
surtax," arguing that retirees shouldn't be singled out to
pay for a social welfare program. The committee urged its
5.5 million members (97 percent of whom voted in the last
election) to write their representatives protesting the surtax.
In a matter of weeks 2 million letters landed on Capitol Hill,
and elected representatives began the ignominious retreat that
culminated in the act's repeal.

It's hard to quarrel with the premise behind the catastrophic
care legislation. The central idea was that the program not lean
on general taxation revenues but be self-supporting by having
better-off seniors pick up the tab for poorer seniors through
a highly progressive income-tax surcharge. Underprivileged
older persons would gain much better access to long-term
medical care, and affluent older persons would pay more for
better benefits. In the wake of the bitter complaints it's hard

to remember that the upper-income elderly would still have been net winners. The data show that even with the surcharge, the most affluent 10 percent of the elderly population would have still paid premiums representing as little as 35 percent of the benefits they received in the improved Medicare package.[74]

At bottom the Catastrophic Coverage Act was an experiment in enlightened public policy in an era of limited resources—and it failed. No one should be proud of this fact. Its repeal is a stunning illustration of the enormous political power wielded by the elderly, particularly those lobbies that represent the affluent elderly. It also sheds an unflattering light on the self-righteous greed of at least some of these elderly activists. Senator Lloyd Bentsen (D-Tex.) described them as "a very vocal minority sounding off. . . . What you have is wealthier people not wanting to pay the additional premium and wanting it to be more heavily subsidized by other taxpayers."[75] The thing is they won.

Letting Posterity Take Care of Itself

Underlying these debates about what should be spent on the old and the young and who should pay the bill is a deeper question, one that has always intrigued and preoccupied economists: the present versus the future, or consumption versus investment. In the words of Yale University economist James Tobin: "How should society divide its resources between current needs and pleasures and those of next year, next decade, next generation?"[76]

It may sound harsh but the money spent on the elderly is basically an expense—a consumption item—whereas money spent on children is an investment, one that enhances our prosperity and ultimately rebounds to the benefit of everyone, including the elderly.

Throughout history the idea that it is appropriate for one generation to make sacrifices for the welfare of the next has been taken for granted—that is, until the rapid and sustained growth of the 1946–1966 period. In those special decades the economy grew at an unprecedented rate, and economists began to assume that rapid growth would roll into the future. In the mid-1960s Princeton economist William Baumol wrote: "In our economy, by and large, the future can be left to take care of itself. There is no need to lower the social rate of discount [standards of living] in order to increase further the prospective wealth of future generations."[77] Given his expectation of buoyant growth into the future, Baumol saw saving for the next generation as some kind of Robin Hood activity stood on its head. This about-face by influential economists became a license to spend rather than save and to consume rather than invest.

A Deteriorating Infrastructure

In public policy one of the first indications of a new consumption mentality was the cutback in infrastructural investment in the late 1960s. The excuse was the Vietnam War, but rather than raising taxes to pay for the war, spending on bridges and roads and other types of physical infrastructure was severely reduced. Public investment in infrastructure fell from 3.5 percent of GNP in the mid-1960s to 2.5 percent in the mid-1980s.[78] In other words, over a twenty-year time span the nation's capital budget fell by a third. Not only was there a reluctance to undertake new projects but there was little maintenance of existing roads, bridges, and airports.

The Reagan years witnessed continued and systematic neglect of infrastructure, with the result that many of our
bridges, roads, and airports are now in deplorable shape. In
1989 the Federal Highway Administration estimated that 23
percent of the nation's 575,000 bridges were deficient and
needed significant repairs.[79] And our highways are hurting.
New highway construction peaked in 1968, and spending on
construction and maintenance has declined steadily since that
time. With the average life of a road estimated at twenty-eight
years, many of the roads constructed in the 1950s and 1960s
have reached the end of their useful lives. Yet net public
investment in highways declined by 0.5 percent a year in the
1980s. The Chamber of Commerce calculates that over the
next twenty-five years "traffic delays caused by inadequate
roads will cost the U.S. $50 billion a year in lost wages and
wasted gasoline."[80]

Public investment in airports and air traffic–control systems
has also lagged. Public spending per passenger mile fell from
a high of 80¢ in 1960 to 20¢ in the late 1980s. The Federal
Aviation Administration warns us that by the year 2000, air-
port congestion will affect 74 percent of passengers, compared
with 39 percent today.[81]

Overall, enormous sums of money are required to make up
the infrastructural deficit. Congress's Joint Economic Committee calculates that from now until the year 2000 the country
will need to spend more than a trillion dollars to repair and
replace existing physical infrastructure.[82] This sum is equal to
half of the national debt, and much of it must be counted as
part of the encumbrance being imposed on the next generation of Americans by their elders.

In September 1989 the CBS news program "60 Minutes" ran
a story entitled "New York Is Falling Apart." The story de-

scribed a commuter named John Burnham, who was driving along the FDR Drive in Manhattan in 1982 when the road simply disappeared.

JOHN BURNHAM: All of a sudden, as I'm pulling into that lane, the whole left side of my car collapsed. And when I looked out the window I just saw nothing and I said to myself, "My God, the road has collapsed." If I had been maybe one foot further to the left, the car would have been in that hole, and who knows what would have happened. You just have to be a fatalist about life in New York and do the best you can.

HARRY REASONER: But hoping for the best doesn't help much in a city where disasters have become routine events. In this case, a water main breaks at Columbus Circle [and] five million gallons of water erupts onto the streets, flooding basements, halting traffic and turning the subway lines into flowing rivers.

SUBWAY OFFICIAL: Attention passengers, attention downtown Sixth Avenue riders. Due to a water main break there is no downtown Sixth Avenue service at this time.

REASONER: Within hours, teams of emergency specialists had rerouted traffic, pumped out the subway lines and identified the problem—a cast-iron water main laid down in 1898. Just one section of pipe in a city that has 6,000 miles of aging water mains. No section of New York is immune from these water attacks. Wall Street has been struck, Madison Avenue, Park Avenue, Broadway. It's as if there were countless time bombs ticking away under the city, certain to go off and flood the streets many times a year. . . . New Yorkers have come to accept these subterranean water attacks much as Filipinos or Thais stoically put up with the annual monsoon.

NARRATOR: But last spring no one was able to be philosophical about the disintegration of another critical part of New York's infrastructure, the city's bridges. Not after Mayor Koch announced that he was closing down the vital Williamsburg Bridge. That bridge normally carries a quarter of a million people back and forth between Manhattan and Brooklyn each day.

MAYOR EDWARD I. KOCH: Better to be inconvenienced and safe than to be convenienced and dead.

REASONER: What New Yorkers saw on their televisions that night was scary. . . . It turned out that most of the bridge had not been painted in 15 years. The new transportation commissioner found he could put his hand through portions of the rusting steel that was supposed to help hold up the bridge. That was enough to unnerve anyone. But then, when the main cables that keep the bridge upright were inspected, hundreds of iron strands that make up the cables were found to be broken.

FIRST BRIDGE WORKER: Scary, man, that's all I can say to you. Scary.

SECOND BRIDGE WORKER: I mean, not one of the bridges here that they didn't know it had to be repaired ten years ago.

REASONER: Now, this city which cannot function without its bridges was acknowledging that decades of neglect had left at least 90 other bridges in a state of extreme disrepair. And, in the case of this six-lane bridge, the conclusion was—nothing can save it.

ROSS SANDLER, TRANSPORTATION COMMISSIONER: The bridges are built to last not decades, not even a century. Bridges should last many centuries. They just need to be maintained.

REASONER: To get them back to a state where you can maintain them reasonably, what's the bill?

SANDLER: Well, it's large. We should spend $2.7 billion over the next 10 years to move all of the poor and fair bridges into the good column. We don't have that money. . . .

REASONER: After we broadcast this report last February, a 500-pound slab of concrete fell from the FDR drive and killed a motorist. And just a week ago, one of those aging water mains broke and unleashed another flood in midtown. This time, millions of gallons of erupting water combined with asbestos from a steam pipe formed a poisonous goo that caused the city to shut down subway lines, close businesses and urge citizens in an eight-block area to evacuate their apartments or stay indoors with their windows sealed.

NARRATOR: In case your reaction to this story is, "Thank God I don't live in New York," we feel obliged to pass on what the urban experts say. The decay overwhelming New York is eating away at virtually every American city east of the Mississippi. And it's heading west, from Boston to Detroit, from Denver to Seattle. . . .[83]

Increasingly the condition of America's physical infrastructure is eating into and compromising the prosperity of the nation. A crumbling infrastructure is inconvenient, even dangerous, for ordinary citizens, but these deficiencies also constrain business activity and depress growth rates into the future. Collapsing bridges, deteriorating roads, and overburdened airports push up the costs of doing business— more gas will be consumed, more overtime will be paid— which in turn lowers productivity and undermines the competitive strength of the economy. Economists at the Federal Reserve attribute a significant part of the recent productivity slump to "neglect of our core infrastructure."[84]

Despite the serious consequences of deteriorating roads, bridges, and airports, the Bush administration is not giving priority to this type of investment. In 1990 we allocated $43.8 billion to infrastructure—about the same as in 1979, even though the economy grew 40 percent in the intervening years. Federal grants to state and local governments for infrastructural projects are down 23 percent since 1979.[85]

A Mountain of Debt

This failure to invest in bridges and water pipes, this unwill-ingness to provide the underpinnings for future prosperity, shortchanges young people because it limits the economic potential of the nation. But these problems pale in comparison with what we have done to our children on the fiscal front. The fact of the matter is that we have not paid for our generos-ity to ourselves—our middle-class entitlements, our high lev-els of consumption—through increased taxation. Indeed, in the mid-1980s we lightened the load by enacting a major income-tax cut. Instead of paying our way we have built a veritable mountain of debt which will have to be paid off by our children.

When Ronald Reagan took office, our national debt was $728 billion, or 26 cents for every dollar the country earned. The United States was also the world's leading creditor nation, with the power and status that goes along with that privileged position. But eight years later—all years of peace—the level of national indebtedness had tripled. In 1988, just before George Bush took office, the federal debt was $2.1 trillion, or 43 cents for every dollar of national income.[86] Worse still, after eight years of large deficits and reckless borrowing, the United States had become the world's largest debtor nation, dependent upon the goodwill of other countries to keep the show on the road.

The speed of the shift from creditor to debtor was breath-taking. As recently as 1981, the United States was $141 billion in the black. By the end of 1988, we were $440 billion in the red[87]—a particularly distressing transformation given the fact that we didn't create this juggernaut of debt to build new bridges or educate young workers, but merely to finance higher and higher levels of personal consumption. A goodly proportion of the $500 billion we burned up in the 1980s—almost half—went toward enhanced middle-class entitlements and those "frills and services and top-of-the-price-line merchandise" so enjoyed by our active, affluent senior citizens.

Pete Peterson has an interesting spin on the glittering "feelgood" 1980s, a decade in which our president told us to "go for the gold" and almost everyone thought that "greed was good." Behind the scenes, this is what was going on.

Consumption per capita rose by $3,100 during the 1980–89 period, but only $950 of this extra consumption was paid for by an increase in what each of us produced; the other $2,150 was funded by cuts in domestic investment (low-income housing is a prime example) and by borrowing huge sums from the next generation. Swollen budget deficits and widening rivers of foreign debt are simply "the mathematical expression of our wish to buy now and pay later" or, more accurately, to buy now and let our children pay later. As Peterson points out, in every previous decade Americans have consumed slightly less than 90 percent of incremental production, but during the 1980s we managed to consume 325 percent of the increase in national production![88] An act of monumental self-indulgence and shortsightedness.

On the simplest level of analysis, at current interest rates every dollar the government borrows will cost taxpayers $24 in interest charges over the next thirty years. Richard Darman, director of the Office of Management and Budget, calculates that the interest charges we have pushed into the future now average $45,000 for every American family of four. "It's like a second mortgage," he says, "but without the house."[89]

On a more fundamental level of analysis, the heavy burden of debt is likely to constrain our economic options into the future. In 1990 interest charges on the national debt consumed 15 percent of the federal budget, cutting into what is available for everything else.[90] Even more serious is the way in which deficits and debt push up the cost of money. In order to finance our burgeoning national debt, policy makers need to keep domestic interest rates artificially high so as to attract sufficient quantities of foreign funds. These high interest rates, in turn, depress business activity and limit growth. It seems that in a variety of direct and indirect ways, our children will spend a great deal of their working lives paying for the 1980s binge.

Now-now-ism

The increasingly massive transfer of income from the young to the old in American society seems to be part of a larger pattern. In recent years our political decisions about how to collect and allocate public money have increasingly tilted in favor of adults over children (particularly elderly adults over families with children), consumption over investment, and the present over the future. Richard Darman calls this collective short-sightedness, or "Now-now-ism." To use Darman's imagery, "Like the spoiled '50s child in the recently revived commercial, we seem on the verge of a collective Now-now scream: 'I want my Maypo; I want it NOWWWWWW!' "[91] Such an approach may work for toddlers at breakfast time, but for adults engaged in the serious tasks of government it is a formula for disaster. (It should be pointed out that despite Darman's profound understanding of the dangers inherent in spoiled child behavior, he has not used his considerable power at the Office of Management and Budget to rein in the deficit or tilt spending away from consumption and toward investment. In the words of *Wall Street Journal*, Darman's analysis is "tarnished by more than a touch of deceit.")[92]

This new level of self-indulgence in the public domain owes much to the ideologies of Ronald Reagan, George Bush, and the Republican party, but ordinary citizens deserve at least some of the blame. Tipping the balance from investment to consumption, and from the future to the present, fits neatly into the materialistic, self-centered mood of the day.

As I discussed in chapter 4, over the last twenty-five years the giving-getting compact in society has undergone a sea change. Starting in about 1965, the focus of adult attention shifted from responsibilities to "other" to responsibilities to "self," and large numbers of Americans became increasingly caught up in behavior patterns that glorified individualism. Robert Bellah tells us that this new preoccupation with self has grown "cancerous" and is destroying family and community, leaving individuals suspended in "glorious, but terrifying, isolation."[93] At the very least it has skewed political decisions so as to emphasize adult rights to consume in the here-and-now. Older American have been the big winners. Demographic trends and voting patterns have given elderly Americans a great deal of political clout, and it has become easy to persuade Congress to spend twice as much money on military pensions as on AFDC.

But government has not always been so passive, meekly reading the opinion polls, figuring out what voters might need or want next. Just a generation ago, in the days of President Kennedy's new frontier, a confident, activist government had no problem telling us all what was just and good. John Fitzgerald Kennedy put his fellow Americans on notice in his 1961 inaugural address: "Ask not what your country can do for you—ask what you can do for your country."[94] The central, inspiring message of the Kennedy administration was that government can lead, government can make a difference. Such an attitude spawned the civil rights movement and the War on Poverty, which went some distance toward closing the gap between the "haves" and "have-nots" and producing a greater measure of social justice in American society.

In the 1980s we lost our way. The Reagan revolution succeeded beyond its fomenters' wildest dreams in discrediting government, and we are now left with a permissive, minimalist state timidly following along in the wake of a self-absorbed electorate increasingly fixated on its own immediate desires. When groups of well-heeled seniors kick and scream and browbeat Congress into repealing a particularly progressive piece of legislation, we all know we have a problem with the "vision thing."

To some extent the void left by the retreat of government has been filled by free enterprise. But, as we have discovered, in spheres as diverse as television programming and juvenile psychiatric care, unfettered markets tend to exacerbate rather than contain the self-indulgence and materialism of our age.

Where do we go from here? How do we persuade government to reassert itself not just as the guardian of children but as the counterweight to Now-now-ism? How do we turn government into a force that promotes investment and compels us to acknowledge our collective responsibility for the future?

The Power of the Public Purse

Chapter 4 ended on a note of hope. It demonstrated that changing the rules of the game can make a difference. New legislation has a chance of turning the tide, of tipping the balance in private decision making so as to protect better the interest of the child. But if new rules beget new ways of living, allocative decisions are even more potent. Deciding how much public money to spend on what, and how to finance such spending, sets up powerful incentives and disincentives in society.

Government can condition behavior in two ways. It can pass laws that establish new rules, and then back these rules with civil and criminal sanctions. Or it can use its financial capability to reward and penalize private behavior. If government provides generous financial backing for an activity, this will often increase enthusiasm for such an activity. If, on the other hand, government starves a project of funds, this will generally dampen enthusiasm for such a project. Rewards and penalties reverberate through society, conditioning what we do and how we think.

In modern times the American government has massively subsidized the life-styles of elderly people—to the tune of $363 billion in 1990. We call these subsidies entitlements and give them to all elderly people whether they need them or not. We don't tax most of these benefits and, in the wake of the fiasco surrounding the Catastrophic Coverage Act, we have given up the idea that the affluent elderly should help defray the costs of benefits for the elderly poor. In other words, we don't expect older people to pull their weight or contribute to the collective good. The message communicated by government spending is that older people have paid their dues and no longer owe anything to anyone.

In direct contrast, young people have been starved of public funds. In 1991, families with children are having a rough time. Not only are they dealing with falling wage rates and disappearing fathers, but government has pulled the rug out from under them. They have been squeezed on at least two fronts. Benefits levels have fallen (AFDC, Medicaid, day care, and housing subsidies were all cut back during the 1980s) and, to make matters worse, *taxes have gone up*.

Despite the acclaimed Reagan tax cuts—which did bring

income-tax rates down—taxes were not cut in the 1980s; the burden was merely shifted from income tax to payroll taxes (chiefly Social Security taxes), which were jacked up by more than 23 percent during this decade.[95] As a result the burden of taxation now falls much more heavily on low- and middle-income working families and much less heavily on wealthy individuals. This is because Social Security taxes are highly regressive—an identical rate of 7.6 percent is levied on all workers, and income above $51,300 is exempt. *The Economist* estimates that with payroll taxes included, the "true" marginal tax rate is now higher for a married couple making $14,000 a year (30 percent) than it is for a couple making $326,000 a year (28 percent).[96] Senator Moynihan has one bitter comment: "If you had told Franklin D. Roosevelt that the day would come when we'd be financing a quarter of the federal government with this payroll tax . . . he'd have used the word . . . thievery."[97]

Thus allocative decision making has become very skewed in American society. Financial obligations to the old have become almost fully socialized, while the cost of raising the next generation continues to fall on individual families.[98] In fact, by cutting benefits to children we have returned even more responsibility to the family despite "the manifest erosion in the family's ability to shoulder these responsibilities." There probably is no way policy makers can protect children from the earthquake that has "shuddered through the American family" over the past thirty years,[99] but rather than compensating for the difficulties imposed by both parents at work, divorce, and single parenthood with generous benefits, successive administrations have tightened the purse strings and increased the penalties attached to child raising in our society. Many young couples now feel that they cannot afford to raise a family. Birth rates have declined 50 percent in a generation and children across the board are at risk.

Clearly, government possesses levers for change: it can alter the rules of the game to make it harder to abandon or otherwise off-load a child, and it can transform financial incentives to reward rather than penalize families with children. In the end it is a question of volition. Where is the trigger that will prompt us to reorder priorities on Capitol Hill? In the final section of this book I will attempt to demonstrate that the economic and human costs of child neglect have reached such intolerable levels that we may be ready both to protect and to invest in our children. We are at the point where we finally understand that, to save our own skins, we have to create the conditions that allow youngsters to flourish.

But before turning to the good news, it is important to understand the forces that could impede such initiatives. In the following chapter I will show how the private and public choices of recent decades have produced a mindset in government that is extraordinarily careless of children. If we are planning to save our children we need to appreciate the depth and scope of official antagonism.

6

Government Policy and the Beginnings of Life

Cinde Guzman never dreamed she would have to pay a thousand dollars for a prenatal checkup. Not that the actual fee for the exam was that much, but that's what several doctors wanted up front before accepting her into their prenatal program. The young Los Angeles graphic artist was in a bind: She was uninsured, but had been told she earned too much to qualify for public medical aid [Medi-Cal]. Her husband, Berto, was in school, and her meager wages from a freelance design job had to support both of them—and their one-year-old daughter, Angel.

It was a tough time to be having a new baby. Some evenings Cinde would spread her bills on the kitchen table and just sit and worry. . . . "It was the worst time in my life, with my paycheck not due for weeks, my rent late, and the utility company about to turn off the lights," recalls Guzman, a tall slender woman of 33 with straight blonde hair.

Guzman was six months pregnant before she had enough money to schedule her first checkup. Then, two nights before her appointment, she felt cramps and sharp pains in her abdomen, but she wearily dismissed them as a sudden case of the flu.

"I was sure it wasn't the baby because I wasn't even showing yet or wearing maternity clothes," says Guzman. But the pain soon grew so intolerable, she recalls, "that my husband said, 'Don't argue with me, get dressed,'" and rushed her to the hospital. Fifteen minutes after she was wheeled into the maternity ward, she gave birth to Carina Guzman, a tiny infant who was three months premature and weighed only 2.6 pounds.

Like many very small, dangerously premature babies, Carina was born fighting for her life. Within 24 hours of her delivery, she suffered a brain hemorrhage, a seizure, and a collapsed lung. A worried doctor told the distraught Guzmans that their infant was likely to die. "I was so stricken with grief *I* wanted to die," says Cinde. ". . . I felt so guilty for working under so much stress, for not having seen a doctor . . . for everything."

To everyone's surprise, Carina Guzman survived, although it was five weeks before nurses could unhook the wires so that her mother could hold her.

If a doctor had examined Cinde early in her pregnancy, he or she might well have noticed a change in the cervix indicating that she was in danger of preterm labor. . . . The doctor could then have prescribed bed rest and intravenous fluids—a strategy of treatment successful in almost half of potential preterm-labor cases.

Prenatal care, at a cost of approximately $1,000 . . . could have prevented Carina's health problems. As it was, the baby's hospital bills alone totaled nearly $150,000, paid for . . . ironically by Medi-Cal.

Carina's traumatic entry into the world may have exacted another kind of cost as well—she has cerebral palsy and cannot walk, a condition that some doctors have linked to premature and underweight births. She also has had heart surgery and may eventually need leg surgery. And doctors warn that she may have sustained additional neurological damage that will not show up for years.

Carina, now four years old, is a bright and loving child who delights both her parents. The Guzmans are struggling, however, with the financial hardship and sacrifice posed by their daughter's cerebral palsy, including three visits a week to physical therapists. Cinde Guzman says they must also contend with the pain of watching Carina try, in vain, to walk like other children. "It's devastating to me," she says, "there's not a day I don't think about her not walking. I wish she could run through the grass and play like the other kids."[1]

For all that they have endured, the Guzmans are still luckier than many parents. Carina could easily have died. As I described in chapter 2, 40,000 American babies die each year before their first birthday and half of these deaths are a direct result of mothers' receiving little or no prenatal care. Women who don't receive adequate prenatal care are forty times as likely to lose their baby in the first month of life than those who initiate prenatal care in the critical first three months of pregnancy. They are also three times as likely to have premature, low-birth-weight babies.[2] Infants who weigh less than 5.5 pounds at birth often need a great deal of expensive medical attention and are much more likely than full-term babies to suffer lifelong disabilities such as cerebral palsy (like Carina), seizure disorders, blindness, and mental retardation.

None of this pain and suffering comes cheaply. In 1989 the Congressional Office of Technological Assessment estimated the cost of caring for dangerously premature babies at $2.4 billion annually. Initial hospital costs average $54,800 per child, and the price tag of a lifetime of care and treatment for these children averages $389,800.[3]

Despite the enormous savings inherent in effective prenatal

care, it is more difficult to obtain today than it was in 1975. Seventeen percent of American women of childbearing age don't have medical coverage—up from 12 percent ten years ago—and the results can be seen in public hospitals across the nation.[4] At King General in Los Angeles, Cook County in Chicago, and Kings County in New York City, 30 percent of pregnant patients arrive to deliver their babies having had no prenatal care—three times the 1981 rate.

> Sonya Johnson lies in delivery room E of Martin Luther King Jr. General Hospital here, cursing. . . . She screams at the medical intern: "Stop that, girl. Leave it *alone,* girl." The exhausted intern snaps at Ms. Johnson to shut up and push. Finally, Ms. Johnson gives birth to a baby girl.
>
> But this is no blessed event. There is no movement; no first cry. The infant is dead—one of the 40,000 U.S. newborns this year who will never see a first birthday. Like the mothers of so many of these babies, Ms. Johnson had no medical care before arriving at the hospital.
>
> Here at the gray concrete Los Angeles County facility where Ms. Johnson gave birth, infant mortality has been on a grim and steady climb to 17.4 babies per 1,000 births, up from 12 in 1983. Fetal deaths are so common that the labor and delivery unit harbors an isolation room—No. 3—to keep grieving would-be mothers from hearing joyous parents nearby.[5]

If Sonya Johnson had received prenatal care, the odds are her baby would have lived. Medication, bed rest, and induced labor could have made all the difference. The main reason so many pregnant women fail to find medical care is financial: some 15 million women of childbearing age have no private health insurance and for one reason or another fail to qualify for Medicaid. Women are far less likely to seek prenatal care early in pregnancy when they must pay for maternity services out of their own, often meager resources (Cinde Guzman is a case in point). According to a 1988 Institute of Medicine study, "financial barriers—particularly inadequate or no insurance and limited personal funds—were the most important obstacles reported in 15 studies of women who received insufficient care."[6] The requirement for a deposit or down payment to obtain prenatal services is particularly onerous.

A handful of states are attempting to make prenatal care more accessible to poor women. In 1987 New York funded a public health program called Personal Care Assistance Program (PCAP) to provide services to low-income pregnant women who lack health insurance and are not eligible for Medicaid. And in 1989 New Jersey started a program called Maternity Outreach and Managed Services (MOMS), which aims to provide comprehensive health and nutritional services to uninsured pregnant women.[7]

These state programs are important steps in the right direction, but it is hard for one or two modest state initiatives to make a dent in what has become a mammoth problem nationwide. The number of uninsured young families grew rapidly in the 1980s as private health insurance became a more expensive and scarcer commodity, and as federal funding for Medicaid was cut back and eligibility standards for poor families became more stringent. The net result: by the end of the decade, 800,000 pregnant women had no medical coverage.[8]

The Story Told by Policy

The harrowing childbirth experiences of Cinde Guzman and Sonya Johnson raise some extremely uncomfortable questions about the values underlying American public policy. If we treat pregnant women in such a profoundly careless manner, how can we pretend to "honor" parents or "value" children? If we squander the lives of newborn babies in such a thoughtless fashion, how can we claim to respect human life?

Harvard Law School professor Mary Ann Glendon describes how the laws and policies of a nation tell a story that projects "certain visions about where we come from, where we are now and where we'd like to go."[9] Our policies in and around childbirth tell a multidimensional story of carelessness and neglect. They tell the tale of a self-centered people supremely uninterested in the fate of other people's children—particularly if these children happen to be poor or black. And they tell a tale of personal culpability. If you have a child, you are on your own. If you can look after it, fine. If you can't, don't expect Uncle Sam to bail you out. You made your bed, you lie in it. The spirit of these tales is uncaring, even spiteful, and the thrust of the story is to deny any form of collective responsibility for children.

These tales are ugly but they are also powerful—so powerful, in fact, that they get in the way of self-interest. We have such a short attention span when it comes to uninsured pregnant women and problem-ridden premature babies that we fail to focus in on these problems long enough to figure out that this stunting of lives is a very expensive business—and we're footing the bill! When an issue is number 33—or thereabouts—on everyone's list of priorities, it becomes extremely hard to get together the energy to determine what a rational policy might look like. Rather than deal with such a tiresome, tedious matter, we shoot ourselves in the foot.

The business community is increasingly disturbed by our public policies in this area. In the fall of 1989 the Washington Business Group published a study called "The Corporate Perspective on Maternal and Child Health." The central message was that it's time to concern ourselves with the health of mothers and babies, that we all have an enormous stake in this problem because we're already paying the bills for neglected pregnant women and critically ill infants. In the words of this report: *"Someone* pays the bills of the sick babies born to mothers who received inadequate care. Government programs such as Medicaid pick up some of the tab and millions of dollars of bad debt are shifted by hospitals onto the bills of paying patients. Eventually these costs are paid by individuals and businesses through higher taxes, higher prices and higher insurance rates."[10] Prenatal and maternity care are simply good investments.

The economic rationale for an aggressive and comprehensive program of prenatal care is especially compelling in the case of drug-exposed babies. As we discovered in chapter 4, there has been an alarming rise in the use of crack by pregnant women; some 375,000 babies are now born each year with severe physical disabilities as a result of exposure to this drug in the womb. The medical costs for crack babies are staggering. The Joint Economic Committee of Congress estimates that it will soon cost this nation $15 billion a year to prepare drug-exposed babies for kindergarten.[11]

Despite these enormous costs we haven't begun to provide residential drug treatment for drug-addicted pregnant women, although it would be much cheaper than dealing with the long-term needs of their crack babies. In New York State the cost of several months of residential drug treatment for a pregnant woman is estimated at $15,000 to $20,000.[12] This investment is only a fraction of the initial costs of caring for one crack-addicted baby. Besides which, preventing damage to a child avoids untold human misery.

Prenatal and Maternity Policies

American policy with regard to prenatal and maternity care combines the worst of two worlds: it is neither compassionate nor cheap. We are unfeeling, even callous, when we deny prenatal care to pregnant women such as Cinde Guzman, because in doing this, we are causing her unnecessary anguish and condemning her child to a lifetime of pain and struggle. And we are foolishly reckless when we squander $150,000 of public funds on neonatal intensive care rather than spend $400 to $1,000 on preventing the tragedy in the first place.

The United States is unique in having created this calamitous policy mix. In all other rich nations pregnant women and newborn children are treated with much more generosity and humanity—which is a large part of the reason why infant mortality rates are so much lower in France, Japan, Sweden, and Canada than they are in the United States. Consider some of the supports and strategies other countries use to reduce their infant mortality rates and generally improve the well-being of mothers and babies:[13]

- Britain offers free health care to all pregnant women through the National Health Service. France completely reimburses women for the expenses involved in pregnancy and childbirth. But whatever the funding arrangement—which does vary from country to country—the governments of all other developed countries have "removed all financial barriers to maternity care."
- In addition to free medical care, many countries offer incentives, financial and otherwise, to encourage pregnant women to attend prenatal clinics. In France, for example,

the government provides monthly payments of approximately $34 to all pregnant women who complete four prenatal visits to a doctor. Fewer than 1 percent of women fail to respond to this *allocation au jeune enfant.*

· In several countries continuity of care is facilitated by having pregnant women carry their prenatal records with them. Then, if there is an emergency, the attending medical staff will have most of the pertinent information they need to care for a woman they may never have seen before. In Japan, for example, every pregnant woman has a *bolshi techo* (mother-child handbook), which records the mother's prenatal care information and exhorts her to attend prenatal classes. Her book is stamped at each class.

· Home visiting is a common feature of maternity care systems in many developed countries. In the Netherlands, Britain, Ireland, Costa Rica, and Belgium, all new mothers are visited at home by either a midwife or the general practitioner who attended the delivery. Home visiting is not just a medical checkup, but is used as an opportunity to assist and educate new mothers in infant care, breast feeding, health and safety issues, family planning, and immunization. In some countries, for example the Netherlands, home visiting has developed into a more elaborate program, in which a specially trained maternity nurse stays at home with the new mother for eight hours a day for up to ten days postpartum.

· Some countries respond to the special needs of families with new babies by providing publicly funded home helpers. In France, for example, maternity aides are offered to new mothers who have experienced high-risk pregnancies on the theory that these women may run into medical complications if they are not able to rest. The French authorities recognize home helpers as a cost savings over rehospitalization of the mother.

- Most European countries offer a one-time cash grant to families when a child is born to help defray the costs associated with a new baby and "to actively express the value of that child to society." Countries as diverse as Spain, Germany, Belgium, and Sweden offer cash birth allowances. In addition, almost all these countries provide a universal child benefit—called a child or family allowance—based on the number of children in a family. Such allowances are equal to 5 to 10 percent of average gross wages and continue until a child is eighteen years old.

The United States is the only advanced industrial country to leave the important matter of childbirth to the vagaries of the private market and an inadequate patchwork of public clinics. The financial barriers to prenatal care remain high and very few women have insurance coverage for the expenses associated with delivery. Doctor's and hospital fees for delivery and immediate postpartum care in the United States now average $4,334 per birth, and even the best medical plans fail to cover the full cost of this care.[14] Most new parents face considerable out-of-pocket expenses. In addition, American public policy provides none of those social supports so common in other countries—home visits, home helpers, cash grants to help pay for a crib or a stroller. The thought that a new parent might be entitled to some hands-on help with a colicky baby—or grocery shopping—is a stunning notion to most Americans. We are so used to dealing with public indifference, to coping on our own, to paying through the nose for our babies, that we expect little help from government.

European attitudes and strategies are clearly more humane, but they are also more cost-effective. As we now know, from a strictly economic vantage point prenatal and maternity care are excellent investments—every dollar spent on prenatal care saves more than $3 in medical costs during the first year of life.[15] American policies in and around childbirth not only place women and children in unnecessary jeopardy for what should be one of life's most rewarding experiences but they are remarkably wasteful of public resources.

Thus the story told by the maternity policies of France, Japan, Italy, Canada, Sweden, and Germany is very different from that told in America. The public policies of these other nations demonstrate that babies are treasured and that childbirth is an event of enormous national significance. There are obvious differences among the specific programs of, say, Sweden, France, and Japan, but if there is variation in the detail of the plot, the basic story line is the same: in these other countries children are societal blessings to be protected and cherished by the nation at large.

In contrast, the maternity policies of the United States denigrate parents and devalue children. Childbirth is a private affair with inconsequential social import. Government steps in—grudgingly—if there are catastrophic medical problems; otherwise individual parents are expected to shoulder the load and pick up the tab.

Workplace Policies

The story does not end with issues of prenatal and maternity care. Over the last twenty years America's careless attitude toward the beginning of life has conditioned workplace policy and dramatically limited the amount of support offered to working parents.

For Marcia Levine, the changes at work started almost immediately after she announced she was pregnant. As she tells the story, her boss at Odeon, a trendy Manhattan restaurant, hounded her about when she would quit work. About three months into her pregnancy, Marcia claims he asked her to walk in front of him to "show profile," to see if she was showing yet. "He said it was totally inappropriate for a maitre d' to be pregnant, that the customers wouldn't like it," recalls Marcia.

Within weeks, she says, the owners informed her that she couldn't work the door beyond her sixth month. She would have to answer the phones in the back, and her pay would be cut from $14 an hour to $9. She refused the phone job, and sued the Odeon's owners for discriminating against her because she was pregnant.[16]

Marcia Levine's case—which is still pending—is not unusual. Each year, thousands of working women report being harassed, demoted, transferred, or fired when they announce that they are pregnant, even though such actions are ostensibly illegal. In other cases, women work through their pregnancies only to lose their job (or their seniority) while on leave with a newborn. In America, no group of women seems immune from such treatment. In a three-month investigation in the winter of 1989–90 *Working Woman* magazine turned up architects, engineers, saleswomen, and secretaries whose earning power and career prospects deteriorated rapidly once they became pregnant.[17]

The only federal provision for pregnancy or maternity is contained in the 1978 Pregnancy Disability Amendment, which decrees that an employer cannot fire a worker *solely* because she is pregnant and that a pregnant woman is eligible for the same fringe benefits as workers with "other disabilities." This seems to boil down to the right to use temporary disability insurance for childbirth.

Despite the fact that the 1978 amendment was hailed as a

major victory for women's rights, it affords pregnant women
and their newborn children very few protections or benefits.
For starters, pregnant women can still be fired on other
(trumped-up) grounds. According to Sharon Kinsella, coordinator for the Office Survival Hotline run by 9to5 (a branch of
the National Association of Working Women), many cases
follow a typical pattern: "A woman might be employed for
four years—getting raises and good reviews. Then, after she
tells a supervisor she's pregnant, all of a sudden she starts
getting bad evaluations and being told she's inefficient. The
company builds a paper record on her, and then they fire her,
and claim it's because she's a bad worker."[18] Craig Gurian, of
the New York City Commission on Human Rights, agrees
with Kinsella: "An employer doesn't say, 'Hey we're firing
you because you're pregnant.' He comes up with another
reason that's within the law."[19]

During the 1980s rulings by the Supreme Court made it
harder for a pregnant woman worker to win a case—or even
to bring one. The deadlines for filing a case were tightened;
it became harder to win a settlement that included attorney's
fees, and the standards of proof became substantially stricter.
"Increasingly conservative rulings by federal courts have undermined the law which . . . now appears to favor the employer, and any woman who tries to sue runs the risk of getting
trashed in court," says Joan Bertin, attorney for the Women's
Rights Project of the American Civil Liberties Union.[20]

The 1978 law not only fails to protect a pregnant worker,
it does little to help a new mother. Specifically, it does not
guarantee any leave from employment for a mother (or father) to spend time with a newborn child, nor does it direct
employers to reinstate women in their jobs after they have
recovered from childbirth. The only thing it does is provide
six to eight weeks of partial wage replacement at the time of

birth, if a working woman is covered by temporary disability insurance.

This provision is of limited use, however, because *federal law does not require employers to provide disability insurance.* In fact only five states—California, Hawaii, New Jersey, New York, and Rhode Island—require disability coverage. But even those women lucky enough to live in the right state might still not be covered by disability insurance. For example, in New York State government workers, farm workers, and workers in firms with fewer than fifteen employees are all excluded from the disability insurance requirement. Experts estimate that nationwide only 40 percent of working women have disability coverage for pregnancy and childbirth.[21]

The United States is the only advanced industrial country that has no statutory maternity or parenting leave. One hundred and seventeen countries (including every industrial nation and many developing nations) guarantee a woman the following rights: leave from employment for childbirth, job protection while she is on leave, and the provision of a cash benefit to replace all or most of her earnings.

All Western European countries, whether they are welfare states or traditional Catholic societies, provide a generous package of rights and benefits to working parents when a child is born. Sweden provides a parenting leave of fifteen months at the birth of a child, which can be taken by either parent, and replaces 90 percent of earnings up to a specified maximum, protects seniority on the job, maintains fringe benefits, and guarantees that a parent can go back to the same or a similar job. In Italy a pregnant woman is entitled to five months' paid leave at 80 percent of her wage, followed by a further six months at 30 percent of her wage. Her job is guaranteed for both periods. Perhaps the most remarkable fact about the Italian system is that a woman worker is entitled to two years'

Cathy copyright © 1986 by Cathy Guisewite. Reprinted by permission of Universal Press Syndicate. All rights reserved.

credit toward seniority each time she gives birth to a child. In Italy working women get "brownie points" for having a child; in the United States they get fired.

The only decent policies in the United States are to be found in large corporations as part of their employee benefits package. As I will describe in chapter 7, 70 percent of the 500 largest companies now offer some type of maternity or parenting leave. The median length of parenting leave in these companies is twelve weeks, and in most cases it carries a job-back guarantee. Unfortunately, fewer than 20 percent of working women are employed by these large corporations; the majority must suffer the consequences of our failure to mandate national standards.

Recent attempts to improve on the 1978 Pregnancy Disability Amendment have ended in dismal failure. In the mid-1980s Pat Schroeder (D-Colo.) in the House of Representatives and Christopher Dodd (D-Conn.) in the Senate spearheaded an attempt to get a parenting leave bill through Congress. Since I testified on behalf of this bill three separate times as an economist and as the director of the Economic Policy Council, I am only too familiar with its dreary history.

I first became involved with the Family and Medical Leave Bill in the spring of 1986. At that time its central goal was the provision of an eighteen-week, unpaid, job-protected leave for both male and female employees to care for a newborn, newly adopted, or seriously ill child. Not a strong enough proposal, I remember thinking at the time. It neglected to provide any paid leave and therefore failed to ease the lives of low-income parents. It was clearly better than nothing, however, since it did provide a significant degree of job protection.

This weak measure did not make it through Congress. President Reagan threatened a veto, and hundreds of small- and medium-sized businesses, alarmed at the thought of an expensive new benefit, mobilized the Chamber of Commerce and the National Federation for Independent Businesses, who then lobbied strenuously against the bill. Its congressional sponsors backed off, and the bill was watered down. By early 1990 the family leave time had been reduced to twelve weeks, and businesses with fewer than fifty employees had been exempt (meaning that 95 percent of all employers and 44 percent of all employees were now excluded from the provisions of the bill). This extremely weak measure still failed to make it onto the statute books. In the spring of 1990 the House and the Senate finally passed the bill, only to have it vetoed by President Bush. Congress failed to override the president's veto.

All this despite the fact that this kind of policy pays off in cost-benefit terms. As I will demonstrate in chapter 7, parental leave can dramatically reduce attrition rates among women workers and it often makes sense for a company to provide this benefit rather than foot the bill for high rates of attrition and labor turnover.

But if these facts and figures increasingly inform the actions of large corporations, they are unknown to millions of small employers. A large part of the reason is that no one in the White House or on Capitol Hill has made it their business to spread the good news, to tell the business community at large that they can have their cake and eat it too. Family leave is a win-win proposition: good for the working parent, good for children, and good for company.

Instead of leading the charge, on June 29, 1990, George Bush vetoed the Family and Medical Leave Bill. He gave two reasons for his decision: He "strongly objected" to Washington mandating how employers should treat their employees, and was "dismayed" at the cost of the bill, which would add to the deficit and make it harder for America to compete in world trade.[22]

Both reasons are spurious. The cost argument cannot be taken seriously. The General Accounting Office has estimated the up-front cost of family leave to be $188 million a year—which boils down to $4.5 per employee![23] It's hard to imagine that saving such a sum would make much of a dent in our deficit. Not only is the direct cost trivial, but due to its effect on absenteeism and labor turnover, over the long run family leave is a cost saver. We should also remember that all of our chief trade competitors—including Germany and Japan—have mandated family leave programs that are far more expensive per employee than the bill vetoed by President Bush.

Bush's objection to regulating employers also fails to ring true. The Family and Medical Leave Bill is completely consistent with established labor standards that give us such protections as child-labor laws, anti-sweatshop codes, health and safety regulations, and the minimum wage. We have always adjusted our labor laws to meet the needs of a changing society. With 50 percent of all mothers with babies under twelve months old in the work force, up from 31 percent fifteen years ago,[24] childbirth is now an urgent (and appropriate) candidate for labor legislation.

It seems that President Bush gave in to the demands of a noisy (and ill-informed) business lobby led by small employers at the National Federation for Independent Businesses. Despite the fact that on the campaign trail Bush promised that "no woman should have to choose between her job and the needs of a sick child,"[25] when push came to shove it was much easier to give in to the demands of long-time business supporters than to stand up for what is right. Childbirth is, after all, way down on everyone's priority list, so the president could count on it not being a very costly political decision.

A few days after the presidential veto, Lawrence Perlman, chief executive officer of Control Data, contributed a thoughtful article to the *Washington Post*. In it he rebukes George Bush for his "ill-advised" decision and points out that Minnesota has had parental leave since 1987 for firms with twenty-one or more employees and yet he knows of "no problems that this state law has caused Minnesota businesses." In Perlman's opinion "the President needs to hear a different busi-

ness voice from the one to which he apparently listened."
Perlman is worried about issues that go beyond the economic.
In his view, this veto has the unfortunate effect of perpetuating
"the public perception that well-managed businesses are inconsistent with the enhancement of human values and the
empowerment of employees."[26] This particular business
leader seems fully aware of the fact that family leave is about
"values and a standard of decency"[27] as well as federal man-
dates and benefits packages. Would that President Bush had
tapped into Perlman's constructive (and well-informed) vision
rather than the fearful vision of the more active business lobbies.

Ideological Barriers

Behind America's careless and neglect-filled policies toward
childbearing and child raising lies a particularly destructive
form of "ideological warfare." Fought by factions on the right
and the left of the political spectrum, these battles have produced gridlock in Washington, repeatedly derailing constructive action on the family support front.

The notion that government should play a major role in
underwriting children or strengthening the family has never
been popular in right-wing circles. Conservatives have generally assumed that parents can and should look after their own
children, that we don't need policies to deal with "regular"
families or "normal" kids.

Right-wing antagonism to state interference in the family is
rooted in deeply held beliefs about the importance of self-
reliance and personal responsibility. In the middle years of this
century, these fundamental conservative values were reinforced by the geopolitics of superpower relations. The con-

frontation between socialism and capitalism, between the Soviet Union and the United States, was about ways of life as well as economic philosophy, and on the right, much political capital was made out of contrasting stereotypes of domestic life. The Soviet Union was described as a place where "motherhood and birth control were established by law and children were taken from their Mother's arms and turned over to public officers."[28] In direct contrast, in the "free world" individual parents raised their own children in a manner they saw fit.

Twentieth-century history is dotted with examples of conservative ideologues using the communist threat as a weapon in the battle to keep government off the backs of the family. When senators Morris Sheppard (D-Tex.) and Horace M. Towner (R-Iowa) introduced the Protection of Maternity and Infancy Act in 1921, the American Medical Association (AMA) opposed it vociferously, branding the policy an "imported socialist scheme." Congressional conservatives joined the chorus, denouncing the ideas behind the bill as "bolshevistic philosophy."[29] And in 1948 when New York's Governor Thomas E. Dewey discontinued wartime support for child care, he accused working mothers of being "communist sympathizers" and told them they were "contaminating" our free society. The cold war had just gotten off the ground and any type of group care for children smacked uncomfortably of "commie baby-raising techniques" on the other side of the Iron Curtain.[30]

These sentiments have pursued us into more modern times. When President Nixon vetoed the Comprehensive Child Development Bill in 1971, he declared that the federal government should not plunge headlong into supporting child development because this would "commit the vast moral authority of the national government to the side of communal approaches to child rearing over against the family-centered approach." In Nixon's view it was OK to have day care "for the children of the poor so that their parents can leave the welfare rolls," but it was simply unacceptable for an American government "to encourage or support middle-class mothers who leave the home."[31] He was applauded by his right wing, who saw the Child Development Bill as the "boldest and most far-reaching scheme ever advanced for the Sovietization of American youth."[32] Nixon seemed not to know—or to care— that a third of these mothers had already left home for the workplace, and that most of these women were propelled by economic pressures. His veto did not resurrect full-time motherhood; it merely left "thousands of children with no care and hundreds of thousands of others in inadequate and sometimes even destructive care."[33]

If conservatives have derived ideological energy from the cold war, they have looked to the child-rearing establishment to justify their "hands-off" approach to the family. During the postwar period, child-rearing experts heavily backed the notion that mothers should stay out of the labor force to better perform their maternal duties. For thirty years Benjamin Spock told us that the children of working parents may grow up neglected and maladjusted. Unless a mother absolutely must work, he said, it makes no sense for her to "pay other people to do a poorer job of bringing up [her] children."[34] Psychologist Selma Fraiberg stressed the dire consequences of maternal deprivation before a child is eighteen months old,[35] while Burton White, director of the Harvard Preschool Project, warned parents of the dangers of out-of-home care: "As one who has specialized in the study of the development of children for more than 20 years I firmly believe that most children will get off to a better start in life when they spend the majority of their waking hours being cared for by their parents."[36]

Interestingly enough, White discounts the importance of parenting leave. Given his conviction that the first six months of life are absolutely critical and that the child "has to be responded to intensely in this period,"[37] you would think that he would urge government to guarantee job-protected leave for working parents that lasted at least this long. Not so. White concentrates on advising mothers to stay out of the labor force. As he told me in an interview, "I am not too interested in advocating parenting leave, as this might encourage the mothers of young children to stay in the work force"[38]— almost precisely the words of Richard Nixon.

Right-wing glorification of the self-reliant, traditional family can be counterproductive in a modern world where only 11 percent of American families approximate the Norman Rockwell ideal of breadwinner husband, homemaker wife, and one or more dependent children. Most obviously it impedes the development of sensible family support policies. Half of all babies under one year old now have mothers in the labor force, and a quarter of all children are growing up in households with a mother but no father. What these nontraditional families need is free access to prenatal and maternity care, generous parenting leave, and a host of other rights and benefits—not another set of pressures. The misguided notion that government should not meddle in family affairs has made it extremely difficult for millions of American children to get a decent start in life.

But the left of the political spectrum has been equally unhelpful in supporting families with children. Over the last thirty years liberals have been much more comfortable promoting individual rights—women's rights, minority rights, old people's rights—than pushing to strengthen the family. In the words of Senator Moynihan, only in the rarest of circum-

stances have social reformers "defined the family as the relevant unit . . . American public policy has been directed to-
wards . . . and pertains to the individual."[39]

In progressive circles, discomfort with the family enterprise
became particularly pronounced in the 1960s with the emer-
gence of a women's liberation movement. Modern feminism
began as a critique of the family. Betty Friedan's *The Feminine
Mystique* was about middle-class housewives and their discon-
tent with the cloying brand of family togetherness that characterized the 1950s. For Friedan and other leaders of the
movement, liberation meant moving out of the domestic
sphere—leaving behind house, husband, children—into the
world of work "where, supposedly, more important things
were going on."[40] The goal was to become independent and
compete for jobs, income, and power on the same terms as
men. It is easy to see that in a brave new world where women
were attempting to "clone the male competitive model," family became part of the problem, not part of the solution.[41]

It is very hard, this business of reconciling self-fulfillment
and autonomy with the bearing and rearing of children, and
some committed feminists have not even tried. In a recent
interview, Gloria Steinem described her own life choices in
the following stark terms: "I either gave birth to someone
else," she explained, "or I gave birth to myself."[42] She opted
for herself.

It is not just feminists who have displayed a lack of enthusiasm for families and children. Most of the progressive social
and cultural movements of the 1960s and 1970s shared this
mindset. For obvious reasons the gay rights movement was
uninterested in the conventional family; the various therapeutic cults of personal self-realization saw the family as a nest of
oppression and pathology;[43] the New Left was highly critical
of American society as a whole, and the family in particular;

and a rising tide of black separatism dismissed the bourgeois family as yet another imposition of white society. In avant-garde elite groups, it became chic to dismiss the family as an outmoded relic of the past and to experiment with "alternative life styles" which ranged from open marriage to communal living. Within a small but powerful academic set, the view that the family was on its last legs gained wide credence. For example, Harvard sociologist Barrington Moore thought the time had come "for advanced industrial societies to do away with the family and substitute other social arrangements that impose fewer unnecessary and painful restrictions on humanity."[44] In 1968 he announced—with evident satisfaction—that the family was dying if not already dead; the only thing left for society was to ensure "a decent burial."[45]

Given this backdrop, it is not surprising that the liberal left has had a great deal of trouble creating a coherent family policy. If you are not sure that marriage is a good idea, if you are not convinced that two-parent families should be strengthened or encouraged, then it is extremely hard to strengthen family ties or create a better environment for raising children. Thus the Democratic party, the political force that has spawned most of the progressive social legislation in America, has never committed itself wholeheartedly to programs of family support. In the recent ruckus over family leave, 57 Democrats in the House of Representatives joined 138 Republicans to sustain the president's veto.[46]

In a 1990 article Betty Friedan berated her colleagues on the left for their lack of enthusiasm for family policy. To use her words, "the Democratic leadership doesn't understand that choice, as it relates to child care or parenting leave, is every bit as important as abortion." If Democrats are short-sighted so is "the current leadership of the women's movement . . . It horrifies me that NOW, the organization I helped found, has not supported Rep. Schroeder's parental leave bill. Leadership in feminist organizations has not expanded choice to include the choice to have children; they have not given the same priority to the child-care and parental leave bill that they've given to abortion."[47]

Thus, for very different reasons, the right and left wings of American political life have both failed to support contemporary families. The Right doesn't believe in interfering in the family, and during the 1980s this hands-off conservative approach left many single mothers and working parents hanging on by their fingernails, barely coping. The Left believes in intervention but isn't at all sure what kind of family to support to what ends. Given this confusion, liberals have tended to concentrate their best efforts on the enhancement of individual rights—and in so doing, have often succeeded in weakening our already brittle family structures, further undermining the life chances of children. For example, as I have already discussed, the progressive liberal establishment was the architect of a free and easy system of no-fault divorce which has had extremely serious consequences for children.

All of which helps explain why paralysis and gridlock have reined in Washington on the family policy front. Neither the Right nor the Left has wanted to move forward. Instead they have channeled their energy into a variety of ideological confrontations—abortion is a good example—that have served to absorb energy and deflect attention from what is really happening to children in this society. The ideological standoff has sometimes reached farcical proportions. In 1980 when President Carter convened a White House Conference on the Family, the participants (from both sides of the political divide) could not even agree on what constitutes a reasonable definition of the family. Instead of one great celebratory gathering at the White House as had been originally envisaged, the

Conference was spun off in two regional meetings with results that even its most committed supporters saw as meager.[48]

Cumulative Causation at Work

During the 1980s official neglect of families and children deepened. Ronald Reagan was a vigorous proponent of the right-wing view that families are best left to their own devices, and during his time in office he systematically cut the amount of public money going to poor families with children: Medical care, child care, school meals, housing subsidies were all slashed. At the same time, he resisted attempts to help middle-class families by mandating parental leave or regulating day care. One of the few pieces of legislation Reagan did support was the 1983 Family Protection Act, introduced by Senator Paul Laxalt (R-Nev.). Laxalt's bill attempted to revive school prayer and ban abortion; it had nothing to say on such matters as prenatal care or parental leave. The president's refusal to back any policies that actually helped children caused Representative Barney Frank (D-Mass.) to remark that "Ronald Reagan seems to believe that life begins at conception and ends at birth."[49]

In a classic demonstration of cumulative momentum, this new level of governmental neglect of children fed off, and was reinforced by, a populace caught up in its own private quest for self-fulfillment. As I explained in chapter 4, adults of both sexes have become absorbed in their own inner worlds and ambitions. Sixty-five percent of all households are now "child-free," other people's children have been relegated to the low end of the list of personal priorities, and government has been allowed, even encouraged, to get out of the business of protecting children and supporting parents. The result: a deterio-

ration in our already fragile family structures. No one should be surprised. "No-responsibility" divorce is very likely to lead to the widespread abandonment of children. And major cuts in federal support for low-income housing virtually guarantee that hundreds of thousands of American children grow up not knowing the security of a home. During the 1980s we looked on—or tuned out—as more than 2 million additional children slithered into poverty.[50]

While the private and public choices of the last decade certainly contributed to child neglect, it is important to stress that this shafting of children predates the 1980s. The recent flowering of conservatism in the public realm and self-absorption in the private realm grew out of a political culture that was already reluctant to help families or children.

Forging a Public Morality

Mary Ann Glendon tells us to be wary; we need to be very careful about the "stories we tell," the "symbols we deploy," and the "visions we project"[51] in our public policies, because these ciphers forge the aspirations and identity of the nation and, in so doing, help construct a public morality. This is bad news for those of us who care about the welfare of children. The stories told by our policies in and around the beginnings of life are fraught with negative symbolism and laden with an intensely private vision of who should take responsibility for children in this society.

There is some heavy-handed symbolism embedded in the language of our labor laws. It's striking that the only legal provision we have for childbirth—the most miraculous event in a human life—is some weak (and demeaning) language that defines pregnancy as just another disability in the eyes of the law. Employers are not supposed to fire a woman solely because she is pregnant; instead, they are instructed to provide her with the same fringe benefits as workers with other disabilities. In 60 percent of all cases these benefits amount to—nothing!

And there is some poignant symbolism wrapped up in what our policies do not address. It's astounding that in an age when half of all new mothers are in the labor force, "our laws are silent about any period a mother or indeed a father may wish to be at home to care for an infant child."[52] In most other countries (all rich nations and many poor nations) childbirth receives prominent treatment in the law, and is the subject of elaborate legislative support. When Brazil rewrote its constitution in 1988 one of the provisions was the right of all Brazilian women to paid leave when they give birth to a child.[53] The notion of paid parenting leave becoming a constitutional right boggles the American imagination. We cannot even get unpaid leave, for restricted groups of workers, onto our statute books. While there are powerful groups pushing for a constitutional amendment to protect the flag, no one has suggested that the constitution concern itself with protecting pregnant women or newborn babies.

Finally, our policies promote a destructive, almost punitive vision of personal accountability. In the United States a baby is seen as a private consumption item, a little like a winter vacation or a second car, and we have privatized large portions of the costs of child raising. In no other civilized country do parents pay such a high price for their children. There are a multitude of direct expenses. Prenatal and maternity care, measles shots and vitamin pills, day care and preschools often need to be purchased in the marketplace. And there are significant indirect costs tied up with forgone earnings. Because women are not entitled to job protection when they give birth to a child, they are often redefined as "new hires" when they return to work after childbirth, routinely losing seniority, benefits, and pay. This is a large part of the reason why working mothers lose 13 percent of their earning power in the aftermath of a first child.[54] Needless to say, all these "penalties" serve to weaken family structures and further undermine the life circumstances of children.

In extensive interviews in the 1980s Vance Packard found that "the decision to have a child is met with perhaps less enthusiasm than at any time in our history except possibly the depression years. . . . Having a child has changed from being part of the natural flow of life to an apprehensive act—or even an act of courage."[55]

In other rich democracies the incentive structure (and the

vision) is quite different. Charles de Gaulle once said that motherhood should be regarded as "a social function similar to military service for men, that has to be financially supported by the whole community."[56] This statement dramatizes the French view of children as precious national resources that deserve the resources and attention of the community-at-large. Nations as diverse as Italy, Japan, and Canada have a profound appreciation of the child as the worker of the future and the citizen of the future. Thus the health, wealth, and security of the nation are wrapped in making sure that each baby gets a good start in life, in guaranteeing that societal conditions permit children to flourish. This sense of collective responsibility for children is the source of those elaborate social supports—prenatal care, home visits, maternity and parenting leave—described in earlier sections of this chapter. These policies demonstrate a clear commitment to children and contribute to the stability and security of family life.

Thus, the careless, neglect-filled American story about the beginnings of life is laden with penalties on the substantive front and denigration on the symbolic front. Indeed, in certain policy areas, childbirth is deemed to be such a trivial event that it doesn't even make it into the law of the land. Such a destructive public morality reinforces and exacerbates private decision making. The momentum of cumulative causation builds relentlessly. When we fail to recognize the importance of childbearing and child rearing in our public policies, it becomes much easier to shaft children in our private lives. When government treats parenthood as some kind of expensive and expendable private hobby, adults are discouraged from investing prime time in this endeavor—to the detriment of our children and our nation.

Despite this depressing tale, there are voices of sanity in the wilderness, and, surprisingly enough, at least some of them belong to the private sector. Increasingly, business executives recognize that parenting leave and flextime are essential if they are to recruit and retain those high-caliber workers needed to survive in the fiercely competitive environment of the 1990s. But can corporate self-interest, no matter how enlightened, be relied upon to solve the enormous problems of American children? To this question we now turn.

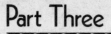

Part Three

Picking Up the Pieces

7

The Private Sector
and Win-Win Scenarios

I n the summer of 1988 James D. Robinson III, the chairman
of American Express, had a lot on his mind. He had just come
to terms with some startling demographic projections put together by the company's human resource team and was beginning to realize that American Express, along with the rest of
corporate America, was about to face a serious shortfall in the
supply of skilled labor.

Not one to beat about the bush, Robinson decided to use
an October gathering of senior management in Tucson, Arizona, to mobilize his company on these issues. In a keynote
address Louis V. Gerstner, Jr., then president of the company,
conjured up a daunting picture of what deteriorating educational standards and a shortfall in skills mean for American
Express:

- 40 percent of today's fourth-graders actually believe the
  world is flat, and 20 percent of sixth-graders cannot locate

the United States on a world map. *Will they be our travel agents of the future?*

· One out of every three ninth-graders can't compute change for a two-item meal. That's a Big Mac and fries! *Can we expect them to understand the difference between whole-life and single-premium life insurance?*

· 40 percent of high school seniors can't name three South American countries. *Will they be the right people to advise Platinum Cardmembers on a $20,000 Amazon journey?*

· 25 percent of U.S. college freshmen are enrolled in remedial math classes. *Will they be tomorrow's margin clerks?*

· One-third of today's ninth-graders can't write a brief summary of a newspaper story. *Will they be able to take phone messages from important clients?*[1]

A shrinking reservoir of young workers seems to be part of the American Express problem. The pool of twenty-to-twenty-nine-year-olds will contract by 17 percent over the next decade; this is bad news for a company that hires fifteen thousand people for entry-level positions every year. Amex worries about fierce competition for young people: "We will be going up against IBM, Xerox, AT&T, Ford and so on. Not to mention the Hondas, Toyotas, Nomuras, Deutsche Banks, Credit Suisses and National Westminsters who are expanding not only in their own backyards but also in ours."[2]

But more important to American Express than the shortfall in numbers is the falloff in educational standards and the growing mismatch between available skills and available jobs. In the words of one senior manager, "while the work force gets less qualified and our education system gets worse, our products and technologies are growing more complex. We'll have technology able to take voice commands, but people who won't know what they're talking about. We'll have machines

that recognize handwriting, but people who can't write."[3]
Robinson finds these trends particularly distressing because he
knows that a well-educated, motivated work force is the life-
blood of his company—indeed, of any service company.
"Computers don't deliver service. People do. People do it,
one transaction at a time."[4]

Senior executives live in fear of a type of service disaster
recently reported in the *Los Angeles Times.* A woman applied
for a Visa card over the phone. Asked by a Citibank employee
whether she wanted a second card for a family member, she
said, "Maybe later." Two weeks later, she received two shiny
new Visa cards: one for her, the other for Maube Later.[5]
Stories like this send cold shudders down Robinson's spine.

Despite the severity and the significance of the prospective
skills shortfall, all was not gloom and doom at the American
Express gathering in the fall of 1988. Amex was about to
tackle these problems with characteristic vigor. At the Tucson
meeting, senior managers adopted the "Work Force Challenge" as the company's top priority for the 1990s. At the
heart of this challenge is how American Express is going to
find, motivate, and retain high-caliber workers as the labor
pool shrinks, creating an ever-widening gap between the demand for and the supply of well-educated young people.

At Amex, and at five thousand other corporations around
the country, the answer to this challenge involves a new level
of commitment to workers. In particular, it includes creating
a family-friendly workplace that provides greater flexibility
and more generous benefits for working Moms and Dads.

Pre-1988, before the days of corporate enlightenment, American Express had a series of "plain vanilla" programs in place
to support working parents: a twelve-week family leave, a
dependent care salary-reduction plan, adoption assistance, and

an information and referral service for child care. Since 1988, however, company support for families has blossomed as American Express has tried to enhance employee loyalty to the company by providing both time and resources for hard-pressed working parents. While this is clearly good news for parents, what this means for the well-being of children is a more complicated matter—one I will take up later in this chapter.

The company has attempted to listen to what parents want. For example, senior executives point to a poll that shows 60 percent of working mothers preferring part-time work, flexible hours, or stay-at-home jobs to standard full-time jobs. Responding to this finding, the company has designed an imaginative array of part-time, flextime, compressed-work-week, telecommuting, and work-at-home alternatives, all of which carry benefits (today, an employee has to work for the company for only fourteen hours a week to qualify for a full range of benefits). Management knows that in a tightening job market, women are quite capable of voting with their feet; and if American Express doesn't provide flexibility, working mothers will go to companies that do. As one Amex executive explains: "Women want balance between jobs and family, and they'll move around until they find it. We're already feeling the pain; in some areas, our attrition rates are much higher than we can afford." In-house analysis has shown that it can cost American Express up to $20,000 in direct expenses to fill one entry-level position.[6] Given a U.S. work force of 82,500 and an attrition rate of at least 10 percent a year, labor turn-over costs this company at least $150 million annually. Policies that can bring this attrition rate down (or at least prevent it from going up) are clearly good for the bottom line.

The new flexible options have won enthusiastic support on both sides of the corporate divide. Stefanie Gearity and Nellie

Hernandez share a job as administrative assistant at corporate headquarters in New York City. According to Stefanie, "I feel very lucky to have found a position where I can coordinate my work schedule with my husband's and we don't need outside child care."[7] Nellie and Stefanie communicate by leaving notes for each other and by telephone. Nellie says that because of their follow-up system, the job gets done as if the position were filled by one person.

Management is also pleased with the new ways of structuring the work week. Several regional operations, including Amex Life Assurance Company of San Rafael, California, have introduced the option of a compressed work week—(a full-time job compressed into a four-day week)—and find that employees on this schedule are very productive because, after most people have gone home for the day, the remaining workers have many fewer interruptions. Indeed, pilot programs such as the one in San Rafael have worked so well that as far as the company is concerned, "it's open season on four-day work weeks."[8]

In addition to all this new flexibility, American Express is beginning to offer generous benefits to working parents. A child-care subsidy called Kids Cheque is about to go into operation and is expected to be an important tool in attracting and keeping skilled workers. Under Kids Cheque the company will cover $25 to $35 a week of dependent care expenses for employees who earn up to $40,000 a year, as long as total family income does not exceed $80,000.[9]

Innovative support policies are not confined to working parents. In an effort to improve the future supply of skills, American Express has begun to reach out to underprivileged youth. The Academy of Finance was started in 1982 as a pilot project of the American Express Company, Shearson Lehman Hutton, and the New York City school system, with the pur-

250 WHEN THE BOUGH BREAKS

pose of offering financial training to inner-city youths. There were thirty-five students in the first graduating class, most of them minority youngsters from poor neighborhoods. When Amex adopted the Work Force Challenge in 1988, the Academy of Finance was greatly expanded, and today the program serves thirty-five schools in seventeen cities and has a total enrollment of more than two thousand students. American Express now spends $3 million a year on this program.[10]

The Academy of Finance offers a special two-year curriculum for public high school juniors and seniors. In addition to regular academic high school courses, students in the Academy take two or three specialized courses each semester in areas such as "Financial Products and Planning" or "Banking and Credit." After fulfilling the academic requirements of the junior year, students are screened and interviewed for summer internships in local businesses. Many interns are later hired for full-time jobs by their internship companies, and, eventually, 90 percent go on to earn college degrees.[11]

The newly minted policies at American Express are symptomatic of a profound change in corporate attitudes. The looming labor and skill shortages of the 1990s have given increased clout to workers and done wonders to concentrate the corporate mind on the needs of their employees (actual and potential). The next decade will be a seller's rather than a buyer's market if you are in the business of selling skills. As the help-wanted signs in stores and restaurants are beginning to tell us, capable, educated workers are increasingly scarce and are able to exert new leverage in the workplace. They can demand (and expect to win) better salaries and better working conditions. Faced with the prospect of unfilled jobs and high attrition rates, management has little choice but to yield to (or, better still, anticipate) these demands. We are talking about nothing less than a historic shift in the balance of power in our society, from management to labor.

These new facts of life are changing attitudes in previously unenlightened circles. American Express, for example, is a company with no particular track record in avant-garde personnel policies. Unlike IBM or Merck, pioneering firms that have been offering child-care subsidies and generous maternity leave for a decade, American Express had not seen the need to be especially "progressive" in these areas. But times are changing. As Jim Robinson figured out in the summer of 1988, given the demographics of the 1990s it now makes economic as well as humanitarian sense for a company to reach out to working parents and minority youngsters. According to one executive I talked to at American Express, "Robinson's a hard-nosed kind of guy who doesn't normally get upset about these warm fuzzy issues, but this time the numbers really got to him."[12]

American Express is not the only firm that is crunching numbers and running scared. Most business leaders perceive a crisis in the supply of skills, many are gearing up their in-house programs of family and community supports, and at least some are talking about a tilt in the corporate balance of power—toward employees. For example, Jack Welch, the bullet-biting CEO of General Electric (definitely not big on warm fuzzies!), has developed a new take on "people power." "Over the next decade power will go to the people: power and career security will go to employees with adaptable minds, flexible skills and portable pensions; power and profits will go to companies smart enough to make their workplaces, work practices and training programs the most attractive; power and wealth will go to nations wise enough to invest in children and schools quickly enough."[13] General Electric seems to be calling for a major realignment of both corporate strategy and government policy.

The New Demographic Pressures

We are clearly heading into a decade of severe labor shortages. From now until the end of the century, the population and work force will grow more slowly than at any time since the 1930s. Population growth, which climbed 1.9 percent a year during the 1950s, will slump to only 0.7 percent a year by the late 1990s; and the labor force, which exploded by 2.9 percent a year in the 1970s, will expand by only 1.2 percent a year in the 1990s. Overall, the labor force is projected to grow by 19 million between 1988 and 2000, compared with a growth of 25 million from 1976 to 1988.[14]

Behind this slowdown in the rate of growth of the work force is a dramatic demographic shift from the high birth rates of the baby boom years (1946–1964) to the low birth rates of the baby bust years (1965–1980). The odds are that we will have to live with these low growth rates for quite a while, since the baby boom's echo—the babies of the boomers—won't reach working age in large numbers until the first few years of the next century.

The most obvious consequence of these demographic trends is that the pool of young workers entering the labor market is shrinking. The number of young workers age sixteen to twenty-four will drop by almost 2 million a year over the next decade, and companies that have grown by hiring large numbers of lower-paid young workers will find such workers in short supply.[15]

The problems posed by the looming shortage of young

workers are compounded by the changing face and form of the work force. White men, who now make up 44 percent of the labor force, are expected to contribute only 12 percent of net new workers between now and the year 2000.[16] Blacks, Hispanics, and women—demographic groups that have traditionally had either weak educational backgrounds or a relatively unstable attachment to work—will provide the bulk of the new entrants to the labor market. In the words of David E. Bloom and Neil G. Bennett, "new workers will increasingly come from backgrounds not traditionally associated with the most productive skills."[17]

Women will comprise 62 percent of the new recruits to the work force over the next decade,[18] and demands for parenting leave and subsidized day care will certainly increase, as will interest in part-time, flexible, and stay-at-home jobs. Corporations across the nation are very likely to follow the American Express example and move to meet these demands. Mainly due to child-care problems, absenteeism and turnover rates among working mothers are roughly twice that of male workers. In a world where businesses are increasingly dependent on women workers, it may well be cheaper to subsidize child care and institute flexible work options than to tolerate high rates of attrition.

Blacks, Hispanics, and other minority groups are expected to make up 43 percent of new entrants to the labor force between now and the year 2000, twice the current level.[19] Although comprising a larger share of a more slowly growing work force might improve employment opportunities for blacks and Hispanics, realizing this potential will depend on massive new investment in education and other types of social support. As I discussed in chapter 2, many minority youngsters are seriously deficient in the skills needed in the modern workplace. In some inner-city neighborhoods, close to half of all teenagers drop out of school. Indeed, in 1988 half as many young black men were in prison as in college.[20]

But the skills shortfall is not confined to minority groups. Underachievement and educational failure reach deep into the white middle class. According to the National Assessment of Educational Progress (NAEP), as of 1988 only 6 percent of all high school seniors could solve material more difficult than a two-step arithmetic problem, and only 5 percent could read and understand material more difficult than a short, complex article.[21] In international math and science proficiency tests, U.S. students consistently finish last or nearly last when measured against other developed countries.[22] Ill-prepared young people with major learning deficits are unlikely to find employment in the economy of the 1990s. Global competitive pressures and rapid technological change are producing a restructuring of U.S. occupational opportunities so as to give much more weight to "human capital"—the knowledge and skills embodied in people.

The crux of the contemporary labor supply problem is that at a time when *the supply of qualified youngsters is small—and shrinking, the demand for educated, skilled workers is acute—and increasing.*

Corporations are discovering that a large proportion of young workers simply don't measure up to the demands of contemporary jobs. In its Newark operation, Prudential Insurance finds that 44 percent of job applicants can't read at the ninth-grade level, the minimum requirement for beginning jobs. "These kids are seventeen years old and virtually unemployable for life," says Robert Winters, Prudential's chief executive. Campbell-Mithun-Esty, a Chicago advertising agency, finds that only one applicant in ten meets the literacy standard for mail-clerk jobs.[23] And Motorola discovered in transferring workers to its new high-tech cellular telephone plant that many couldn't pass a basic skills test that required an eighth-grade reading level. Much to its chagrin, the company was forced to put these workers through a six-month remedial education course before they could do their jobs. "We spent $5 million on this training last year, and that came right out of profits," says Edward Bales, director of education at Motorola.[24]

Today's jobs demand far greater mental agility than those of twenty years ago. The secretary who once pecked away at a manual typewriter must now master a word processor and sophisticated telecommunications equipment. Even a cashier at 7-Eleven has to operate a computer and do minor maintenance jobs on the Slurpee and Big Gulp machines.

William B. Johnston and Arnold H. Packer of the Hudson Institute have charted this upscaling of the job market. As recently as 1984, the entire pool of 105 million jobs in the American economy required an average language proficiency of 3.0—the level typical of retail salespersons or skilled construction workers. By contrast, the 26 million jobs expected to be created between 1984 and 2000 will require an average level of 3.6. And yet the average young adult in the United States reads at the 2.6 level. According to Packer, "you're talking about a major mismatch of workers and jobs."[25]

Among the fastest-growing job categories, the trend toward higher educational requirements is striking. Of all the new jobs that will be created between 1990 and 2000, more than half will require some education beyond high school and almost a third will require a college degree. Today, less than a quarter of all jobs are filled by college graduates.[26] It seems that in order to remain competitive our schools must graduate a majority of students with achievement levels long thought possible for only a privileged few. In the words of Marc S. Tucker, president of the National Center on Education and the Economy, "we must become a nation of people who can think for a living."[27]

Educational level is only a rough indication of skills required on the job, but analysis of the language, math, and reasoning skills required in various occupations confirms an upward trend. The Department of Labor ranks occupations on a scale from 1 to 6 and finds that there is a direct correlation between the level of skill required in an occupation and the rate of growth of employment in that occupation. Natural scientists and lawyers, who have the highest skill levels (rated at 5.7 and 5.2, respectively), belong to the two fastest-growing occupations, with each field slated to add up to 70 percent more workers over the next decade. In contrast, occupations in decline show some of the lowest skill levels. Machine tenders have a skill rating of 1.8, and this field is projected to decline 7 percent by the year 2000.[28]

Although the overall pattern of job growth is weighted toward higher-skilled occupations, very large numbers of jobs will be created in some low- and medium-skilled fields. In absolute terms, most new jobs will be found in three occupational categories: services (cooks, nursing aides, and waiters); administration (secretaries, clerks, and computer operators); and marketing (salespersons and cashiers). Together, these fields will account for half of all new employment in the 1990s.[29] However, to hold down these service and sales jobs—whose typical skill scores fall in the 2.5–3.0 range—workers will be expected to read and understand directions, to add and subtract, to speak and think clearly, and to deal graciously with customers and clients. In other words, even these low-status, low-wage jobs will present a "skills hurdle" for young people. Given the deficiencies of our educational system, these jobs will be outside the reach of many American youngsters and will go begging. The branch of MCI (Microwave Communications Inc.) in Boston, for example, cannot find enough qualified candidates to fill its telephone sales jobs. "We have 52 job slots but only 38 employees," says Joanne M. Ramsey, the residential sales manager. These jobs will eventually get filled, "but you're talking about lower productivity"—and ultimately a lower standard of living for everyone.[30]

Toward a Family-Friendly Workplace

The convergence of massive demographic change with rapid technological advance creates the potential—*but only the potential*—to give disadvantaged workers (and their children) a new kind of leverage. The fact that women and minorities will constitute almost 90 percent of all new entrants to the work force in the 1990s could achieve, through sheer demographic pressure, what discrimination has historically denied these groups: access to well-paid jobs. But this will happen only if women are provided with an elaborate bundle of family supports, and if blacks and Hispanics are equipped with strong educational backgrounds (as we have seen, technology is pushing up the bar of basic competence that even entry-level jobs demand). In short, sex and race will diminish as barriers to occupational success if women and minorities can gain the wherewithal to take advantage of the new demographic opportunities.

Once upon a time, women anchored a domestic and familial support system that enabled male breadwinners to focus on their jobs for at least forty hours a week. They raised the children, looked after the house, took the clothes to the dry cleaner, and visited Grandma in the hospital. This home-based support system began to recede a generation ago and is now more the exception than the rule. Seventy percent of women with children between the ages of six and seventeen are now in the labor force, as are half of all women with children less than a year old.[31] As we saw in chapter 3, this new reality has produced enormous stress and strain in family life. Almost every day, working parents are faced with wrenching dilemmas: Who will take care of the three-year-old who is running a temperature of 104°? Can the seven-year-old be trusted to look after herself between 3:30 and 6:00 P.M.? Who will let the plumber in so that the leak in the bathroom can finally be fixed?

For companies this strain and stress translates into poor concentration on the job, high rates of absenteeism, and increased labor turnover. It is very easy for worries about a latchkey child or a sick infant to get in the way of an employee's giving his or her best energy to the job.

It should therefore come as no surprise that family-friendly workplace policies are capable of improving productivity. Increasingly there is hard evidence that points to family support policies enhancing the corporate bottom line. One of the most comprehensive studies of the interaction between family supports and profitability is the National Employer Supported Child Care Project, a nationwide study of 415 industrial, service sector, and governmental organizations. In this report employers highlight the following "payoffs" to family benefits: improved recruitment (cited by 85 percent of the respondents in this survey and ranked as the most important benefit in virtually all studies); reduced turnover (65 percent); reduced absenteeism (53 percent); increased productivity (49 percent); and enhanced company image (85 percent).[32] Harder-to-quantify improvements were also reported in such areas as morale, loyalty to firm, and reduced tardiness.

A few companies have analyzed in detail the costs and benefits of specific family support policies. For example, Union Bank has calculated the economic returns to on-site child care; Honeywell has costed out sick child care; Merck has computed the cost savings achieved by parenting leave; and Sunbeam has estimated the financial benefits of in-house prenatal care.

Union Bank

In January 1987 the Union Bank opened its first on-site child-care center in a building adjacent to the bank's operations center in Monterey Park, California. To determine the impact of the center on absenteeism, attrition rates, and other costs of doing business, the bank carried out an elaborate cost-benefit study during the first year of operation. The conclusion was that on a number of fronts the center more than paid for itself.

Take the calculations in and around absenteeism. Unreliable child-care arrangements can cause parents to miss work. The bank compared the number of days absent per year for employees using on-site child care with those who had young children in other types of child care. It turned out that parents using the in-house facility were absent less often (4.6 as opposed to 6.3 days). Savings due to the reduced number of absences among parents totaled $19,000 in 1987.

A similar exercise was carried out in the area of attrition rates. The number of employees using on-site child care who left their jobs at Union Bank during 1987 was extremely small, a mere 2.2 percent. This was substantially lower than the 9.5 percent turnover rate among employees who used other forms of child care.[33] Replacing workers costs money— according to one survey of turnover costs in Southern California, at least $10,000 in direct costs per worker. Using this rather modest cost estimate, the differential in turnover rates represented a savings to the bank of $63,000 in 1987.

The center has also produced a great deal of free publicity. During 1987 the Union Bank Child Care Center was featured in more than twenty-seven newspaper and magazine articles, two evening TV news spots, and a radio program. An independent PR firm estimated the cost of equivalent advertising at approximately $40,000.

Union Bank calculates that during the first year of operation, the Child Care Center produced savings of approximately $200,000 for the company. These savings not only paid for the center's operating subsidy—$105,000 in 1987— but also contributed substantially toward the $430,000 start-up cost. The bank expects this capital cost to be fully recovered within five years.[34]

Honeywell

In September 1988 Honeywell introduced a Sick Child Care program for its employees in the Minneapolis area. Under this program, Honeywell subsidizes 80 percent of the cost of providing care for sick children. It offers parents two alternatives to staying home from work when a child falls ill:

- Chicken Soup, a day-care center for mildly sick children ages infant to twelve years. The fee is $40 a day, of which Honeywell pays $32.
- TenderCare for Kids, a service that provides in-home care for sick children ages infant to fourteen years. The fee is $9.50 per hour, of which Honeywell pays $7.60.

Honeywell calculates that the Sick Child Care program saved the company $45,000 during its first nine months of operation. The savings were determined by subtracting Honeywell's program costs ($27,800) from the cumulative daily salaries ($73,000) of the 161 employees who used the Sick Child Care service.[35]

Merck

Merck has demonstrated impressive returns from its parenting leave policy. The price tag attached to replacing an employee at this large pharmaceutical firm is $50,000. But by permitting a new parent to take a generous six-month child-care leave (cost: $38,000, which includes partial pay, benefits, and other indirect costs), the company succeeds in retaining almost all of its new mothers, thereby achieving a net savings of $12,000 per employee.[36]

J. Douglas Phillips, senior director of corporate planning at Merck, stresses the large cost savings inherent in bringing attrition rates down. In an analysis of turnover costs—duplicated in other companies with similar results—he shows that turnover costs average 1.5 times annual salary. (Phillips includes direct costs such as agency search fees, but also includes indirect costs such as incoming employee productivity—it takes about thirteen months for a new employee to achieve maximum efficiency.)[37] According to Phillips, few companies are aware of how expensive it is to replace workers, but in most firms "avoiding turnover for just a few employees will yield excellent paybacks."[38] His research shows that, while other programs are capable of reducing attrition rates, parenting leave and other types of family support have the biggest impact on turnover. He believes that Merck's family support package helps account for the company's low annual turnover rate of 5.5 percent, against a national average of more than 12 percent.[39]

Sunbeam

Sunbeam Appliance Company discovered the importance of prenatal care the hard way. Four premature babies born in 1984 to women working at the company's Coushatta, Louisiana, plant accounted for fully half of the $1 million the company paid that year in health care for 530 employees. One of the babies required so much care that medical bills exceeded the $250,000 limit in major medical coverage.

Shocked by these numbers, the company did some in-house research and discovered that pregnant women who worked at the plant (Sunbeam's labor force is 80 percent female) were waiting too long to see a doctor. So, in 1986, Sunbeam started a prenatal program. Pregnant employees were allowed to take an hour of company time every other week to attend classes in health care and nutrition taught by a specialist in prenatal nursing. In addition, the plant nurse weighed the women weekly, checked their blood pressure, and ran urine tests.

Since the program started there has been only one premature birth, which didn't entail severe problems. Average medical costs for childbirth have taken a nosedive, falling to $3,200 in 1987 from $27,242 three years earlier. The program has been extended to another Sunbeam plant in Mississippi and is now available not only to employees but to their spouses as well. The total cost of the program at the two plants is less than $20,000 a year.[40]

This kind of data is garnering support for family-friendly policies in boardrooms across the nation. According to Dana Friedman, co-president of the Families and Work Institute, as of 1990, 5,400 employers offered child-care assistance and parenting as part of their benefits package, up from 600 in 1982.[41] Friedman describes recent progress as "phenomenal, particularly since the new initiatives comprise complete packages rather than a token policy or two."[42] In the manner of American Express, companies are increasingly offering a range of family supports: parenting leave, child care, elder care, at-home and part-time work, flexible hours, and job sharing.

Other Corporate Initiatives

On the cutting edge of family policy are corporations as different as IBM (230,000 employees) and the NCNB Corporation, a Charlotte, North Carolina–based bank-holding company (13,000 employees). Over the years both companies have put together impressive track records as firms that support working parents.

For more than a decade IBM has steadily increased its efforts to adapt to family needs. In the early 1980s it pioneered child-care and elder-care assistance programs. A national resource and referral service network put together by IBM in 1984 now serves 900,000 employees in more than twenty-five companies. But, as was the case with American Express, the big push came in 1988. According to a news story published in October of that year: "Big Blue has seen the future. And it is filled with working women, dual-career couples, single parents . . . and a shortage of young, skilled workers. Bowing to the inevitability of these demographic trends, International Business Machines last week broadened an already enviable benefits package to make it easier for its 228,000 U.S. workers to balance their careers and private lives."[43] Under the expanded plan, most employees have the option of beginning or ending their working day an hour earlier or later. In addition, IBM employees (30 percent of whom are women) can take a three-year break from full-time employment—with the option of working part-time in the second and third years—to take care of young children or elderly relatives. With the exception of the part-time component this "career break" is unpaid, but health and retirement benefits continue while workers are on leave, and IBM guarantees a full-time job at the end of the three years. In recent months the company has added work-at-home options and introduced family-issues sensitivity training for more than 25,000 managers and supervisors.[44]

Working on a very different scale, the NCNB Corporation has launched two extremely innovative programs. On the flextime front, NCNB has designed an option called Select Time which allows employees at all levels, including managers, to reduce their time and job commitments for dependent care purposes without cutting off advancement opportunities. For example, a branch manager is now able to work a three-day week without getting off the career ladder. On the benefits front, in 1989 the bank initiated a subsidy program called NCNB Childcare Plus, which makes direct financial contributions to the cost of child care. To be eligible an employee has to earn $24,000 or less and have a preschool child in licensed day care. If these conditions are met, NCNB will pay 50 percent of the cost of care up to a maximum of $35 per week per child. By targeting licensed child care, NCNB hopes to raise the quality of child care in the surrounding community. According to Chairman Hugh L. McColl, Jr., "NCNB began its work-family policies and programs because it made good business sense and because it was the right thing to do. Our goals are to attract quality employees, retain valued employees, increase loyalty to the company, improve productivity by reducing stress, and allow people to achieve in the company while succeeding as parents."[45]

In early 1989 Johnson & Johnson announced an extremely broad work-and-family initiative that includes a one-year family leave (with benefits and job-back guarantees), resource and referral services for child and elder care, dependent care accounts, flexible hours, compressed-work-week options, and on-site child care. AT&T recently negotiated a contract with two of its unions that establishes a dependent care referral service and provides leaves for up to one year, with job-back guarantees for new parents and for workers with seriously ill dependents. Apple computer now operates its own employee-staffed child-care center and gives "baby bonuses" of $500 to new parents. In 1989, Allstate Insurance Company created a package of family support policies called "Work and Family Connections." The package includes employee spending accounts for dependent care, family illness allowances, and options for job sharing, part-time, and flexible work schedules. DuPont has helped establish child-care centers in Delaware with contributions of money and space. And Eastman Kodak has adopted new rules permitting part-time work, job sharing, and informal situational flextime.[46] To quote the *Harvard Business Review,* for reasons that are economic and strategic, "these and scores of other businesses are building work environments that let people give their best to their jobs without giving up the pleasures and responsibilities of family life."[47]

Companies tend to follow a three-step evolutionary process in the development of family support policies. Most start off in what Dana Friedman calls the "no mess, no fuss" stage,[48] seeking a low-cost, high-impact program that will quickly show employees that they care. Resource and referral services (R&R) are very popular in this early phase. In some firms R&R is little more than one employee working with a set of files and a bulletin board, but even such a minimal level of support can be deeply appreciated by desperate parents trying to find affordable child care in the local community.

The next stage brings the company into what Friedman calls the Jane Fonda, or "no pain, no gain," phase. Here it becomes necessary for senior executives to commit serious resources to family benefits and to admit that some basic workplace rules have to be modified, particularly rules relating to the rhythm of work. Predictably, these changes run into managerial resistance, especially at the supervisory level, and companies often find it necessary to offer training programs to change attitudes and prepare management for what Friedman calls "the Cultural Revolution" stage—the point at which companies attempt to transform the nature of their organizations. They reinvent their benefits package, creating a complete menu of family supports. But they also redefine how productive work is done in their corporation, putting much more emphasis on results and much less emphasis on conventional schedules and time spent on the job. IBM and NCNB are both established in this third phase; American Express is almost there.

But before we run away with the idea that corporate America is on its way to solving the problems of working parents and their children, we should back up and recognize that despite considerable progress, family support policies are still far from universal. Too many corporations are stuck in a 1950s time warp, rooted in the assumption that employees have "someone at home" to attend to the house and to the children. Most of them don't.

Of all parents in the work force in 1989, only 20 percent of them were married men with nonworking wives.[49] The other 80 percent were men and women who had to make nontraditional arrangements for child care. A recent survey of high-tech companies in New England showed that at these firms the average working mother logs a total of eighty-four hours a week between her home and her job, compared with seventy-two hours for male parents and fifty hours for married men and women with no children.[50] In other words, employed mothers work the equivalent of two full-time jobs (the second shift discussed in chapter 3), and employed fathers work the equivalent of a job and a half. No wonder these parents are looking for flexible schedules, part-time employment, dependent care assistance, and other family supports. Yet despite an urgent level of need, in 1990 only 10 percent of the nation's employers offered any help with child care—financial assistance, on-site centers, or resource and referral services—to employees with young children.[51]

One reason family support policy has been slow to catch on in corporate America is that labor market conditions in the 1970s and 1980s discouraged employees from making new demands in the workplace. It was hard for workers to ask for additional benefits or more flexibility in the context of abundant labor. The huge increase in the number of women joining the paid labor force coincided with the coming of age of the baby boom generation. Any problems encountered by firms employing this new cohort of working mothers—high turnover, lost productivity—were masked by a large labor surplus. Most employees could be easily and quickly replaced, and there were plenty of young people (as yet unencumbered with children) who were willing to make the standard sacrifices for career success—travel, overtime, relocation.

If abundant labor discouraged innovative personnel policies, the problem was compounded by the corporate restructuring that dominated the decade of the 1980s. During these years there was over a trillion dollars of merger and acquisition activity, triggering a great deal of "churning" in the labor market. According to the Bureau of Labor Statistics, during the 1980s approximately 1 million long-term workers (those on the job three years or more) were displaced each year.[52]

This clearly inspired fear in employees and served to dampen new demands. Shuttered factories and fired neighbors littered the American landscape; it was not a good time to stick your head out and ask for a new set of benefits.

Neither of these demand-inhibiting conditions exists any longer. The merger and acquisition movement has abated. And with the baby bust and the dramatic slowdown in the rate of growth of the labor force, companies now incur high costs when they fail to accommodate talented women (and men) who are trying to act responsibly at home as well as at work. These new demographic facts of life started to bite in the late 1980s and business responded. As we have seen, the big corporate push came in 1988, triggered by shortfalls in the supply of skilled labor.

As we move into the 1990s the pressure on firms is bound to build. Working parents are empowered by labor shortages, and demand for family-friendly workplaces is clearly growing. Over the past several years, Louis Harris Associates has polled American workers to determine which benefits they expect from employers. The key finding is a rapidly rising demand for family support benefits. Eighty percent of American adults now believe that employers should help provide (and pay for) community-based child care, and 90 percent feel that employers should include parental leave as a standard benefit. Support for these policies has grown by 10 to 20 percentage points over the last decade.[53]

Reaching Out to Schools

While 5,000-odd corporations have become involved in creating family support policies for their employees, a smaller but significant group is reaching beyond working parents to intervene directly in the lives of disadvantaged children. Business leaders are concerned that in the 1990s companies will be unable to grow and compete because an expanding educational underclass will be unable to meet the demands of jobs generated by an increasingly sophisticated economy. This concern is a relatively recent one.

To put things in historical perspective, the children of the poor have always been less likely to complete their education than their more privileged middle-class peers; indeed, until the 1950s, fewer than 50 percent of all students graduated high school. In earlier periods, however, our nation could tolerate a sink-or-swim attitude toward those in school because American industry could absorb massive numbers of unskilled laborers. A strong back and a pair of deft hands could secure a decently paid factory job or help run a farm.

Over the last twenty-five years technological advance and intensified global competition have brought dramatic and irreversible changes to the job market. As I have shown earlier in this chapter, factories and offices have come to rely less and less on unskilled manual labor. Production processes increasingly depend on computers, and most manufacturing jobs now demand a significant level of math and reading ability. Likewise, jobs in the growing service sector require more literate workers with good interpersonal skills. Peter Drucker estimates that as many as half of all American workers are unqualified to do the "knowledge work" of the 1990s.[54]

It is concern over this "human resource deficit" that is fueling corporate support of primary and secondary education, particularly in the inner cities. In recent years General Electric, American Express, Xerox, AT&T, General Motors, and scores of other corporations have all gotten into the business of education. Company executives acknowledge that the new interest in children is largely a response to the deteriorating quality of American schools and a tightening labor market. "We read the gloomy education reports and decided that if we were going to make any increases in giving, it should be in pre-college education for minorities as a matter of company interest and our national interest," says Edward Bligh of AT&T.[55] Business leaders, looking at the changing work force between now and the year 2000, see that more than a third of the new entrants to the labor market will be ill-prepared minorities. Many are attempting to reach out and improve the chances of these disadvantaged youngsters.

Patrick F. Taylor might at first seem an unlikely educational reformer. A tough-talking, abrasive Southerner, Taylor has a soft spot for fast cars, cowboy boots, and heavy gold cuff links. He is the sole owner of Taylor Energy, an oil and gas company worth $300 million, and has been enormously successful as an oil and natural gas producer at a time when other independents have been destroyed by soft energy prices. He may well be the richest man in Louisiana.

But he is more than that. Because he left his East Texas home at age sixteen with 35 cents in his pocket and had to scrabble for a petroleum engineering degree, he is a fervent believer in the importance of education. He sees more and better education as the key to this nation's future. In his words "our society decided nearly a century ago that 12 years of education were necessary for people to survive in society. But we were manufacturing buggy whips back then. Now it is time for society to decide that a college degree is necessary, that we need 16 years of formal education, not 12." Taylor's passionate advocacy of better access to college has just led to a reform of Louisiana's system of higher education that will remove financial obstacles for poor youngsters.[56]

Taylor's educational reform was born out of a request, in

March 1988, that he visit a junior high school in a shabby New Orleans neighborhood to serve as a role model. This was a familiar task; Pat Taylor had been delivering inspirational talks to students and teachers on Horatio Alger themes for some time. But he was warned that these kids were different. All 221 of them were either two or three years behind in school, 95 percent were black, the majority came from single-parent families, and all lived in drug- and crime-infested areas of the city. Officials at the Livingston Middle School estimated that 80 percent wouldn't finish twelfth grade. It was considered futile, and maybe even cruel, to talk to these kids about college.

Pat Taylor was appalled at the future these children faced and decided to conduct an experiment. "I laid it on pretty thick," says Taylor. "I told the kids where I had come from and what I had, how I had succeeded—oil fields, gas fields, offshore rigs, racing boats, airplanes, ranches, all that stuff. And I told them that . . . if they stayed in school, if they did their work, they would benefit. On the other hand, if they chose to drop out of school and end up on the streets or on welfare, they could blame whomever they wished but it wouldn't make any difference. They would have to live with the results of that failure.

"I then threw out a challenge. I asked, 'How many of you kids would like to go to college?' The reaction was extraordinary. Every hand went up. Nobody looked around to see what the others were going to do. Every hand went up as if they all wanted to be the first one to get their hand up. There was no lack of appreciation for education. Every kid knew that education was the way to succeed in our society.

"So I said, 'OK, here's how we're going to do this. . . . You kids stay in school and in your four years of high school complete these courses. If you make an A average, you don't need me: the universities will snap you up. If you make Cs and Ds, I don't think you'll be qualified for college, but you'll have a valid 12th grade education and you can get a job. But if you make a B average, I'll see to it you go to college.' "

Pat Taylor kept his word. He reached an agreement with three college presidents to waive tuition and room and board if these youngsters fulfilled the terms of his challenge. He arranged (and paid for) eighty-three eighth-graders to take a six-week summer course on the Loyola and University of New Orleans campuses, attending classes and cultural events, learning personal hygiene, and working part-time at paying jobs. He had "Taylor's Kids" T-shirts and blazers made up to create group solidarity and give the kids some protection on the streets. Two years later, 21 of them had become honor roll students; 172 of the original 221 were still in school; only one student had became pregnant; and there had been no cases of drug abuse.

Inspired by the success of his kids, Pat Taylor began promoting statewide educational reform. In his view, college education in Louisiana should be made much more accessible. The average income in the state is a shade under $20,000 a year; it costs almost a third of this sum ($6,000 a year) to keep a child at Louisiana State University. In Taylor's words, "Look at what this does to people in the lower income ranges. It robs them of an achievable ambition and it robs us of truly productive citizens."

Taylor lobbied hard for a bill that would give financial relief to qualified youngsters. "Almost single-handedly he pushed, pulled, jerked and yanked Governor Roemer, the Louisiana legislature and Board of Regents" until they approved and funded his bill. After being buttonholed by Taylor, one legislator said, "Once Pat gets his paws on you, he doesn't let go until he gets yes for an answer. He won't take no for an answer and he won't take maybe, and he gets real angry if you say you're going to study it."

The Taylor Plan Bill (Senate Bill 280) was introduced in the Louisiana legislature's spring 1989 session and was formally passed on July 10, 1989. The Taylor Plan says that any Louisiana high school senior who has completed 17.5 hours of college preparatory courses, maintained a C+ average, and scores at least an 18 out of a possible 36 on the American College Test entrance exam is eligible for state-subsidized tuition payments if he or she comes from a family with an annual income of less than $25,000. The cutoff is $30,000 for a family with two children and $35,000 for larger families.

Pat Taylor firmly believes that by providing these incentives, Louisiana will not only enhance education but will also reduce drug abuse, crime, teenage pregnancy, and other costly socioeconomic problems.

The Taylor Plan and its New York equivalent, Eugene Lang's I Have a Dream Foundation, are being used as models across the nation. Over the past few years a dozen cities and states, including Boston, Detroit, Baltimore, Milwaukee, New York, and Rhode Island, have adopted versions of these initiatives. In February 1990 Milwaukee Mayor John Norquist pledged to guarantee a spot in college with financial aid for any student in the city who graduates from high school with at least a C+ average. According to Norquist "every youngster in our school system needs to know and believe that somebody is behind them and that hard work and achievement will be rewarded."[57] The Milwaukee guarantee is part of a citywide campaign by business leaders that gives awards of $500 to teachers who have been chosen as superior, and provides one-on-one tutoring for students deemed at risk of dropping out of school.

In Milwaukee, as in other urban areas throughout the nation, the odds facing inner-city students are daunting. Sixty percent of the 98,000 pupils in Milwaukee public schools live at or near the poverty level, 70 percent are black, and 50 percent live in single-parent homes. Starved of resources, lacking role models, and dealing with various types of discrimination, the children in this school system are not doing well. Only 22 percent of black students attain a cumulative grade-point average of 2.0 (a C average), and only 2.2 percent attain a grade-point average of 3.0 (a B average).

With the unemployment rate dipping below the 5 percent level, Milwaukee businesses have begun to complain of a dire shortage of educated workers. "Business has a strong self-interest in seeing that these students are better trained," says Robert H. Milbourne, executive director of the Greater Milwaukee Committee, a consortium of business and civic leaders.

Ideas (and even legislative initiatives) from the private sector are no longer scoffed at by professional educators. Individual business leaders and corporations are increasingly involved in shaping and funding educational reform.

In the mid-1980s General Electric started Project Continued Success at Aiken High School, an inner-city school in Cincinnati. GE committed resources to bankroll better salaries for teachers and an enriched curriculum, but the company also contributed a great deal of personal energy. Hundreds of company employees (from vice presidents to janitors) spent their free time acting as mentors and tutors for these disadvantaged students, and this one-on-one contact seems to have made a critical difference to these youngsters. The program has more than met its goals, boosting the number of Aiken students going on to college from three graduating seniors in

1985 to sixty-three in 1988. Encouraged by the Aiken success story, GE recently launched College Bound, a $20 million commitment to double the number of college-ready students at selected poor and inner-city schools by the year 2000.[58]

In November 1989 RJR Nabisco announced it was giving grants totaling $30 million over a five-year period to school systems that develop innovative yet practical ways of improving education. RJR says it wants to finance programs that bring more control and accountability to the individual school; provide more options for students; make greater use of technology; and employ nontraditional concepts like longer school days and speedier ways to license teachers.

In Chicago, whose schools were once described by former Secretary of Education William J. Bennett as the worst in the nation, a group of companies, including Quaker Oats, McDonald's, Baxter International, and Sears Roebuck, have started their own private school for poor, inner-city children as a demonstration laboratory for educational innovation.

And in Rochester, New York, Eastman Kodak has helped fund reforms that are turning the local school system into a national prototype. Teacher salaries have been sharply raised (to as much as $70,000 a year) and elaborate support systems have been put in place to help teachers do their jobs better. In one of the most significant innovations, Rochester teachers must now take overall responsibility for a small group of students, including making home visits to determine whether problems outside of school are affecting classroom performance. Teachers are held accountable for students' performance and can be dismissed for incompetence.[59]

Reaching Out to Home and Community

Clearly, a great deal of corporate effort is now focused on reforming and improving the educational system. But for at least some business leaders, the problems of America's children are so profound and pervasive that solutions to educational failure must reach beyond the traditional boundaries of the school into the home and the community.

In the mid-1980s, the Committee for Economic Development (CED), a Washington-based research organization comprised of over two hundred high-level executives, published a study on business and the public schools.[60] In preparing this report, the business leaders at CED came to believe that there were real limits to what could be done within the formal educational system. To senior executives such as Owen Butler, retired chairman of Procter & Gamble, the facts and figures seemed to indicate that "the seeds of educational failure are planted early. Children who are born into poverty or overly stressful family circumstances often suffer from a wide variety of physical and emotional problems . . . that impair their ability to function effectively in the typical public school setting."[61] In other words, no matter how much money you pump into schools, no matter how well you pay the teachers, fine-tune the curricula, or enrich the programs, you do not address the critical needs of a substantial segment of students unless you also concern yourself with nutrition, health care, housing, and family functioning—the factors that determine the early development of the child. If children are hungry or abused, if their minds are paralyzed by fear, or if they live in cramped squalid tenements, it is unlikely they will do well in school.

Inspired by these findings, CED launched a project that was

designed to look at what could be done to improve the early environment of the child, and in 1987 published *Children in Need: Investment Strategies for the Educationally Disadvantaged.* A startling document that created a stir in corporate America, *Children in Need* called upon the nation to spend billions of dollars and "give highest priority to early and sustained intervention in the lives of disadvantaged children."[62]

It is eleven o'clock on a Monday morning and nine-year-old Janine Rios is sitting on the stoop of a dilapidated apartment house on East 124th Street in Manhattan, throwing stones into the gutter and watching some hookers ply their trade on the other side of the street.

"I ain't going to school today," she tells me. I asked her why. "I've got these nits in my hair and the school nurse sent me home so that my Mom could get this special stuff and wash the nits out." Janine ducked her mop of curly hair so that I could take a look. A moment later she came up for air and explained, "That was way back last week but my Mom hasn't gotten around to getting the stuff yet so I guess I'll be out of school for a while." Janine sounded philosophical; she didn't mind missing school.

Janine attends a school in East Harlem that has developed an elaborate program aimed at preventing students from dropping out. With funds provided by the city and a variety of private donors, this school offers remedial math and reading, after-school enrichment activities, and big "brothers" and "sisters" who act as mentors to the children. But no one has thought to deal with the head lice problem. During the 1988–89 school year, Janine was out of school for a total of seven weeks because her dysfunctional parents were incapable of buying the shampoo and producing the level of hygiene that, together, would have gotten rid of the lice.[63]

* * *

On the other side of America, in Los Angeles, the entrance
hall of the George Washington Preparatory High School features a handmade plaque bearing the names of five hundred
students, friends, and relatives who have died violently in the
past decade, most of them victims of the ferocious gangs that
rule the local streets.

A demilitarized zone in the gang wars, this high school is
a magnet school offering enhanced math and science. Under
the guidance of its principal, Larry Higgins, 2,700 youngsters
are supposed to be concentrating on getting into college. Most
students are grateful. They are acutely aware that they are
being given a chance to live a very different kind of life.

But for a while last year, Sandra Deas, seventeen, was afraid
even to go to school. Three kids were gunned down in front
of nearby homes, and several more were caught in crossfire
between rival gangs. "For weeks," says Sandra, "I was so
scared." Now, her mother forbids her to walk to school. Some
days Sandra gets rides from family members or friends; other
days she is forced to skip school.[64]

If a child's mind is filled with fear or her hair is full of lice,
it is hard to take advantage of educational opportunity. The
CED estimates that 30 percent of contemporary American
children are coping with problems on the family or community front severe enough to close off most educational options.
Many of these problems are linked to poverty.[65]

As we saw in chapter 2, 20 percent of all children under
eighteen and 23 percent of children under six currently live
in families whose incomes fall below the poverty line. Children in poverty suffer disproportionately from prematurity,
malnutrition, recurrent and untreated health problems, psychological and physical stress, child abuse, and learning

disabilities. Not surprisingly, poverty correlates closely with school failure, especially where family structure has broken down as well. Poor students are three times more likely to become dropouts than are students from economically advantaged homes. The patterns of behavior that lead to school failure begin to appear in early childhood. Teenagers rarely make a sudden, conscious decision to leave school at age fifteen or sixteen; the act of dropping out is the culmination of years of frustration and failure.

In *Children in Need* the CED recommends that the U.S. government intervene directly in the lives of poor families and spend much more money on programs such as prenatal care for high-risk mothers; parenting education for both mothers and fathers; family health care; and quality preschool education for all disadvantaged three- and four-year-olds. The report stresses the cost-benefit arguments for early intervention and points out that every $1 spent on preschool education saves $4.75 in remedial education, welfare, and crime down the road. According to CED's corporate executives, "the price of corrective action may be high, but the cost of inaction is far higher." *Children in Need* suggests that the private sector play a pace-setting role in improving the early environment of the child, and cites the Beethoven Project as a model program that might well be worth copying nationwide.[66]

In early 1987 Victoria Brown was a frightened teenager expecting her first child, worrying about caring for an infant, and lacking plans for the future. Today her baby, Constance, has grown into a healthy, alert toddler and the nineteen-year-old mother exudes new confidence: "I graduate from high school in June. I want a job working with computers and I want to leave Robert Taylor [public housing] and live in a house. I'm happy with the baby but I don't want more kids."[67]

The turnaround in Victoria's life and the improved prospects for her daughter are a result of the vision of businessman and philanthropist Irving B. Harris and his Beethoven Project, an innovative cradle-to-kindergarten program he helped launch at the Robert Taylor housing project in Chicago.

The goal of the Beethoven Project is to improve—by means of a range of social, medical, and educational services—the life chances of children born into some particularly disadvantaged families living in the nation's largest public housing project. The context is grim. The shabby sixteen-story concrete towers known as the Robert Taylor Homes are situated in a desolate, crime-ridden neighborhood on Chicago's South Side. The majority of the 20,000 residents in this housing complex are single mothers who eke out a living on public assistance. Like Victoria, most of them are young, virtually all are black. One community leader calls the Robert Taylor Homes a "breeding ground of despair." Infant mortality, teenage pregnancy, and illiteracy are rampant.

The program targets the kindergarten classes that will enter the nearby Beethoven elementary school in 1993 and 1994, and provides an array of services that have not been available to these children before: comprehensive prenatal care, nutrition and health education, a family drop-in center, parent education, developmental screening, a toddler school, and Head Start. All of these services are designed to prepare these disadvantaged children so that they will enter school "primed for success," and to help their parents build stronger, more self-sufficient families.

For the last thirty years Harris has devoted some of his best energy (and substantial amounts of money) to disadvantaged children. In 1982 he joined with the Illinois Department of Children and Family Services to create the Ounce of Prevention Fund, based on the premise that an ounce of prevention is worth at least a pound of cure. It was this fund that sparked the Beethoven Project in late 1987.

Harris believes strongly that the enormous human and societal cost of a lifetime of poverty can be greatly reduced by early and sustained intervention in the lives of poor children. He is impressed by the cost of wasted lives and estimates that one child's "failure" as a member of society costs the taxpayer about $300,000. That figure represents the cost of *not* preventing problems that are, in many cases, preventable: intensive hospital care for low-birth-weight babies; special education for children who are developmentally delayed or handicapped; AFDC and Medicaid for families in the welfare system; truant officers and corrections services. According to Harris the only way to avoid these huge costs is to invest a much more modest amount of money in the early development of children. The Beethoven Project is not cheap—estimates are in the $50,000 range per child from before birth to kindergarten—but in Harris's view, if this money is not spent the costs are certain to be much greater in the long run.[68]

The Corporate Bottom Line

The impetus behind the corporate embrace of "warm fuzzy" issues is, of course, concern about the shape and form of the American labor pool. Given the looming labor and skill shortages of the 1990s, it now makes economic as well as humanitarian sense for business to reach out to working parents and minority youngsters. Thousands of American companies are now engaged in creating family-friendly workplaces, and hundreds more are getting directly involved in improving the life chances of disadvantaged children.

But what does all of this corporate activity amount to? What are the chances that business initiatives can solve the problems of the second shift or make up the educational deficit of black and Hispanic youth?

It does seem that private sector initiatives can take us a certain distance in lightening the burden on working mothers (and fathers). As we have seen, companies such as IBM, Johnson & Johnson, American Express, Merck, DuPont, and AT&T now offer a significant degree of flexibility and substantial benefits to several million working parents. Indeed, since the early 1980s the number of companies offering family support benefits has increased by a factor of nine, and this rate of growth will only speed up in the 1990s as the competition for the best employees forces the issue.[69] As pointed out in a recent issue of the *Harvard Business Review,* "a smaller labor supply means that workers will no longer have to take jobs in the forms that have always been offered. Companies will have to market their own employment practices and adapt their jobs to the demands of the work force."[70]

Despite these compelling labor market arguments, however, there remains a great deal of inertia and resistance in corporate America. The shift from unencumbered white men to overburdened and disadvantaged women and minorities has happened too quickly for the full significance of this "revolution" to have penetrated the consciousness of at least some business executives.

Dana Friedman recalls a presentation she made to a breakfast meeting of chief executives in Hartford, Connecticut: "I announced that [over the next decade] 80 percent of all women in the work force will be of childbearing age, and that 90 percent of them will get pregnant," she said. "One CEO jumped up and said, 'Well, I just won't hire them!' I said, 'You are not going to have a choice, sir,' and then I gave him the third statistic: that two-thirds of the new entrants to the work force will be women."[71]

A great deal of work needs to be done to close the information gap Friedman discovered in Hartford. We need to publi-
cize the new demographic facts of life, and we need to shout
from the rooftops the cost-benefit data presented in this chapter. For nothing grabs corporate attention more effectively
than hard evidence demonstrating that a family-friendly workplace more than pays for itself. High rates of turnover and
absenteeism incur costs, costs that can be dramatically reduced
by company-sponsored child care, parenting leave, and other
types of family support. The icing on the cake is that many of
these cost-effective policies don't involve large up-front commitments on the part of the firm. Companies can help employees in relatively inexpensive ways, and some accommodations
are virtually cost-free. For example, firms that offer a dependent care assistance account (which provides sizable tax benefits to employees) find that this benefit can be provided at little
or no cost. In a recent survey carried out by *Working Mother*
magazine, 77 percent of readers said flexible hours would
make an enormous difference to their lives, yet implementing
a flextime policy would not cost employers a penny.[72]

An aggressive promotional campaign that aired these facts
and figures in boardrooms around the nation could well trigger an impressive increase in the number of companies supporting working parents. (Ten percent of all workers were
offered child-care assistance by their employers. This number
could easily rise to 30 percent by the year 2000).[73] However,
it is important to realize that there will always be large numbers of companies that cannot respond to the new demographic imperatives. Firms with fewer than twenty-five workers (which employ 28 percent of all working women)[74] will
find it difficult to be generous on the benefits or flexibility
front. A six-month parenting leave can be onerous in a small
office where every worker is seen as indispensable. And companies in declining fields (the apparel industry is a good exam-

ple) will hardly be in the business of designing policies that
retain or attract workers.

With these qualifications, I think it is possible to look forward to a decade where corporate America will get into the
business of helping a significant proportion of all dual-worker
families. The driving force will be enlightened self-interest,
not altruism; but whatever the motive, these private sector
policies will clearly improve the lives of millions of working
parents—and their children. In many cases family support
policies will enable women to avoid those costly career interruptions that—along with discrimination—have so severely
limited female earning power.[75] A study by the Rand Corporation shows that a two-to-four-year break in employment lowers lifetime income by 13 percent, while a five-year break in
employment lowers lifetime income by 19 percent.[76] Economist Eli Ginzberg goes so far as to say that "a continuous work
history is almost a prerequisite for high or even good achievement" in the labor market.[77] In other words, expanded programs of family support will enable more women to hang on
to their jobs—and thus their career ladders—during their
childbearing years, and this should lead to a dramatic narrow-
ing of the wage gap in the 1990s.

But if family support policies enhance female earning
power, they also contribute substantially to the quality of family life. In particular, new forms of flexibility are capable of
easing the strain and stress that permeates the lives of so many
working parents and their children.

Family Time: The Ultimate Win-Win Scenario

When Kathy talks about Mondays and Tuesdays at home, this
efficient down-to-earth business executive can sound down-

right lyrical: "It is a precious time. My little girl can get up whenever she wants—no need to bundle her up in a snowsuit, no need to rush off to the day-care center. We often go out to a long lazy ten o'clock breakfast or just fool around in bed and watch *The Lady and the Tramp* on the VCR. It seems to be such a wonderful gift—two whole days of totally discretionary time.

"Of course, by the time Wednesday rolls around I am quite ready to get dressed up in a suit, go into the office and be with grownups, and Caroline is equally ready to be with playmates of her own age. But changing the balance of my life so that I have four days at home and three in the office instead of the standard two and five is quite simply the best thing I ever did."

Kathy Cruise Murphy works three days a week sharing a middle management job in the card division of American Express in New York City. Job sharing was not something she had in mind when she started out at Amex some eleven years ago. Kathy is ambitious and extremely capable, but becoming a mother changed her priorities in unexpected ways.

"When Caroline was born three and a half years ago, I just took the standard leave and was back at work full-time when my baby was eight weeks old. . . . I guess I just assumed that we modern women can 'have it all' and should 'do it all.' "

For a while things more or less worked out. After a bad experience with a young *au pair* girl who stayed only two months, Kathy put Caroline into a day-care center near their home in New Jersey between 8:00 A.M. and 6:00 P.M. five days a week. The baby seemed to do well, but slowly Kathy began to feel that her life didn't have the right balance.

"If you figure in the commute, my job was consuming fifty-five hours a week. Many evening hours and much of the weekend seemed to be filled with household chores and errands. I felt I was on a treadmill—tired, harassed, and unhappy. I resented the fact that there was no time to enjoy my child, my husband, my family."

Just as Kathy was having these second thoughts, she met up with Jean Gol, another middle-level manager at Amex who had just had her first child and also wanted to work part-time. Kathy and Jean decided to try to share a job. They put together a proposal and together applied for a middle management job in human resources. They landed the job and for the last two years Jean has worked two-fifths' time at 40 percent of her former salary, and Kathy has worked three-fifths' time at 60 percent of her former salary. Both are entitled to full benefits for themselves and their dependents.

Before Kathy goes home on Friday nights she leaves a file folder of pending work for Jean. When Jean comes into the office on Monday, she spends half an hour on the phone with Kathy going over the materials in the file. The same routine is followed Tuesday evening and Wednesday morning, when Jean leaves and Kathy takes over. The two women rarely find they need to talk outside of these two half-hour slots, and the work gets done efficiently and smoothly. According to a senior colleague, "Jean and Kathy really know how to get this job done; by tapping the experience of both of these women in this one job, the company gets a good deal." Kathy and Jean's job share has proved so successful that there are now nine other job shares in the same division of Amex, one of them involving a male employee.

According to Kathy, when they broached their plan to Amex in 1988, not only was the company surprisingly open to a job-sharing arrangement but social attitudes were beginning to change: "The image of the 'supermom' was becoming a little tarnished. For the first time in a while it was OK to admit that you wanted to spend time with your baby, that your worth was not solely wrapped up in working a fifty-five-hour week. This change in perspective helped me get together the courage to change the rhythm of my life.''

Reflecting on her decision to share a job, Kathy says, "If you're ambitious or if your identity is mixed up with being a professional, becoming a part-timer is kind of scary. It's easy to imagine that you will become a second-class citizen, that no one will give you responsibility or take you seriously. I don't feel that has happened to me—at least not yet. My work is valued by the company.'' I asked Kathy how she sees the future. She thought long and hard before replying. "We need a whole new career track for part-timers. I know that I would feel better about my future at Amex if I could identify the next rung on the ladder. With creativity and imagination it should be possible to create part-time or job-sharing positions up to the vice-presidential level."[78]

Job sharing clearly involves sacrificing some income, and this particular type of flexibility might not work for a parent who needs to maximize earning power (single mothers, for example). However, for many dual-worker households—which today account for 24.9 million children—job sharing would seem to resolve a great many problems. The working parent is able to achieve real balance in his or her life; the company retains highly productive employees who might otherwise be forced to leave; and the child gets to see much more of Mom or Dad. It also need not be just a one-shot or temporary solution. Ten years down the road a job-sharing arrangement would allow Kathy (or her husband) to spend extended time with Caroline in her early teenage years—a time when youngsters often benefit from lots of parental attention. As Kathy correctly points out, there is no reason why companies can't build entire career ladders for part-time or job-sharing employees. Most hourly work and a great deal of middle management work are susceptible to being organized this way. There is nothing especially efficient in nine-to-five work-days or forty-to-fifty-hour work weeks. Industry was organized this way to fit the needs of male breadwinners back in the days when Mom was at home to take care of the kids. There is no reason why we can't reorganize the rhythm of work so that contemporary parents can give more time to their children.

Which brings us to a central question. What does a family-friendly workplace mean for the well-being of children? Are family support policies really win-win propositions: good for companies, good for parents, good for kids?

Most of the time corporate supports for working parents do promote the interests of the child. The generous parenting-leave policies of companies such as Merck and Johnson & Johnson (which typically hold a job open for twelve to eigh-teen months and provide benefits and partial pay) make an important difference in a child's critical first months of life. Job sharing, part-time work, compressed work weeks, staggered hours—all those flexible options now offered by companies such as American Express and IBM—are clearly good for children in that they free up parents to spend more and better time with their children. As Cathy Collins's overburdened life demonstrates, mothers working full-time can experience so much stress in their daily lives that quality time with the kids seems like some kind of bad joke.

Finally, on-site child care, or subsidies that permit a parent to opt for higher-quality child care, can upgrade the quality of out-of-home care. This is clearly an important step in the right direction. Many working parents are still forced to put their infants or toddlers in third-rate, unlicensed, even dangerous day care because they simply cannot afford anything better.

But we shouldn't fool ourselves and assume that the needs of the working parent (or the corporation, for that matter) are identical to those of the child: *there is no necessary congruence of interest.* Some working parents may be more interested in getting promoted than in spending time with little Johnny, and companies are mostly interested in easing the lives of working parents so that they can devote more of their best attention to the firm. Because of this divergence of interest, at least some of the new corporate policies, even those labeled "family supports," are not particularly good for children, and a few may actually harm them. For example, out-of-home emergency or sick care for children might reduce absenteeism for the firm and boost earning power for the individual working parent, but such a solution may seem singularly unappealing to a sick child who would much rather stay at home with Mom or Dad. "Over the long term we need a solution like the one in Sweden, where mothers have a certain number of days off when their children are sick,"[79] says Edward Zigler, Professor of Psychology at Yale University and a long-time children's advocate.

In 1989 Wilmer, Cutler & Pickering, a prominent Washington law firm, set up an on-site child care center for emergencies—to cover a situation where a child is sick or a regular baby-sitter fails to turn up. Despite the fact that this facility proved to be expensive (start-up costs were in the $300,000 range), the law firm expects it to more than pay for itself.[80] The reason is that the firm's (high-priced) female lawyers are now much more available to work late into the night and on weekends. This may make a lot of sense for Wilmer, Cutler & Pickering; it may even make some sense for individual women lawyers at the firm who can now log fourteen-hour days and work full-tilt toward partnership. But is it actually good for the children who now see even less of their mothers?

Time is the crucial issue here, or more specifically the lack of it. As I demonstrated in chapter 3, millions of mainstream American children are failing to thrive because they do not receive sufficient parental time and attention. In the over-loaded contemporary world of disappearing dads and length-ening work weeks, corporate policies that give parents the gift of time so that they can devote more and better time to their children are "pro-family" in an extremely clear-cut way. The same cannot be said, however, of those new policies—on-site care for sick children being one example—that seek solely to free parents from parental obligations so that they can spend more of their time and energy at work.

Despite these limitations, private sector policies do seem able to ease the problems of the second shift. Jack Welch is right: The looming labor shortages have tilted the balance of power in society toward skilled labor, and working parents (particularly working mothers) are the prime beneficiaries of this move.

The Limits of Self-Interest

It is much less clear how much of a difference corporations are able to make when they reach out to disadvantaged young-sters. Initiatives such as College Bound and the Academy of Finance are clearly laudable, but they are a drop in the bucket. American Express now contributes $3 million a year to the Academy of Finance, which currently enrolls 2,000 students. This is a whole lot better than nothing, but it only skims the surface of our problems. The dimensions of our educational deficit are gigantic. In 1989 New York City alone spent $6 billion on education—and yet this was a long way from being enough: the city still generates 45,000 dropouts a year.[81]

Business executives know that they face a huge problem. David T. Kearns, chairman of Xerox, talks about the lack of qualifications among U.S. workers, "putting this country at a terrible competitive disadvantage." Owen Butler describes "a

Third World within our own country," while J. Richard Munro, CEO of *Time* magazine, warns that "there just are not enough new skilled workers to go around," with costs to the economy that will soon be "staggering."[82] And yet despite anxiety and concern, there is one very important reason why corporate America will not devote massive resources to the problems of underprivileged youth: *it is impossible for an individual company to reap the rewards of this type of investment in any direct way.*

General Electric spends a few million dollars preparing Aiken High School students for college, Eastman Kodak devotes some resources and energy to reforming the Rochester school system; but both companies know that while their efforts may "improve" the pool of labor from which they draw, they cannot expect to employ very many of the graduates of these programs and reap the benefits of their largesse. Which is precisely why they are spending millions rather than billions on these programs. An executive at American Express told me that only a handful of the graduates of the Academy of Finance are with the firm; these well-qualified young people are now "scattered all over Wall Street."[83]

Unlike family support policies, where companies can expect to see an immediate return on their investment (attrition rates go down, productivity goes up), high school enrichment programs or early childhood education cannot be counted on to pay off for the firm, even in the long run. These investments clearly pay off for the community and the nation. But executives are not in the business of promoting the national good. Some companies will still choose to undertake these programs; they improve the general business environment and are good for company image. But in the aggregate, few companies will get involved with schools or children, and when they do it will be on a modest scale.

In other words, we cannot look to the private sector to

provide the bulk of the resources necessary to upgrade the life prospects of disadvantaged youngsters. Government cannot pass the buck and pretend that business can somehow "fix" the problem of underachievement and failure among our children. The public sector is uniquely qualified to undertake this mammoth task.

Business as Pacesetter

But if the private sector cannot be expected to bankroll secondary schools or prenatal care, it can play a critical role in providing a cost-benefit rationale for significant new public investment in children. When Irving Harris founded the Ounce of Prevention Fund and initiated the Beethoven Project, he was driven by the commonsensical notion that in the Chicago slums relatively small investments in young children yield handsome returns. Similarly, Pat Taylor figured out that in Louisiana it is much cheaper to pay for college than to pick up the tab for welfare and crime. Precisely because business leaders are ruled by the need to make a profit they have an accurate and urgent understanding of what is at stake. In the eloquent words of the Committee for Economic Development, "The United States is creating a permanent underclass of young people for whom poverty and despair are life's daily companions . . . The nation can ill-afford such an egregious waste of human resources. Allowing this to continue will not only impoverish our children, it will impoverish our nation—culturally, politically and economically."[84]

The private sector is rarely in the vanguard of social policy, but here the statistics and trend lines speak with an urgency that is hard to ignore. CED's corporate executives understand that on the backs of our children rides the future prosperity of the nation.

8

A Call to Action

Imagine the scene: it's sometime in the early 1990s and a new president is delivering a special address to a joint session of Congress, televised on prime time. His subject: How to Save Our Children and Recapture the Greatness of America.

Mr. Speaker, distinguished members of the House and Senate, fellow citizens. For more than two hundred years, presidents have come to this chamber in times of national crisis. Tidings of war, depression, nuclear threat, and natural disaster have reverberated around these walls.

Tonight I am here to alert you to an impending American tragedy that is threatening to bring this great nation to its knees.

The problems of our children—America's most precious asset—have reached catastrophic proportions. Across the face of this nation children are failing to thrive. Black kids, white kids, poor kids, privileged kids deal with risk and neglect on

*a scale unknown in previous eras. With results that are calami-
tous—for us and for them.*

One-fifth of our children are growing up in poverty; more
than a quarter drop out of school; and 25 percent are abandoned by their fathers. The number of American teenagers in
psychiatric hospitals has quintupled over the last five years,
and a baby born in our nation's capital is now more likely to
die in the first year of life than one born in Singapore or Costa
Rica. Deprivation, rejection, and anguish sown on this scale
will surely yield a harvest of failure and violence.

I issue a solemn warning: a nation that allows large numbers
of its children to grow up in poverty, afflicted by poor health,
handicapped by inferior education, deserted by fathers, cut
adrift by society—this nation asks for, and gets, chaos. And it
is richly deserved.

Our mammoth task in the 1990s is to create conditions that
will allow children to flourish. We must support parents and
reconstruct the family as the cornerstone of society; then and
only then can we heal the wounds of our young and knit
together the fabric of this nation.

Tonight I am presenting you with an Action Plan for Children that will accomplish this purpose and ensure this country's strength into the future. It has four key ingredients:

- Give top billing to families with children.
  *Let's shout it from the rooftops and write it into the laws of
  this land: America honors parents and cherishes children.*
- Invest in the future.
  *Treat kids as capital. It is time we put our money where our
  mouth is and devoted more resources to children. For the
  longer our graduation lines today, the shorter our unemployment lines tomorrow.*
- Hold parents accountable.

Let the word go out: any man who fathers a child in this society will acquire enduring responsibility for the welfare of that child. We will create the sanctions to make this stick. Marriage might not be "till death do us part," but parenthood surely is.

· No new taxes.

We can accomplish all of these goals without further burdening the taxpayer. In borrowing from business a cost-benefit logic, we can intervene where we get the "biggest bang for our buck." Early childhood education for poor youngsters pays for itself seven times over. And money spent on early childhood education has a 30 percent rate of return. These programs will wind up saving us money!

I want to stress this economic dimension. If we are interested in the size of our paychecks in the future, we have to get out there and take better care of our children.

Business executives tell me that they are facing a serious crunch in the labor market. The pool of qualified youngsters is small—and shrinking—and the demand for educated, skilled workers is acute—and increasing. A company like New York Telephone finds that only 4 percent of job applicants are able to pass its basic skills test, which is pegged at an eighth-grade level. If we can't do a better job in preparing our youngsters, the engine of economic growth will falter and all of us will face a lower standard of living.

But this is not the end of the story: badly educated young people not only undermine the prosperity of the nation; they drain the public purse. A wasted life costs upward of $300,000 when you add in welfare charges and the expenses of the penal system. These costs, my friends, are paid for by you and me.

If we cherish our children, they will add to the wealth and strength of our country; if we neglect our children, they will

drag this great nation down. Either way, they have an enormous impact on our well-being.

One way to look after children is to invest more in education, but while this is important, no matter how much we
spend on our schools, they will continue to fall short of the
mark unless we also strengthen families. One-half of what a
human being learns from birth to age seventeen is learned
before the age of four. For any child the first and most important teacher is the parent.

If we want to compete with the Japanese and the Germans
in the twenty-first century, we must upgrade our educational
system, but we must also empower families by providing parents with additional resources so that they can do a better job
by their children. This is what my Action Plan will attempt
to do.

Back in February of 1909, Theodore Roosevelt delivered
a special message to Congress: "Each of our children represents either a potential addition to the productive capacity and
the enlightened citizenship of the nation, or, if allowed to
suffer from neglect, a potential addition to the destructive
forces of the community. The ranks of criminals and other
enemies of society are recruited in an altogether undue proportion from children bereft of their natural homes and left
without sufficient care. The interests of the nation are involved
in the welfare of this army of children no less than in our great
material affairs."

Of course, back in Teddy Roosevelt's day, presidents
couldn't cost it out; they didn't have a staff of economists
crunching numbers, proving to us all that it really is much
cheaper to pay for day care on the front end of life than jail
care on the back end of life.

Which brings me to what I call the icing on the cake.

Saving our kids is not just the compassionate thing to do and

the moral thing to do; it also happens to be the fiscally respon-
sible thing to do. For once in political life, conscience and
convenience go hand in hand. Doing what is right by our kids
builds up our competitive strength and knits together the
raveled sleeve of this society, but it also produces a kinder and
gentler nation.

Just last week I received a letter from Amy Fenton, a young
mother who lives in Cleveland, Ohio.

"Please, Mr. President," she writes, "find a way to help.
We are expecting our second child in four months, and I
haven't seen a doctor yet. There's no way we can come up with
the down payment for another baby. We still owe $2,100 for
Tracy, and she will be two in September.

"We don't know where to turn. We both have decent jobs
working in restaurants downtown, but neither of us has medical coverage. We don't take vacations, we don't eat out, and
we don't pay for sitters because we work back-to-back shifts
and take care of Tracy ourselves. But still, we're real close to
the edge.

"We lie awake at nights thinking about how we're going to
provide for two kids—whether we can afford Pampers,
whether we can pay the rent on a two-bedroom trailer.

"You know, we're not whiners or welfare cheats. We're
just a regular, hard-working couple. We obey the laws, pay
our taxes, and fly the American flag on holidays.

"So I don't get it. Why is it such a hard, grinding struggle
for working folks to raise a family in America?

"I guess we just don't shout and scream and make a whole
lot of noise.

"I think maybe we're tired.

"But we can't hack this next baby. We need your help, Mr.
President."

* * *

Well, if Amy Fenton doesn't get medical care soon, it could cost us taxpayers a pretty penny. Prenatal care costs $400; preemies cost $1,000 a day. And which would we rather have: a healthy, full-term, inexpensive baby, or a sickly, low-birth-weight, expensive baby who may well face a lifetime of heartache as a result of being born too small and too early?

Tonight I make a pledge to families throughout the length and breadth of this land. This month my administration will introduce legislation that will underwrite the expenses of pre-natal and maternity care for all mothers and newborn babies. From here on in, the gift of life will be freely given in America—not grudgingly, but in a spirit of great rejoicing, as befits the miracle of birth. I can think of no better way of demonstrating how much this nation values its children.

To my fellow Americans watching in your living rooms tonight, I say hold fast to your dreams. You will be succored and supported in your endeavor to build strong families. Your lonely struggle is over. Amy Fenton and her unborn baby will not have to hack it alone.

To my colleagues in this chamber, I ask for your energetic help in moving forward with my Action Plan despite debt and deficits. Leadership is passed from generation to generation, but so is stewardship. The time has come to fulfill our responsibility to the future. Let our descendants look back and say that at the end of the twentieth century we had the wisdom and foresight to invest in our children and, in so doing, revitalized the body, recharged the spirit, and recaptured the soul of this great nation.

It is to this broad mission that I call all Americans. We are a God-fearing, moral people and understand that to find fulfillment in life we need to form an attachment to something larger than the lonely self. Let us find this larger purpose in our children and our children's children.

I need your help. Government cannot accomplish these tasks alone. Bureaucracies cannot soothe the shuddering body of a crack baby or act as mentor to a throwaway child. If we are to succeed in saving our children, we need the resources of the public purse but we also need the hands-on compassionate energies of an army of volunteers. Let us reach out together and offer a place in the sun to the children of the shadows.

Thank you and God bless you.

It's compelling, plausible stuff, this imaginary speech concocted for a phantom president. It comes across as a guaranteed vote getter. One can almost imagine politicians lining up for blueprints of this Action Plan for Children. Sure, it needs fleshing out (inspirational speeches by presidents on prime-time TV are often short on substance), but it does extremely well on three fronts.

In the first place, this speech connects with the self-interest of the voting public. Whether you are a sixty-seven-year-old bachelor or a thirty-four-year-old DINK, you will sit up and take notice. Until this moment you had always yawned and flipped channels when the subject of poverty-stricken children came up. You couldn't be less interested in the problems of other people's kids, especially other people's brown or black kids. But this speech will get you thinking.

You mean, neglected, rejected, throwaway kids turn into angry, alienated, gun-toting criminals, which is why I just spent $3,000 on an alarm system for my condo?

You mean, the fact that one out of three ninth-graders can't figure out change for a two-item meal is going to bring this nation to its knees and eat into my standard of living? It's one thing for inner-city kids to be unemployed and down and out; it's something else to contemplate a cut in my own paycheck.

Secondly, getting a "big bang for your buck" is definitely

the way to go in the 1990s. Thinking of kids as capital grabs the attention of the most self-absorbed yuppie or recalcitrant retiree. Whether you're a Democrat or a Republican, an indiscriminate let's-throw-some-money-at-the-problem approach won't work any longer. We all realize that given the size of our deficits, public policy making in the waning years of the twentieth century is likely to be a cutthroat competition for vanishing funds. To gain public support for any policy initiative, it is increasingly necessary to demonstrate that a program will be cost-effective, that it will constitute an efficient use of public funds.

It is important to show that neglecting kids is an extremely expensive proposition. Very few taxpayers understand that we are already picking up the tab for those drug-exposed babies; that each class of high school dropouts costs you and me $242 million; and that Head Start ($3,000 a year per child) is much less expensive than prison ($20,000 a year per inmate).[1] Compassion, it turns out, is a whole lot cheaper than callousness.

And finally, this speech touches all the right emotional chords. It sounds hokey, but it turns out to be refreshingly true. Americans like to think of themselves as a generous, idealistic, moral people, and respond well when appealed to in this fashion. Despite the excesses of the 1980s, when this nation built a great "bonfire of the vanities," most Americans treasure their families, and understand that self-indulgence and greed are not heroic values and should not form the basis of our private or public morality. With the right kind of leadership, we might be ready to rediscover a half-forgotten language of generosity and commitment and reach out together to save our children.

An Action Plan for Children

This plan is built around six principles.

- Government should tell the nation how much it values children by guaranteeing certain *universal rights or entitlements.* The problems of our youth are not limited to disadvantaged groups within the population. We need to design a comprehensive system of supports that upgrade the life chances of all American children. Free access to prenatal and maternity care and state-mandated parenting leave are excellent examples of how government can demonstrate commitment to families with children across the board.
- Government should put its money where its mouth is by *increasing the amount of public money invested in young people.* We spend very little money on our children: a mere 4.8 percent of the federal budget goes to programs that support families with young children—compared with 22.9 percent for the elderly.[2] The time has come to redress the balance between old and young, between consumption and investment, between the present and the future, and, in so doing, build a stronger America. Education and child care should be primary targets for new public spending.
- Within a framework of significant new resources for children, government should adopt a *bottom-line logic.* We should focus attention and resources on high-priority prevention programs and intervene where we get the biggest bang for our buck. In other words, government should borrow the principle of cost-effectiveness from the private sector. Head Start and WIC command particularly high rates of return and should be central components of the new Action Plan.

- While resources are important, government's commitment to children should go beyond dollars and cents to tackle the *family time famine.* In dual-income families where parents between them work a ninety-hour week, children often find the shortage of parental time to be a significant problem. Government should therefore encourage employers to design family-friendly workplaces that offer working parents the gift of time. Flextime, compressed work weeks, job sharing, and career sequencing are time-enhancing options for parents that can be cost-effective for the firm.

  (A word on the intermingling of factors. To a certain extent time is money. For many families additional resources are readily transformed into more time with the kids. For example, if government were to subsidize housing for families with children, a significant measure of choice would be restored to parents. Working Moms and Dads would be under less financial pressure and would be able to choose to spend less time on the job and more time with the kids. However, this kind of choice cannot be exercised unless employers offer part-time and flextime work options.)

- Our legal and regulatory systems should be restructured so that *the rules of the game are more protective of the interests of children.* Television programming—particularly in the late afternoon hours—and juvenile psychiatric care are areas where there should be a greater measure of regulation to safeguard children from the excesses of profit-maximizing entrepreneurs and freewheeling markets.

  Even more important are the rules that govern marriage and divorce. In these areas government policy should construct a more potent set of rewards and penalties to create incentives for parents to stay together or, in the event of marital breakdown, to ensure that children are not abandoned or impoverished.

· Finally, government should strive to *empower families* rather
than supplant them. We should remember that the state
cannot take direct responsibility for the young. Children
cannot live alone and do not thrive in institutions; there is
no substitute for the parent(s) and the home. The main task
of policy is therefore to help parents succeed so they can
help their children succeed. Government should intervene
at critical junctures—particularly in the early years—with
carefully tailored programs of support. Bill Clinton, the
governor of Arkansas, put it well when he described government "not as savior—nor certainly as spectator, but as a
catalyst and partner with families."[3] The Beethoven Project
in Chicago and the New Futures School in Albuquerque,
New Mexico, are examples of family empowerment at
work.

Certain programs are particularly central to this policy
agenda because they satisfy more than one of the six principles
listed above. For example, a program that provides free access
to prenatal and maternity care proclaims a new level of commitment to children. At the same time it makes a highly cost-
effective investment in our children.

Let me now take a more detailed look at my Action Plan
for Children. Specifically, I will describe ten key policy initiatives that are capable of improving the life chances of children
in multidimensional ways.

1. A National Task Force on Children

A first task is to *set up a National Task Force on Children* co-
chaired by the president and a prominent business leader. Its
purpose would be to galvanize the nation, to produce that
massive infusion of political energy that will help us rearrange

priorities so as to tilt private and public choices toward children. We need the political and economic leadership of this country to impress on us the urgent need to invest in the next generation. We need our president on prime-time television warning us that this shafting of children is threatening to transform the American Dream into something approaching a nightmare.

Once we have put children center stage we can move on and enact the components of my Action Plan.

2. Parenting Leave

Government should *mandate job-protected parenting leave for a period of twenty-four weeks*—thought by many experts to be the minimally adequate period of time for a parent to bond with a new child.[4] This leave would be offered to all working parents for the purpose of looking after a newborn baby, a newly adopted child, or a seriously ill child. Workers unable to obtain income replacement through company benefits policy or disability insurance would be entitled to the minimum wage for this six-month period. This pay would derive from Social Security funds to ensure that employers would not suffer financial hardship—or be tempted to discriminate against young parents. In the case of small firms (less than twenty-five employees), government would also pick up the expenses involved in carrying health insurance and other employee benefits during the period a worker is out on parenting leave.

Mandating parenting leave would help vulnerable families on the edges of the modern economy. Workers in small companies and workers in declining fields, who have little leverage in the labor market and little prospect of winning addi-

tional employee-sponsored benefits, would be the prime beneficiaries of this legislation.

Given the severe problems encountered in enacting parenting leave at the federal level (see discussion in chapter 6),
individual states should be encouraged to develop policies in
this area. Indeed, in recent years several states have moved to
provide parenting leave to their own residents. In Connecticut, for example, a 1989 bill sponsored by the state senate's
president pro tempore, John Larson, now guarantees state
employees sixteen weeks of family leave to care for an infant,
child, or other close relative.[5]

3. Prenatal and Maternity Care

Government should *guarantee free access to high-quality prenatal
and maternity care* to all American women. Medicaid should be
extended to pregnant women not covered by private insurance, and government should set up a special fund to cover the
considerable out-of-pocket expenses currently associated with
delivery and postpartum hospital care. To insure that pregnant
women actively seek out prenatal care, *cash grants should be
offered to those women who complete at least six prenatal visits to a
doctor.*

In addition, we should set up a system of postpartum *home
visiting* in the manner of other developed countries (see discussion in chapter 7). This would provide medical care for
new mothers, but would also offer concrete help with infant
care, breast feeding, immunization, and family planning.

4. Child Care

Government should *vastly improve access to quality child care* for working parents. Low- and middle-income families face enormous barriers when they attempt to find quality care for their children. "A lot of what we have today in commercial day care is kennels," says Cornell psychologist Irving Lazar.[6] Obviously, we do not want kennels for our children, but we will continue to get them unless we adopt policies that both boost parental buying power (through earned-income tax credits and vouchers) *and* improve the standard of care through regulation and subsidies to day-care providers.

As we discovered in chapter 7, this policy area has been fraught with ideological confrontation. Conservatives and liberals have found it difficult to agree on what child care should look like, and even more difficult to give this issue any real priority. During the 1980s, more than a hundred unsuccessful child-care bills blanketed Capitol Hill. Finally, in 1990, after much controversy, we made a little progress.

In March 1990 the House passed the Early Childhood Education and Development Act. This bill provided block grants to the states to expand day-care programs; vouchers to parents to pay for the child care of their choice; and earned-income tax credits for low-income working parents. It also planned to create programs in the public schools for "latchkey children"; offered tax breaks to employers who provided child care; expanded Head Start; and enforced new health and safety standards for child-care facilities. By and large this was a good bill, since it provided a significant subsidy to child care (the total package is estimated to cost $27 billion over a five-year period) while boosting standards and preserving a considerable measure of parental choice.[7]

Despite this, President Bush threatened to veto the bill. His objection was partly one of cost: the Office of Management and Budget circulated a letter calling the child-care bill "an exercise in fiscal irresponsibility."[8] Congress wanted to spend up to $5 billion in 1991, and more in later years. Bush's preferred bill—which relied heavily on tax credits—would have cost approximately $2 billion in the first year.

The sharpest clash between the administration and Congress, however, was over ideology, not cash. Citing a recent National Research Council study, congressional leaders pointed to the need for regulating child-care providers, and the House bill stressed quality-control and regulation measures. The Bush administration was strongly against all this, arguing that while it may be appropriate for the federal government to stimulate the supply of child-care services by increasing parental income, government should not get into the business of dictating standards as this would "improperly interject the state into families' affairs."[9]

In the end the budget reconciliation forced a compromise, and in October 1990 Congress and the White House agreed upon a child-care bill that comprised four elements:

- *$2.5 billion over three years to help states subsidize day care for working parents.* States will issue vouchers to parents that will pay part of the cost of child care.
- *$1.5 billion over five years to provide day care for families receiving public assistance.*
- *$15 billion over five years in tax credits for low-income working families with children.* This will allow families with children to reduce the amount they pay in federal income taxes.[10]

- *New licensing and training requirements for child-care providers.*
  Since the bill does not require states to enforce these regulations it is unclear how effective they can be.

This package is clearly better but it falls short of the House
bill. It adds up to $9 billion fewer dollars and the regulatory
component is much weaker. It is unclear how much is really
happening with this new child-care bill. Press reports in January 1991 indicated that the plan was stalled, with the Bush
administration "dragging its feet" on the funding front.[11]

In my opinion an adequate child-care bill would comprise
the 1990 Early Childhood Education and Development Act
plus the following items:

- *A method of policing* licensing and training requirements at
  the state level.
- *A restructuring of funding,* to help pay for the benefits included in the House bill. At the moment child-care subsidies go to those who need the money least. Close to half the
  $6.9 billion the government spends on child care goes to
  families earning more than $50,000 a year, via the depen-
  dent care tax credit. In contrast, low-income families can
  rarely take advantage of tax credits—only 3 percent of the
  dependent care tax credit goes to the poorest 30 percent of
  American families—and have been stung by federal budget
  cuts. Child-care block grants to the states, currently frozen
  at $2.7 billion a year, have lost half their value since 1975.
  Limiting dependent care tax credits to families earning less
  than $50,000 a year would free up $1 billion, which could
  then be spent on direct subsidies to child care.[12]
- *Parenting leave* should become a central component of child-
  care policy. The emotional and financial arguments are compelling. Out-of-home infant care can be bad for families: it

is of crucial importance for a new baby to spend a considerable portion of the first months of life with a parent. It is also bad for the bottom line: high-quality infant care is tremendously expensive—in many cities such care hovers around the $150-a-week mark,[13] a sum that equals the minimum wage! A parenting-leave policy that replaces income at the minimum-wage level would therefore be no more expensive than out-of-home care—and would enable a baby to get a much better start in life.

· Finally, we should *integrate child care into our schools.* This is not only cost-effective—it uses existing overhead—but helps children make good early connections to the educational system. One such program is the School of the 21st Century, pioneered by Yale psychologist Edward F. Zigler and already in operation in some parts of Missouri, Wyoming, and Connecticut.[14] Included in Zigler's school-based program are year-round child care for preschoolers from age three through kindergarten; after-school and vacation care from kindergarten through sixth grade; and outreach services that involve and support parents in the educational process. In Kansas City these programs are already self-supporting. Parents pay $45 a week for all-day care and $18 for programs before and after school. "We expected to turn a profit in two years," says school superintendent Robert Henley, "but we were self-supporting after one month."[15]

5. Educational Reform

Government should *significantly increase educational investment.* American education is in deep trouble, and a large part of the problem is that we are not spending enough money on our schools, particularly in the inner cities.

In Los Angeles, some 24,000 students are being bused each day, not because of a mandate to desegregate but because there is no room for them at their home schools. Most of these students are immigrants who need help with English. But they often fail to find bilingual instructors at the schools they are taken to. Bilingual teachers are expensive, and these schools are in the red.[16]

In Chicago, inner-city high schools don't have the money to offer day care, and most teenage mothers (sometimes 20 percent of the class) are forced to drop out.[17] In New York City, many public schools cannot afford to air-condition classrooms in July and August, which makes it hard for them to offer remedial and enrichment programs to disadvantaged kids during the summer vacation.[18]

Despite all this, the Bush administration believes that we are throwing plenty of money at education. At the Education Summit in September 1989, the president declared that the United States lavishes "unsurpassed resources" on our children's schooling. Therefore "our focus must no longer be on resources. It must be on results." And John Sununu, President Bush's chief of staff, tells us that "we spend twice as much [on education] as the Japanese and almost 40% more than all the other major industrial countries of the world."[19]

In fact, we don't compare favorably to our competitors. A recent study by the Economic Policy Institute shows that public and private spending on preschool, primary, and secondary education is lower in the United States than in most other countries. The United States ties for twelfth place among sixteen industrialized nations. To bring our primary and secondary schools up to the average level found in the other fifteen countries, we would need to increase spending by over $20 billion annually. It is only because the United States spends a great deal of private money on higher education that we look good in international comparisons—overall, we tie for second place among these sixteen industrialized countries.[20]

The spending gap between America and the rest of the advanced world is especially wide for small children. The United States devotes very little public money to preschool education. In the mid-1980s federal, state, and local government spent $264 billion a year on education for those age six and older, but only $1 billion on those age five and younger.[21] Thus, fewer than half our three-to-five-year-olds are in preschool.[22] Most nursery schools are private—and expensive— and Head Start enrolls only a quarter of eligible children. Many of our competitors demonstrate a much stronger commitment to early childhood education, and some of them— France, Japan, and Italy, for example—have underwritten nearly universal preschool programs.

The ways in which our educational budgets shortchange the very young is particularly distressing given an impressive body of data that show early childhood education to be tremendously cost-effective. The Perry Preschool Program is a case in point.

It was started in 1962 by David Weikart, who recruited three- and four-year-old children from low-income black families on the south side of Ypsilanti, one of the poorest areas in the state of Michigan. Participating children were randomly assigned to either the experimental program or a control group; all came from families with incomes below the poverty line and all had IQs in the 60 to 90 range. Almost half lived in single-parent homes, and fewer than 20 percent of the parents had completed high school. The program consisted of a daily two-and-a-half-hour educational session extending over two school years, with a ratio of one adult for every five or six children. Teachers also spent one and a half hours a week visiting each mother and child at home.

The results of this rather modest program have been remarkable. If you take the graduates of the Perry Preschool
Program at age nineteen and compare them to the control
group, they are twice as likely to be employed, attending
college, or receiving further training. Their high school graduation rate is one-third higher, their arrest rates 40 percent
lower, and their teen pregnancy rates 42 percent lower than
those of their peers. Their lives have changed for the better,
and the community in which they live has also reaped benefits
in terms of lower crime rates and lower welfare charges. Weikart estimates the economic returns to this program to be
seven times the cost.[23]

It was this kind of data that convinced the Committee for
Economic Development that preschool education was an "extraordinary economic buy . . . it would be hard to imagine that
society could find a higher yield for a dollar of investment than
that found in preschool programs for at-risk children."[24]

For any program of educational reform to succeed, it must
take account of the following needs:

· We need significant *new money for programs that target disadvantaged youth.* Our schools barely have the resources to
  teach reading, writing, and math. In neighborhoods scarred
  by poverty, drugs, and homelessness, schools do not begin
  to have the resources to make up for what is wrong or
  missing in their students' lives. The reforms of the 1980s
  did not change or improve the system but merely "tightened the screws," says David R. Mandel of the Carnegie
  Forum on Education and the Economy.[25] He is particularly
  concerned that the first wave of reform either ignored or
  underplayed the plight of the disadvantaged.
    If we were to restore federal spending on education to its

pre-Reagan level, with 2.5 percent rather than 2.0 percent of the budget going to education, we would have money for classrooms, libraries, air-conditioning, and bilingual teachers.

- But we also need to *tilt the balance of educational expenditure* so as to spend relatively more in the early years, where society gets a very high rate of return. Let's fund Head Start and reap the kinds of rewards demonstrated in the Perry Preschool Program. At the moment only a quarter of this country's 1.8 million poor preschool children are enrolled in Head Start; for about $1.2 billion more a year, this program could be expanded to cover all eligible children.[26]

We should also serve every child entitled to aid under Chapter One of the 1965 Education Act. Eight million children are theoretically eligible to receive the compensatory education called for under Chapter One, but due to funding shortfalls, fewer than 5 million are currently enrolled. Under Chapter One, children who are at risk of repeating a grade receive remedial teaching at a cost of $700 per child per year. Since repeating a grade costs $3,500 per child per year, this program saves tax dollars.[27]

- We should also *make it easier for poor qualified students to go to college.* During the 1980s economic barriers to college entrance were raised considerably. Private as well as public colleges increased their tuition charges, while financial aid plummeted. In 1979 Pell grants paid for 50 percent of a poor recipient's college costs; they now cover only 29 percent.[28] These monies should be restored and enhanced. As Pat Taylor discovered in Louisiana (see chapter 7), if you eliminate financial hurdles, a large proportion of disadvantaged kids will strive to make the grades necessary for college entrance.

- Finally, we should *lengthen the school day and the school year* so as to provide a more rigorous education for American youngsters. In Japan and Germany schools are in session 30 to 40 percent longer than in the States. An expanded school day and school year also eases the problems of the "latch-key" child.

Spending more money is not all we need to do if we want to revitalize education in the United States. We also need to enrich the curricula, upgrade the status of teachers, introduce accountability into the administration of schools, and increase expectations for student performance. But while it is clear that money does not guarantee excellence, adequate resources are an essential ingredient of any first-rate system. It is hard to teach a love of reading without a library; it is difficult to teach summer school in Harlem without air-conditioning; and it is almost impossible to attract superior teachers without competitive salaries.

6. Housing Policy

Government should *provide substantial housing subsidies for families with children.* Finding adequate housing is an extremely difficult problem for many American families. As we discovered in chapter 2, 600,000 to 3 million people are homeless and a further 10 million are living near the edge of homelessness, either doubled up illegally with other families or paying more than 70 percent of their income in rent.[29]

But it's no longer just the poor and the near-poor who are squeezed. In recent years all young households have had trouble affording housing. The basic problem is that the price of housing has risen much faster than wages. A recent study by Arthur Andersen & Company shows that the median price of a new home in 1978 was $58,100, or 3.2 times the median income. By 1989 the price of a house had risen to $149,900, or 4.2 times income.[30] For the first time since the Great Depression, the rate of home ownership is declining. In 1989 only 35 percent of those aged twenty-five to twenty-nine owned a home, down from 42 percent in 1976.[31]

The sharp increase in the cost of housing and the decline in the male wage rate are the main reasons so many mothers with young children have flooded into the work force. A Gallup poll shows that only 13 percent of working women with dependent children want to work full-time, although 52 percent of them currently do so.[32] Most believe they cannot fulfill their responsibilities to their children and work a forty-hour week. In many cases what keeps these mothers at work are high rents or heavy mortgage payments. Young couples today face a painful choice: either a decent place to live or time with the kids.

Karen wants to know how she and her husband are supposed to buy a house. She is a twenty-six-year-old housewife living in the Chicago area with her husband and two children. According to Karen, "You can't buy a house any more on a single income. . . . It seems that young couples starting a family are just in a hole. There is no way out. You either buy a home, both of you work and your kids suffer, or one of you works and you live in a rental. Paying rent for an apartment feels like digging a hole and crawling right in."[33]

David Glaser bought a modest house in Teaneck, New Jersey, in 1987. He now has second thoughts about that decision: "If I didn't have such high mortgage payments my wife might be able to stay home when we start a family," he says. "We love this house, but our regret is whether it might affect how we bring up a child."[34]

A government program that subsidized housing for middle-

and low-income families would have tremendous potential for improving the circumstances of children. It would banish the specter of homelessness that today haunts millions of low-income families. It would also remove the most pressing financial constraint on middle-class lives. Joseph J. Minarik, executive director of the congressional joint economic committee, estimates that the typical thirty-year-old man buying a median-priced home in 1973 incurred carrying costs equal to 21 percent of his income. By 1987 this had risen to 40 percent.[35] If housing once again were to consume 21 percent rather than 40 percent of a thirty-year-old's wage, many more parents would be able to choose to spend more time with the kids and less time at work. You wouldn't need to be a high-earning professional to make the kind of choice Kathy made at American Express when she decided to share a job (see chapter 7).

Any new housing policy initiative helpful to parents would need to include the following elements:

- Some type of meaningful *mortgage subsidy* to make home ownership a realistic ambition for many more young families. This subsidy should be related to income (mortgage rates would rise along with family income, and the subsidy would disappear when income reached $50,000 a year), and the program could be partially paid for by limiting the tax deductibility of mortgage payments to those earning more than $50,000 a year. In 1988 tax deductions for home mortgages totaled $53.9 billion (up from $11.2 billion in 1976), and two-thirds of these tax benefits went to people in the $50,000+ income bracket.[36] These benefits could be recast as mortgage subsidies to families in lower-income brackets.
- We also need many more *rent vouchers* for low-income fami-

lies. HUD is already moving away from construction subsidies toward rent vouchers, which pay the difference between 30 percent of household income and the prevailing market rent. This policy shift makes a lot of sense. Vouchers can boost the purchasing power of poor families while stimulating the production of moderate-priced rental accommodation. Vouchers have the added advantage of giving mobility and choice to low-income American families. Instead of confining the poor to blighted ghettos, they allow recipients to decide where they want to live. In Chicago, James Rosenbaum, a sociologist at Northwestern University, tracked 114 black inner-city welfare mothers who used vouchers to relocate in mostly white suburbs where they could send their children to good schools.[37]

The only problem with rent vouchers is that there are not nearly enough of them. In 1990, only 82,000 additional families were offered assistance—a drop in the bucket of the 11 million low-income families that urgently needed help in finding affordable housing. The government should vastly expand this program. At an average yearly cost of $3,500 per household, vouchers are much less expensive than paying to warehouse homeless families in shelters.[38] In many American cities, homeless families are housed in squalid "welfare hotels" such as the Prince George—home to Fatima and her family (see Prologue). These hotels provide no permanent solution to homelessness and are very expensive, costing more than $2,000 a month per family.[39]

One further point. The first half of this housing program will help the second half, in that once more middle-class families are able to buy homes, the rental market will be freed up for low-income groups. The supply of rental housing will expand, and rents will go down.

The last time housing was a major national issue was when

the G.I.s came home from World War II, and "public officials broke their backs getting them into housing."[40] Under the loan provisions of the 1944 G.I. Bill, the Veterans Administration guaranteed 6 million home loans to returning servicemen. These mortgages required no down payment and carried a maximum interest rate of 4 percent a year.[41] Designed to furnish homes for veterans for as little as $25 a month, these low-cost mortgages triggered the great postwar boom in home building that provided good, affordable housing for American families until the 1970s. According to one contemporary analyst, G.I. home loans had "more impact on the American way of life than any law since the passage of the Homestead Act in 1862."[42]

My program of mortgage subsidies and rent vouchers would underwrite family homes in a fashion similar to the G.I. Bill. It is desperately needed. The housing crunch of 1991 is actually worse than the one following World War II. In 1946, 5 million families were on the brink of homelessness; today over 10 million are.

7. Tax Reform

Government can do *much more with tax policy* to support families with children. Despite the acclaimed Reagan tax cuts which reduced income tax rates, taxes were not actually cut in the 1980s; the burden was merely shifted from income taxes to payroll taxes (chiefly Social Security taxes) which rose 23 percent during this decade. As a result the burden of taxation now falls much more heavily on low- and middle-income working households (most young families with children) and much less heavily on wealthy households (mostly older and child-free). This is because Social Security payroll taxes are highly regressive; an identical rate of 7.6 percent is levied on all workers, and income above $51,300 is exempt.[43]

A pro-family tax package would need to include the following elements:

- We should *reduce the cost of Social Security* by taxing the now-exempt half of the benefit and raising the retirement age. If these measures were coupled with lowering the initial benefits to the well-off elderly, we would save up to $50 billion a year.[44]
- We should *make military and civil service pensions self-supporting* and save another $50 billion a year.
- We should *redistribute the tax burden* so that relatively more is paid in the form of income tax and relatively less is paid in the form of payroll taxes. Such an exercise would shift the burden of taxation away from young families.
- We should *limit the dependent care tax credit*. Not only has this tax credit become an expensive subsidy to relatively affluent parents, but, because it links benefits to the amount spent on child care, it redistributes income away from families who make little or no use of paid child care toward those who make extensive use of such services. Thus, it both penalizes families in which one parent stays home full-time to care for children, and shortchanges parents who seek to minimize their use of substitute care by working part-time, working at home, or staggering their work shifts.
- Finally, we should *create a $2,000-per-child family allowance,* which would be subject to taxation and therefore more valuable at the lower end of the income scale.

Similar to the child allowance proposed by Ed Zigler, this would expand the Social Security system to provide an annual stipend for the families of all children under three.[45] The stipend could be used to help defray the cost of child care, but it could also be used as replacement income for parents who choose to care for their infants and toddlers at home. Unlike President Bush's refundable tax credit (which targets the poor and is capped at $1,000 per child), this family allowance trust fund would be a cash benefit available to all families who have contributed to the Social Security system. At $2,000 per child it would be generous enough to supplement the income of parents significantly.

8. Workplace Policy

As I discussed in chapter 7, corporate America is developing elaborate family support policies, which will soon reach a significant proportion of all working parents in America. The role of government in this area is to *shape and complement private sector efforts.*

- Government should encourage corporations to address the *family time famine.* This is a critical task because of the divergence of interest between what is good for employers and what is good for children—both want more of a parent's time! Government should therefore weigh in and persuade firms to provide "time" as well as "resources" in their family-friendly benefits packages. Companies as different as IBM and the NCNB Corporation have shown that it is possible to create a more fluid, less rigid workplace that gives workers with family responsibilities significant discretion over how they structure their careers, how many hours they work each week, and when and where work is performed. Government can encourage these family-friendly policies by granting tax breaks to companies that offer flexible hours, compressed work weeks, part-time work with

benefits, job sharing, career sequencing, extended parenting leave, and home-based employment opportunities.

In some states companies that offer on-site child care already qualify for tax concessions. Why not extend this concept? If carefully tailored tax incentives prompted companies
to extend flextime to a majority of employees, many more
parents would be able to work 7:00 A.M. to 3:00 P.M. and be
home in time to catch up with the kids in those important
after-school hours.

Time-enhancing workplace policies have impressive win-
win properties. Take the issue of *career sequencing*. The ability
to take extended parenting leave without losing one's job; the
ability to share a job for two or ten years; the ability to construct a challenging and remunerative part-time career—these
are tremendously attractive options for professional parents
who are often faced with the choice of working a fifty-hour
week or getting off a career ladder designed for men with
at-home wives. In the contemporary economy, conventional
career structures can be unfair and inefficient. Not only do
rigid career trajectories discriminate heavily against women
(who tend to take time out to have children) but they are
wasteful of human capital. With mothers comprising more
than half of all labor market entrants over the next decade, it
is in the self-interest of companies to use their woman-power
well, to make sure that some of their best educated and most
valuable workers are not cast aside or thrown away because of
a career interruption. In other words, given the demographic
pressures of the 1990s, government should find it relatively
easy to prod corporations into being responsive to the needs
of working parents and their children, rather than attempt to
make parents and children fit into the rigid structures of established business practice.

9. Divorce Reform

Government should *seek to bring down the rate of divorce* by constructing a set of rewards and penalties that encourage parents to stay together. In the event of marital breakdown, the role of government is to create a legal framework that ensures children are not abandoned or impoverished in the wake of divorce. Prompted by the federal Child Support Enforcement Amendment of 1984, many states have tightened their collection procedures and some have attempted to increase the value of child-support awards. Indeed, since the Family Support Act of 1988, courts have been required to use state guidelines in setting child-support levels. Innovative policy initiatives in Wisconsin have served as a model nationwide.

In the 1983–1987 period Wisconsin drew up guidelines for child-support awards using a flat percentage-of-income standard.[46] The new standards are generous—17 percent of the noncustodial parent's income for one child, rising to 34 percent for five or more children—and they have dramatically increased the monetary value of child support. At the same time, Wisconsin instituted a system of routinely withholding child-support payments from the paychecks of noncustodial parents, which has brought delinquency rates down. The net result: custodial parents are granted much larger child-support awards, and these awards are much more likely to be paid.

A powerful aspect of the Wisconsin initiative is that it treats never-married fathers (where it is possible to establish paternity) just like divorced fathers, using identical guidelines and collection procedures. Irwin Garfinkel estimates that as many as 90 percent of never-married fathers will eventually be forced to contribute child support.[47]

If the Wisconsin model were adopted throughout the United States, it would greatly improve the financial security of custodial parents (generally mothers) and their children. Such a move would also increase the economic penalties attached to divorce and make divorce more expensive, and, at the margin, discourage husbands (or wives) from leaving a marriage.

But is the Wisconsin model enough? Easing financial hardship and increasing economic penalties are worthy goals, but since these reforms are not expected to bring divorce rates down appreciably, they will not heal the psychic wounds of divorce. No matter how prosperous the context, abandoned children still yearn for their fathers and underperform in school.

One thing we have learned in this book is that if you care about the welfare of children, you cannot be agnostic on the issue of divorce. When marriages break down children often become separated from their fathers—in almost half of all cases there is no contact at all in the wake of divorce—and this can be extremely harmful to children. As I demonstrated in chapter 3, the research evidence is overwhelming: children derive a great deal of intellectual stimulation and emotional sustenance from day-to-day contact with Dad. It seems that fathers are not readily expendable.

Deciding that a father's presence as well as his paycheck is important to the well-being of children complicates policy making. We can no longer "fix" the divorce problem with bigger and more reliable child-support payments but must attempt to bring divorce rates down, and, in the event of marital breakdown, create a legal framework that maximizes contact between the noncustodial parent and the child.

In 1991 it's extremely hard to get back into the business of enforcing the value of marriage as a long-term commitment.

It seems old-fashioned, even quaint, to reintroduce morality, but we must *for the sake of the children.* The thing is, government cannot be neutral. Like it or not, the state has enormous moral suasion. In moving toward no-fault divorce, we thought that we were relinquishing the responsibility of arbitrating private morality. In fact, our new policies, by giving a green light to much easier methods of ending marriage, produced a major shift in private values. As we found out in chapter 4, no-fault divorce tells a very powerful story: that no one is to blame when a marriage breaks up, and no one need take responsibility for the consequences. As Cherlin shows in his research, the new legislation changed public attitudes toward divorce, and, in the end, both weakened the institution of marriage and undermined the life prospects of children.[48] We need to undo this damage and once more bend the vast moral authority of the state to the task of strengthening families and protecting children.

Thus, any new initiative in the area of divorce should encompass both economic and ethical dimensions. I recommend some version of the Wisconsin model plus the following items:

- When a noncustodial parent evades the withholding system and fails to pay child support (and this will continue to happen in a minority of cases), *the state, rather than the custodial parent, should absorb the risk.* In practical terms this means that if a father is delinquent, a government agency rather than the mother tries to collect, in the meantime advancing the amount of child support owed, up to a limit set by law.
- *The economic obligations of the noncustodial parent should not stop when a child turns eighteen* but continue until the child has completed his or her education.
- Couples with dependent children should be *encouraged to stay married* and to live together as a family. The process of

divorce has become too easy and too automatic. Couples experiencing difficulties very quickly find themselves in a one-way street leading to divorce. In the spirit of a 1990 British Law Commission report that advocated "throwing sand in the machinery of divorce,"[49] parents seeking divorce should face an eighteen-month waiting period, during which time they would be obliged to seek marriage counseling. In addition, they should be legally obliged to safeguard their children's future before winning a final divorce decree. Without getting involved in allocating blame in the manner of the extremely flawed pre-1970 system, government can encourage parents to think long and hard before breaking up a family. Such a policy has a moral dimension since it sends a clear signal that this society values marriage and believes that families with children are worth preserving.

· Finally, we should institute *guidelines for visitation,* backed up by an appropriate set of sanctions. If a noncustodial parent (normally the father) has not seen his child in, say, three months, that parent should be fined or otherwise put on notice that such conduct is unacceptable. Even if it were impossible to enforce this kind of provision fully, its very existence would communicate the message that society acknowledges the importance of fathering, and is prepared to go to considerable lengths to encourage contact between fathers and children.

10. Volunteer Efforts

Last but not least, we need to *complement government policy with a new level of personal commitment* to this nation's family of children. As our phantom president correctly points out, "bureaucracies cannot soothe the shuddering body of a crack baby or act as mentor to a throwaway child."

For example, *senior citizens should be encouraged to reach out and help children,* particularly underprivileged children. Reading stories to a learning-disabled toddler, being a grandfatherly presence in the life of a boy who has never known a father, taking an inner-city child on a Sunday outing to a beach or a state park, are opportunities and connections that can be enormously helpful to a needy child. In modern America many older persons can expect to have twenty years of health and prosperity *after* retirement. Is it too much to ask that some of this huge reservoir of time be devoted to neglected, rejected youngsters?[50] Tapping the energy and compassion of seniors might go some distance toward filling the enormous parenting deficit in our society.

But *volunteer efforts should not be limited to the elderly.* If we rearrange personal priorities in the way suggested in my Action Plan, all of us will have more and better energy for children. Parents and nonparents, yuppies and suburbanites, young women and middle-aged men can all participate in this campaign to save our children. In the summer of 1990, when 490 volunteers from Teach for America fanned out into classrooms across the country, they put themselves on the cutting edge of this effort. Founded just two years ago by Wendy Kopp, a twenty-three-year-old Princeton University graduate, Teach for America is a program that infuses some of America's poorest school districts with bright, dedicated college graduates who have signed on to spend at least two years teaching in understaffed, overburdened schools.[51] Kopp's program may be a drop in an ocean of need, but it shows that leadership and energy can summon forth altruism and commitment even in a generation of college students who have extremely materialistic ambitions. Small-scale personal efforts can be surprisingly powerful, a fact that I newly appreciate.

In the spring of 1987, I helped start a Children's Task Force at All Souls Unitarian Church in Manhattan. The idea was to involve this rather privileged congregation in the bleak lives of needy children in a city where 40 percent of all youngsters grow up in poverty. The program has developed a remarkable following. Over the last four years, hundreds of volunteers have cuddled boarder babies, tutored homeless children, formed scout troops, and organized a children's theater. But church activity on behalf of children has not stopped at hands-on help. Volunteering has triggered a type of consciousness raising that in its turn has led to political action. Congregants have staged demonstrations in front of City Hall demanding more funds for children's programs, and in January 1991 All Souls Church helped launch an Inter-Faith Partnership for Children, which brings together the entire religious community of New York City in a concerted effort to ease the lives of children.[52] As part of this initiative, churches and synagogues will pledge a proportion of their budgets to programs that help needy children.

I can take no credit for the cumulative and ongoing effort at All Souls Church. After the initial planning stage, others took up the leadership roles in the Children's Task Force and I became a foot soldier in the volunteer force, concentrating my efforts on forging links with individual children—like Fatima.

Despite my new appreciation of volunteerism—particularly when it politicizes the comfortable classes—I would like to stress that private efforts cannot begin to replace a massive new public commitment to America's children. Even a thousand points of light "spread like stars in a broad and peaceful sky" will not be enough; the afflictions of our children are just too great. In 1991 these enormous problems need the deep pockets and vast moral authority of the state. Individual efforts can help at the edges, however, and even, in the spirit of the Inter-Faith Partnership, go some way toward creating new political momentum.

So there we have it. A highly cost-effective Action Plan for children that conforms to American values and vastly improves the life circumstances of children.

Can we afford such a plan?

The simple answer is, *Of course we can.* As should be quite obvious from the analysis in this book, looking after our children is a bargain when compared to the current costs of neglect.

But the policy-making process is more complicated than this. Despite the "no-new-taxes" promise of our phantom president, it is clear that in the short run some of the programs contained in the Action Plan will involve up-front money. For example, there is no way to upgrade the quality of child care significantly without enlarging budgets. Some of this money can be recovered by phasing out the dependent care tax credit, and all of it will be recouped in the long run—children will ultimately be more productive—but there will be some requirement for new expenditures. Where will this money come from? Given all the red ink sloshing around Washington, will we be able to underwrite even a modest amount of new investment in children?

The 1990 debate over the peace dividend throws a particularly harsh light on this question of which programs we choose to afford and which we choose to throw to the winds. In the winter of 1989–90 there was a massive downward shift in the tensions between the superpowers. Within the space of a few short months freedom and democracy broke out all over "the Evil Empire." Russian soldiers were thrown out of Eastern

Europe, the Warsaw Pact collapsed, and the cold war became a relic of the past. For the first seven months of 1990 (up until August 2, when Iraq invaded Kuwait) almost no one thought the United States needed to spend $300 billion a year on its military any longer; we simply didn't have a very convincing enemy.

Estimates of the size of the peace dividend varied. President Bush was on the cautious side of the debate, saying that by 1995 savings would be in the region of $40 billion a year. Others were more aggressive. For example, former Secretary of Defense Robert S. McNamara believed that the military budget could safely be cut in half by the turn of the century. In his view, savings could amount to $75 billion a year by mid-decade, and $150 billion a year by the year 2000.[53]

If the peace dividend was seen as "a fabulous fortune," the line of people with claims on these monies stretched "around

the block.''[54] There were basically three alternative uses for this windfall: we could cut taxes; we could use the revenue to reduce the budget deficit; or we could spend the money on new domestic programs (like child care or mortgage subsidies). Many conservatives favored a tax cut. Senator Phil Gramm (R-Tex.) argued that "the American people paid for the superiority of our system to emerge" and should now be rewarded in kind. "I don't think the benefits from winning the cold war should go to the Government," he declared.[55] In January 1990 the Heritage Foundation, a conservative research institute, published a paper listing eleven different ways to cut taxes.

Economists, for the most part, preferred using the money to lower the federal budget deficit. Such a policy, said Charles Schultze, director of the economic studies program at the Brookings Institution, would lead to lower interest rates, more national savings, greater investment, and a higher standard of living for all Americans.

There is little doubt where the American public stood. A poll in January 1990 found that 62 percent of Americans would spend the money "to fight problems such as drugs and homelessness"; only 21 percent would use the peace dividend to reduce the deficit; and a mere 10 percent would cut taxes.[56]

The American people seem to have a better handle on national priorities than either the political establishment or the academic elite. Without having a very clear idea about how to tackle drugs or homelessness, ordinary men and women are acutely aware of how rapidly the social fabric of this nation is unraveling, and would much prefer to do something about the misery and violence in our streets than cut their own taxes.

Which brings me to my main point. The presence of a windfall such as the peace dividend will not on its own provoke political action. (Indeed, the peace dividend itself seems to have been a transient phenomenon. In 1991 it was already fast disappearing, a casualty of the war in the Persian Gulf.) We have not failed our children because there has been a shortage of cash. America is an immensely rich country; our federal government spends $1.3 trillion a year on programs of one sort or another. If we give an issue or a program priority, we can always find the money for it, despite seemingly severe budget constraints. A Stealth bomber is a pricey item—$530 million per plane[57]—and yet we continued to build Stealth bombers during the 1980s, a decade when we slashed programs for children in an attempt to reduce the deficit. In a similar vein, we have no problem finding public money to pay for capital punishment ($1.7 million a case), to bail out the savings banks, or to provide income supplements for prosperous senior citizens.

If we wanted to we could easily find additional money for children—we could raise taxes, scrap a weapons program, or trim Social Security benefits (Pete Peterson has shown that we can save $50 billion a year on entitlements to the elderly *without* cutting into the incomes of the elderly poor).[58] The reason we have failed our children is not because we cannot afford to look after them, but because they have been at the bottom of our list of priorities.

In a recent speech, Governor Mario Cuomo of New York staged an imaginary conversation with President Bush.

In the campaign, Mr. President, you said there was no money for housing or child care or educational programs. . . .

Now suddenly you've come up with $166 billion for the S & Ls. . . . You said you didn't have it. Where did you get it? Is it there for banks but not for babies?

$166 billion to protect investors but not $20 billion to educate kids and teach them the fundamental values that could save a generation?

It's there, Mr. President . . . if you want to do it.[59]

It seems that in the end, whether or not we save our children has very little to do with debt and deficits. It all comes down to political will and private volition.

9

Saving Our Children, Saving Ourselves

We now understand the depth and scope of child neglect in America. We can spell out the enormous disadvantages attendant upon being born to an impoverished single mother. Dr. Samuel Proctor, former pastor of the Abyssinian Baptist Church in New York City, says it's like "being born without a skin."[1] And we can grasp the equally real agonies of a middle-class child derailed and betrayed by marital disruption, parked in front of "Geraldo" or dumped in psychiatric care, cut adrift or thrown away by overburdened parents intent on other agendas. These youngsters do not play by the rules generated by people for whom society works. It's hard to defer gratification, sexual or otherwise, for a good future everything they know tells them will never come.

Furthermore, we now know how to ameliorate these enormous problems. The techniques and the strategies exist. We know how to step in and strengthen families and reverse the momentum of cumulative causation so that it spirals up instead of down, strengthening rather than weakening fragile families, transforming the destinies of vulnerable children. This book offers hard evidence: systematic intervention and support early in the life cycle can dramatically improve the life prospects of children growing up at risk.

The great unanswered question is, *Will we do it?* Can we conjure up the resolve to move on this front?

The barriers are formidable. We need to turn around a political culture that has become deeply antagonistic to helping families with children. And we need to break into a self-absorbed culture that has consistently screened out any notion of collective accountability. Are we capable of turning away from the "Now-now-ism" of the 1980s and taking responsibility for our children's future?

Abraham Lincoln once said: "Few can be induced to labor exclusively for posterity and none will do it enthusiastically. Posterity has done nothing for us, and . . . we shall do very little for it unless we are made to think we are, at the same time, doing something for ourselves."[2] In the 1990s, two powerful forms of self-interest will conspire to force this issue:

- What we have done to our children has let loose a surging tide of violence that is destroying the fabric of our society and threatening the life and limb of you and me.
- What we have done to our children has produced a heavy burden of educational failure that is undermining our competitive strength and eating into paychecks in households across the nation.

The human and economic costs of child neglect have become so overwhelming that, enthusiastic or not, we shall be driven to pay our dues to posterity. As our phantom president pointed out in chapter 8, there are painful, intimate connections between child neglect and our own life circumstances. A white skin and middle-class status no longer protect us from what we have wrought in our children. The chickens are coming home to roost in our very own backyards.

Tearing the Social Fabric

Take the issue of personal safety, which American adults consider the single most important factor in determining the quality of their lives—more important than job satisfaction, financial security, marriage, or health. Americans murder, assault, rape, and rob one another at a truly astounding rate. In 1989, 1,905 people were slain in New York City—a rise of 30 percent since 1979 and 600 percent since 1959. And the Big Apple is only the thirteenth most violent city in the nation! Dallas, Seattle, San Antonio, Boston, and Detroit are all much more dangerous places to live. Washington, D.C., ironically, is the murder capital of the United States, with a homicide rate twice as high as New York's; and Cleveland wins first prize for sexual assault, the incidence of rape in this city being four times as high as that in New York.[3]

We've become inured to these bleak statistics, and are not sufficiently aware of how very much more violent America has become in recent years—and of how badly we stack up against other rich industrial countries. The risk of being robbed is 208 times greater in the United States than in Japan, and the homicide rate among young adults in the United States is 36 times higher than in Great Britain. More people are murdered in Los Angeles in an average month than in Great Britain during the course of a year.[4]

For most of us, these dreadful facts and figures boil down

to an ever-present fear and anxiety that distorts and constrains the way we think and live. Ronald White of the *Washington Post* describes the consequences of not being able to trust anyone on the streets at night: "Every time I realize that I have not enjoyed the cool night air nor marveled at a full moon, I know that one does not have to be robbed at gunpoint to be a victim of a crime."[5]

Occasionally some particularly brutal crime forces us to face the dangers squarely. "NONE OF US IS SAFE" screamed the front-page headlines of the *New York Post* on April 24, 1989. A young investment banker jogging in Central Park had just been savagely raped and beaten by a gang of marauding toughs. The newspapers called it *wilding*.

The whole city was up in arms. Mayor Koch demanded the death penalty; Cardinal O'Connor prayed; Donald Trump threatened vengeance; and a visibly shaken Governor Cuomo pondered the significance of the attack: "Are we a society out of control? To me, a person who's lived in this city all of his life, this is the ultimate shriek of alarm."

Who were these toughs who so outraged the sensibilities of New Yorkers?

They were children.

All eight males charged with the crime were under eighteen—two of them were fourteen, four were fifteen.

In videotaped and written statements to the police, these teenagers described how they had hunted the woman jogger, chased her down a path, beaten her with a lead pipe, smashed her with bricks and rocks, stripped her naked, and then held her down while at least four of them raped her. All eight confessed to being involved in the crime, although each blamed the others for the more heinous acts.

Raymond Santana, fourteen, said he "felt her breasts while the others raped her." Kharey Wise, sixteen, claimed he "only played with the lady's legs." Yusef Salaam, fifteen, admitted whipping the woman with a lead pipe about the head, then "grabbing her breasts while the others raped her." Steve Lopez, fifteen, acknowledged that he had participated in the wilding, but said he left before the rape. But his friend Santana told police that Lopez had beaten her, ripped her clothes off, gagged her, and then raped her.

These teenagers showed little remorse, laughing and joking while in police custody. "She wasn't nothing," said one; "I did it because it was fun," said another. Only Clarence Thomas, fourteen, showed any regret: "It got to me when her blood started to squirt, I freaked out."

All these kids are black and grew up in the bleak wasteland of East Harlem. Although four lived in a building with a doorman, their lives "bore daily witness to an abounding pathology" of drugs, drink, absentee Dads, teenage childbearing, and poverty. In this environment, life is cheap and violent crime commonplace. The attack on April 24 became newsworthy only because the violence spilled out of the ghetto. The victim was an elite white woman who lived in the East eighties and worked on Wall Street. She was someone the news media could identify with.[6]

But the experts were not surprised by the gang rape in Central Park. "Wilding may be a new term, but it's hardly a new activity," said Peter Reinharz, chief prosecutor in New York's Family Court. There were 761 wolf-pack attacks in New York City in 1988, three-quarters of them committed by children age eleven through eighteen. Disturbing as these figures are, they are a drop in the bucket of the 1,905 homicides, 93,377 robberies, and 3,254 rapes reported that year in this city of just over 7 million people.[7]

All of this exacts a huge toll. We cower behind triple-locked doors and spend $5 billion a year on home security systems;

we take karate lessons and carry handguns in our purses; and we incarcerate a million people in our jails. Yet we still live in fear and trembling. If we are lucky, the violence that pervades our lives will not kill or maim us, but it is guaranteed to produce an oppressive level of anxiety, distrust, and suspicion. This emotional burden dulls our spirits and wounds our souls. It poisons our lives as effectively as PCB or acid rain.

It is that time of year for the community gardeners in Greenwich Village: time to plant, mulch, prune and adjust the chains around the shrubs. Growing things sometimes need a little extra slack. But not too much.

"The Cytisus still seems to have enough room," says Mary Emma Harris, eyeing the steel links entwined in the stems of a Scotch broom shrub. Next to it is the spot from which an identical shrub, naively left unchained because it was five feet high and four feet wide, was stolen last August.

There's a new wave of larceny in New York City and its object is living plants.[8]

Casual theft has always been a problem for city gardeners—Mother's Day and Easter are particularly risky times of year—but in the last few years plant theft has become systematic and widespread. Pansies in windowboxes, rhododendron trees in wooden tubs, tomato seedlings in community gardens—all are disappearing.

On the Upper East Side, gardeners are planting root balls under wire lattices and cabling six-foot trees to underground cinder blocks and devices called duckbill anchors. On the Lower East Side, the azaleas are wearing barbed wire this spring. Some stolen plants have later been spotted for sale on the streets. Gardeners hold youthful crack addicts responsible for the thefts.

* * *

The problems of our cities run the gamut from the horrific to the slightly ridiculous—from gang rape to floral bondage. One thing is for sure. Wolf-pack attacks in city parks and rhododendron trees in chains serve to rub our noses in the fact that something quite terrible is happening to the social fabric of this nation—and this dreadful unraveling has a lot to do with the aching anger of neglected kids. To use Senator Moynihan's words, "it would appear that the process of making human beings human is breaking down in American Society."[9]

"The Extravagance of Vengeance"

Angry, alienated youths not only detract from the quality of all of our lives; they also constitute a heavy drain on the public purse. Irving Harris estimates the cost of one wasted life at $300,000.[10]

By far the largest element in his calculation is the expense of the criminal justice system. During the 1980s the number of persons in federal and state prisons doubled. There are now 1 million people behind bars and another 2.6 million on probation or parole. This is a very expensive business. The cost of building a new prison is $60,000 per inmate, and it costs $15,000 a year to keep each prisoner in jail. Nationwide, prison costs total $20 billion a year, much more than we spend on Aid to Families with Dependent Children.[11]

As the crime rate surges, so do prison expenditures. California is planning to spend $2 billion on additional cell space in ten new facilities, Texas $500 million, and New York State $700 million.[12] Given tight budgets at the state and local levels, the billions spent on incarcerating criminals means that much less is available for hiring teachers or repairing bridges. According to one study, "for every person who goes to prison, two people don't go to college."[13] San Francisco allocated $8 million for a new jail in 1989, the same year it reduced its education budget by $10 million—an almost dollar-for-dollar trade-off.[14] City officials openly acknowledge that juvenile crime is very likely to increase as extracurricular activities and sports programs are cut from the education budget.

The *Washington Post* calls it "the extravagance of vengeance."[15] And it's true: when it comes to punishing criminals we have no problem waiving budget constraints and spending all kinds of money we don't have. Take the issue of capital punishment. Fifteen years ago, when the Supreme Court ruled on the death penalty, Thurgood Marshall noted that "when all is said and done, there can be no doubt that it costs more to execute a man than to keep him in prison for life." It now costs between $1.8 and $7 million to prosecute each capital case, in comparison with the $602,000 it costs to imprison someone for forty years.[16] The reason for this very high price tag is that in our legal system capital cases are treated differently from noncapital cases. Very often more than one attorney is appointed for the defendant, judges search painstakingly for reversible error, and there is a lengthy and elaborate appeal process. With almost 2,000 individuals currently on death row, the resurrection of capital punishment is costing a tidy penny.

Although we seem willing to go to extraordinarily expensive lengths to punish criminals, we are reluctant to spend money on programs that have proven effective at preventing youngsters from slipping into a life of crime in the first place. In the 1980s we more than doubled the amount of money we spent on prisons while slashing programs that underpin poor children—housing subsidies, Pell grants, and measles vaccinations were all cut back. This kind of shortsighted economy will undoubtedly feed our surging crime rate into the future. It's no coincidence that more than 80 percent of inmates in state prisons are high school dropouts, and most can't read and write well enough to fill out an application form, much less hold down a paying job. "Crime is easy when you have nothing to lose."[17]

Government needs to understand that it's cheaper to create the conditions that allow youngsters to flourish than to deal in the miserable currency of vengeance and damage control.

Undermining America's Economic Strength

Aside from costing us tens of billions of dollars every year, neglected, alienated youngsters also depress the productive capability of our nation. Deprived children grow into problem-ridden youngsters who are extremely difficult to absorb successfully into the work force. Yet with the looming labor shortages of the 1990s we will need to employ these youngsters. Over the next decade, labor markets will be tighter and there will be a smaller reservoir of qualified workers than at any point since World War II. We can no longer tolerate a high school dropout rate of 27 percent. We can't afford to throw away more than a quarter of each generation.

The stakes are enormously high. I am not talking about whether domestic industry will grow at 1 percent versus 3 percent a year, but about whether a shortfall in skills and in labor productivity will trigger a decline in American preeminence in the world. To quote a 1989 report by a blue-ribbon panel of business and labor leaders, "America's ability to shape the course of the 21st century will depend largely on the productivity of the American workforce."[18] Human capital seems to have replaced military might as the principal source of global dominance. Yale historian Paul Kennedy calls it America's "unattended frontier." In a 1989 analysis of the causes of economic decline, Kennedy was much more worried about the "long term education and social health of the people" than about military overreach or any type of external threat.[19] In his view, a deficit on the human resource front may well prove to be America's Achilles' heel.

For much of the postwar period, the U.S. economy led the world. During the 1950s and 1960s, America was No. 1, producing an extraordinary 40 percent of the world's wealth. During these years it had the world's best-educated and best-trained labor force, the most modern plants and equipment, the newest technology, and superior management. It also had a clear head start over the war-ravaged economies of Europe and Asia. The net result: American citizens enjoyed the world's highest living standard—twice that of Europe's leading contenders.

After 1970, the United States became increasingly integrated into the world economy, obliged to compete head-on with nations such as Japan and Germany, who were investing heavily in physical and human capital. By the 1980s, America's share of the world's wealth had fallen to 23 percent. It had become a leading member of a community of advanced industrial nations, rather than a giant looming over all.

Harvard political economist Robert Reich has pointed out that as economies become international, a nation's most important competitive asset becomes the skills and cumulative learning of its work force. The very process of globalization makes this true, since every factor of production other than work-force skills can now be duplicated anywhere around the world. In Reich's words: "Capital now sloshes freely across international boundaries, so much so that the cost of capital in different countries is rapidly converging. State-of-the-art factories can be erected anywhere. The latest technologies flow from computers in one nation, up to satellites parked in space, then back down to computers in another nation—all at the speed of electronic impulses. It is all fungible: capital, technology, raw materials, information—all, except for one thing, the most critical part, the one element that is unique about a nation: its work force."[20]

In fact, because all the other factors of production can move so easily around the world, a work force that is knowledgeable and skilled at doing complex things is capable of setting up a virtuous spiral of cumulative causation that results in ever-increasing prosperity. High-caliber workers attract global corporations, which invest and add to the number of well-paid jobs; an expanding pool of high-productivity workers, in turn, attracts additional investment. New companies are drawn in, and the economy shifts into a higher gear.

Reich makes a compelling case for a much higher level of investment in human capital, but he does not take his analysis far enough. He forgets that our ability to educate and train young people is critically dependent upon strong, functioning families. We clearly should invest more in our educational system. Schools can and should do more to prepare youngsters for productive employment, but they will continue to fall short of the mark unless we support parents and give them the time and the resources to do a better job by their children. As I have amply demonstrated in the pages of this book, our educational system cannot compensate for the tasks that overburdened parents no longer perform. Middle-class children whose parents jointly work a ninety-hour week and disadvantaged children on the brink of homelessness have the cards stacked against them. In the words of a recent Labor Department study, "the school is clearly second to the family in its importance as source of the education that forms the foundation for a lifetime of career options."[21] Some of the most important labor market skills—punctuality, reliability, self-control—are best learned at home, before a child enters the educational system. In other words, unless we make up deficiencies on the home front, all kinds of educational dollars can be thrown down the drain at ages six, nine, or twelve as we fail to motivate youngsters undermined by a myriad of family problems.

The Japanese Model

Analysts rarely appreciate the degree to which the economic miracle of postwar Japan has hinged on the family. In an immediate sense, Japan's highly educated work force has been a key driving force behind this country's rapid growth. We are all familiar with the comparative figures that put the American educational system to shame. Japanese students in science and math seem to outperform American children at every grade level and at every stratum of ability and background. However, much of this school success rests on an exceptionally strong family structure, and on the degree to which Japanese family life is centered on and geared to the needs of children. Only one in five marriages in Japan ends in divorce, and an extremely small percentage of families with children fall below the official poverty line. Japanese parents devote an impressive 20 percent of disposable income to education and are heavily involved in the educational process. Not only do most mothers stay out of the labor force to devote more and better time to their families, many of them cater to the educational needs of their children in ways which are startling to an American observer.

Yuki Sasaki, a forty-five-year-old Kagoshima housewife, is a typical "education mama" who pushes, pressures, and cajoles her son in order to get him into a good college. "I help my son prepare for his exams by arranging my schedule around his schedule," she says. "I take care of his meals, his bath and anything else he requires because he doesn't have much time. I try to cook his favorite foods like teriyaki steak (very thin) and fried vegetables. I buy him chocolate ice cream and kiwi, apples, oranges and pears."

Michiko Tanaka is equally devoted to her four-year-old son, preparing him for a test he must take to enter private elementary school: "After nursery school we both go the juku [an after-school tutoring program] from 2:00 P.M. until 6:30 or 7:00 P.M. I watch and watch and make notes about his weak points." If her son is sick and has to miss juku, she attends for him, crammed behind his tiny desk, writing down what the children are doing and saying so that her son will not fall behind.[22]

It's silly to imagine that American parents can or should mimic these Japanese mothers, but within the constraints of the American cultural reality we can rearrange values so as to give children much higher priority. This would mean devoting many more resources to families with children, and motivating and empowering parents so that they can devote more and better time to their children. These changes are essential prerequisites to educational reform, which in its turn will lead to high-caliber workers and the virtuous circle of ever-increasing prosperity that Reich describes so well.

The argument builds logically, cumulatively, and remorselessly, leaving us with the overwhelming conviction that each and every citizen has an enormous stake in avoiding damage to children. "We all pay to support the unproductive and incarcerate the violent."[23] We all live in fear of crime in our homes and on our streets. We are all diminished when large numbers of parents are incapable of nurturing their young and wolf packs roam city parks. If we fail to save our children we will pay through the nose—and put our own lives on the line. In the words of Marian Wright Edelman, "our children are either going to be invested in . . . or they're going to shoot at us."[24]

Epilogue

The Limits of Freedom

As we head into the last decade of the twentieth century, our minds are filled with extraordinary political images: Chinese students carving a styrofoam Goddess of Democracy in Tiananmen Square; the Berlin Wall being dismantled slab by slab; Poles voting Solidarity in and communism out; hundreds of thousands of Czechs swarming in Wenceslas Square, pressing their claims to freedom; Violeta Chamorro being vested with the sash of office by a Sandinista leader defeated in a free and open election.

At a general strike in Prague in November 1989, Zdenek Janicek, a Czech brewery worker, climbed up on a platform, looked out at his audience, and recited the following words: "We hold these truths to be self-evident, that all men are created equal, that they are endowed by their creator with certain unalienable rights and amongst these are life, liberty and the pursuit of happiness. . . ."[1]

Every schoolchild in the United States knows these lines. It's hard not to feel proud and puffed up, hearing them shouted by people on the other side of what was the Iron Curtain; seeing the words *freedom* and *democracy* hoisted on placards by crowds the size of small cities. We seem to be on the brink of a worldwide victory for a type of economic and political liberalism that is quintessentially American. In April 1990, London's *Financial Times* noted approvingly that for "millions around the world, the American flag is a symbol of an economic and social system that works. No country is more committed to personal freedom and the market economy than the U.S. and no country offers the enterprising individual greater opportunity."[2]

This is heady, spine-chilling stuff.

It should also be chastening.

The United States finds itself in a curious, even embarrassing position. Here are Poles, Nicaraguans, Czechs, even Russians, intoxicated by our slogans about equality and freedom, "reaching for the ideas at America's core."[3] And yet we who know the American reality have much to be ashamed of. Just think about it. The United States ranks last among rich nations in infant mortality; one in four children under the age of six is poor; more than a quarter of all teenagers drop out of school; close to 1 million American families are homeless; 25 percent of children are growing up without fathers; the national debt stands at $2.9 trillion, three times what it was in 1980; and there are more homicides in the United States during an average week than in Japan or Britain during an average year.

These statistics readily translate into the lives of the children we have met in this book. In midtown Manhattan, a small homeless boy tortures a pigeon, acting out the slow, bitter death of his baby sister; on the campus of the University of

Southern California in Los Angeles, a beautiful blonde coed bites at bloodied fingernails as she tells the story of her father's betrayal; in a Tallahassee hospital, a one-and-a-half-pound crack baby twitches in his incubator, tubes sprouting from every part of his pain-wracked body; in Seattle, a seven-year-old latchkey child sits motionless in front of a TV, watching "G.I. Joe"—his sixth show of the day—hoping that the noise from the set will scare off the "bad guys" on his block; and in Newark, girls of thirteen use crack as an abortifacient or shop for maternity wear.

All these disparate types of agony share a common root: the failure of our society to cherish and support its children. You don't need to be a criminologist to realize that abused and neglected children often become violent themselves. You don't require a Ph.D. in education to grasp that poverty-stricken children living on the edge of homelessness might well fail in school. You don't have to be a psychologist to understand that betrayal and abandonment can undermine a child's ability to trust. And you certainly don't need to be an economist to figure out that if you triple the national debt in a single decade, you are likely to produce a bitter burden for the next generation.

Thus, as we celebrate the victory of economic and political liberalism around the world, as we hail the "triumph of the idea of freedom,"[4] it is important to recognize that independence and autonomy can get out of hand. Indeed, in America we may be reaching an appreciation of the limits of freedom at precisely the same time that millions of oppressed people around the world are crying out for a much greater measure of self-determination. As we install our security systems and chain down our rhododendron trees, many of us wonder whether the society that "takes self to the max"[5] has run into serious trouble.

The last few decades, particularly the 1980s, have been extraordinarily free in America. Free not only in the conventional sense of providing access to an elaborate set of individual rights and economic opportunities (for women and blacks as well as for white males), but also free in the deeper sense of offering freedom from internal monitors. We have cut ourselves loose from most moral and religious constraints and acquired a new range of emotional and sexual liberties. We have given ourselves permission to do whatever feels good in the here and now: to spend more than we produce or earn; to abort or abandon our children; to pick and choose television programs, life-styles, and sexual partners. Many of us revel in a new and unparalleled range of choice. We may not quite be ready to emulate Garrison Keillor's Ron and Nancy, who sell the kids in order to discover the joys of selfhood in Biafra, but, like Tom Wolfe, we have tasted our new freedoms and find them "quite glorious."[6]

There is of course a dark side to this degree of freedom. Remember Sherman McCoy, the main character in Tom Wolfe's 1988 novel *The Bonfire of the Vanities*? McCoy is the ultimate symbol of the 1980s, the biggest producer on the trading floor of his Wall Street firm, an immensely successful cad with terrific curb appeal who spends his time "baying for money on the bond market."[7] But McCoy's life is wrecked by a group of alienated black youths from the South Bronx. Even this "Master of the Universe" fails to avoid the alienation and violence that lurk at the edges of his glittering world.

There are two sides to the coin of freedom. On the one side is the enormous potential for prosperity and personal fulfillment; on the other are all the hazards of untrammeled opportunity and unfettered choice. Free markets can produce grinding poverty as well as spectacular wealth; unregulated industry can create dangerous levels of pollution as well as rapid rates

Expanding the boundaries of personal liberty.

of growth; and an uncluttered drive for personal fulfillment can have disastrous effects on families and children. Rampant individualism does not bring with it sweet freedom; rather, it explodes in our faces and limits life's potential.

One thing we can be sure of: these negative spinoffs will come back to haunt us. If, by dint of freely pursuing our own selfish ends, we damage our environment, our communities, or our children, we will most surely pay a price in the quality and possibilities of our own private lives. Sherman McCoy ultimately does not get away with the economic disparities and racial tensions he and his class spawned and heightened.

Toward a Better Balance

Once upon a time we didn't have to worry about constraining freedom or limiting choice. No matter how self-centered or predatory the behavior of men, women could be relied upon to stay quietly in their separate sphere, looking after children, family, and community, providing the needed balance to the aggressive individualism that dominated the outside world.

In the 1830s, Alexis de Tocqueville wrote, "No free communities ever existed without morals and . . . morals are the work of women." In his view, women provided a counterpoint to the relentless competitive pressures of capitalist societies. Men "rushing boldly onward in pursuit of wealth" led "tumultuous and constantly harassed lives," and were apt to relinquish ideals for profit.[8]

Women, on the other hand, not being governed by the marketplace, presided over a domestic universe where an entirely different set of values held sway. In Tocqueville's upper-middle-class nineteenth-century world, wives and mothers were engaged in the creation of a comfortable home; the care and nurturing of husband and children; the handing on of a cultural tradition; the teaching of values; and the maintenance of a complex web of social and familial relationships. These tasks clearly required a great deal of selfless labor, but they also encompassed a moral dimension. In woman's domestic sphere, life was about tenderness, beauty, compassion, and responsibility to others, as well as scrambling for a buck.

In a much more modern context, psychologist Carol Gilligan talks about the difference between the "voices" of men and women. In her 1982 book *In a Different Voice,* she describes how men gravitate toward the instrumental and the impersonal and emphasize abstract principles, while women lean toward intimacy and caring and give priority to human relationships. Gilligan points out that the female "care" voice is not inferior to the male "instrumental" voice, as it is often treated in psychological theory; it is simply different. In her opinion, the voice of care plays a critical role in producing a needed equilibrium between individual and community in American society. Because it balances "self" with "other," and tempers material aspirations with those things spiritual, it goes some distance toward redeeming the ugly, urgent greed that is the spirit of capitalism.

Back in the days when families were organized along traditional lines, women provided the energy and vision that knitted together family and community. At least in the prosperous classes, a clear division of labor between the sexes allowed women to devote considerable time to nurturing and home-making tasks. Under these conditions the voice of care rang out loud and clear through the land and children flourished. But in America (and to a lesser extent in Europe) these traditional patterns were broken by a liberation movement that urged women to get out into the world and seek money and power on the same terms as men, and by a set of economic pressures that increasingly required both parents at work to sustain any semblance of middle-class life.

According to Gilligan the main change wrought by feminism was that it "enabled women to consider it moral to care not only for others but also for themselves." She quotes Elizabeth Cady Stanton telling a reporter in 1948 "to put it down in capital letters: SELF-DEVELOPMENT IS A HIGHER DUTY THAN SELF-SACRIFICE."[9] Modern women have struggled with this lesson. In recent years some elite women have achieved considerable status and earning power in the marketplace, the most successful being those who have traded the care voice for the instrumental voice and cloned the male competitive model. Many less privileged women have gotten bogged down in debilitating divorces, single parenthood, second shifts, and plain, old-fashioned poverty. One thing is clear: with women preoccupied with the search for self and/or the fight for economic survival, there is often no one at home to look after the children or worry about the moral tone of society.

But before we get nostalgic about traditional roles and start dumping the blame on that easy scapegoat, liberated women, we must remind ourselves of some contemporary realities.

It's become a risky, thankless task, this business of raising children and building families. Risky in that divorce can quickly destroy a lifetime of investment in family, leaving a displaced homemaker teetering on the edge of poverty, struggling to earn a living in a labor market that exacts large penalties for career interruptions. Thankless in that we no longer seem to value these activities. The story told by our public policies is that almost any endeavor is more worthy of support than child raising. We discriminate heavily against pregnant workers and fail to provide parenting leave or prenatal care; under our tax code a couple would be better off breeding race horses than raising children; and most states do a better job regulating kennels than day-care centers. To use the words of Germaine Greer, "if the management of childbearing in our society had actually been intended to maximize stress, it could hardly have succeeded better. The childbearers embark on their struggle alone; the rest of us wash our hands of them."[10]

No wonder individual women find it increasingly difficult to place children at the center of their lives. In the titanic struggle to get ahead, to earn money and accumulate power— the only yardsticks that count in contemporary society—children are increasingly relegated to the margins of life.

As we move through the 1990s, we have to learn how to increase the rewards and spread around the sacrifices of parenting. There is no sensible alternative. It would be foolish to expect wives and mothers to assume a more traditional role and somehow find the resources to take up, once again, the entire family burden. Modern women are intent upon a fair measure of self-realization; besides which, the economic facts of life preclude a return to a 1950s division of labor. With plummeting wages and sky-high divorce rates, it's hard to spin out a scenario where large numbers of mothers have the option of staying home with their children on a full-time basis. Tighter divorce laws, job sharing, and mortgage subsidies might well be part of the solution, but whatever the precise mechanisms, we simply have to bend the rules of the game so as to free up many more resources and much more time for children. The critical task of building strong families can no longer be defined as a private endeavor, least of all a private female endeavor. It is time to demonstrate in our laws and policies that we, as a nation, honor parents, value families, and treasure our children.

Redrawing our public policies so that children may thrive has one enormously important additional characteristic—it will greatly improve the economic status of women. Enhancing and enforcing child-support awards eases the lives of the children of divorce but also bolsters the standard of living of ex-wives; mandating parenting leave improves the life circumstances of infants but also protects the earning power of women and reduces the wage gap; job sharing and career sequencing provide time and flexibility for children but also allow a mother to work part-time and then get back on the career ladder with her promotional prospects intact. In other words, family support policies, because they *reduce the price mothers are asked to pay for their children,* contribute significantly

356 WHEN THE BOUGH BREAKS

to achieving equality of economic opportunity between men and women. Not because they necessarily produce a 50-50 split in nurturing or breadwinning tasks in any given day or week, but because they compensate mothers for childbearing and child raising and promote a greater measure of equity over the life span.[11] When we place a high value on children, modern women benefit enormously.

Beyond Self-Interest

Whatever the material advantages of my Action Plan, there is more to this business of saving children than enlightened self-interest.

Yes, we need to invest in our children to save our own skins.

But we also need to devote new and better energy to our children because *it is the right thing to do.*

Throughout the ages people have striven for meaning that goes beyond the narrow scope of individual lives. No amount of material success or personal gratification ultimately satisfies the human soul. Beyond some level of achievement, earning power and self-realization become poor substitutes for the higher values of compassion, communion—and charity toward others. "Though I speak with the tongues of men and angels, and have not charity, I am become as a sounding brass or a tinkling cymbal. . . . I am nothing."[12]

The 1980s were years when the oldest tensions in American society, between old and young, consumption and investment, present and future, got way out of whack. We journeyed far along the road of self-indulgence and discovered—not much of anything at all! The core of this narcissistic version of the American Dream was hollow and void. We rediscovered that the individual is a very poor site for finding meaning and that a necessary condition for finding fulfillment in life is an attachment to something larger than the lonely self.

As we head toward the twenty-first century, we may well be ready to temper our autonomous, self-absorbed drive with a concern for others. Nothing is more worth doing than easing the pain and improving the life chances of vulnerable, blameless children. In the final analysis, enriching and enhancing the lives of Fatima, Brian, and Becky might be the nearest we mortals come to reaching beyond earthly limits to touch the face of God.

Notes

Prologue. Fractured Childhoods

1. In the 1980s, New York City used substandard welfare hotels to house homeless families. In 1987, at the peak, there were 3,600 families in 62 hotels, the Prince George and the Martinique being among the largest. The conditions in these hotels caused a public outcry, and in 1989 many families were resettled in apartment houses and small shelters scattered throughout the boroughs. In 1990, however, due to increased levels of homelessness, the welfare hotels staged a comeback. In September 1990, there were again 427 families in midtown hotels.

   One of the most ironic facts about these welfare hotels is that they have always been immensely expensive, costing approximately $2,300 per month per family. This cost is shared by the city and federal governments. Editorial, "The New Crunch for Welfare Hotels," *New York Times,* September 21, 1990, p. A30.

2. I am indebted to Gretchen Buchenholz, executive director of

the Association to Benefit Children, for giving me access to her notes on Brian.

3. *A Vision for America's Future, An Agenda for the 1990s: A Children's Defense Budget* (Washington, D.C.: Children's Defense Fund, 1989), p. 91.

4. Frank F. Furstenberg, Jr., and Christine Winquist Nord, "Parenting Apart: Patterns of Childrearing After Marital Disruption," *Journal of Marriage and the Family* 47, no. 4 (November 1985): 874.

5. Quoted in *A Vision for America's Future,* p. xiii.

Chapter 1. A Matter of National Survival

1. Select Committee on Children, Youth and Families, *U.S. Children and Their Families: Current Conditions and Recent Trends* (Washington, D.C.: U.S. House of Representatives, September 1989), p. x.

2. National Commission on the Role of the School and the Community in Improving Adolescent Health, *Code Blue: Uniting for Healthier Youth* (Washington, D.C.: National Association of State Boards of Education and the American Medical Association, 1990), p. 3.

3. Fordham Institute for Innovation in Social Policy, *Measuring the Social Well-Being of the Nation: The Social Health of Children and Youth* (New York: Fordham University Graduate Center, 1989).

4. "Money, Income and Poverty Status in the United States: 1989" (U.S. Bureau of the Census, Current Population Reports Series P-60, No. 168, September 1990), p. 59, table 20.

5. Homelessness is, by definition, almost impossible to measure precisely, and estimates of the number of children who are homeless on any given night range from 35,000 (the Urban Institute) to 500,000 (National Coalition of Homeless). A middle-range estimate prepared by the U.S. Department of Education in 1990 (covering October 1, 1988, through September 30, 1989) claims there are 272,773 school-aged homeless children (plus more than 56,783 preschool children). See discussion in Select Committee on Children, Youth and Families, *U.S. Children and Their Families,* p. 31.

One thing we are sure of is that the number of homeless

people has increased in recent years, and the characteristics of the homeless population have changed to include significantly more children. Today 31 percent of the homeless are families with children, up from 21 percent in the early 1980s. See "A Report on the 1988 National Survey of Shelters for the Homeless" (Washington, D.C.: U.S. Department of Housing and Urban Development, Office of Policy Research, March 1989), exhibit 12. One in every four homeless persons in cities is a child. See "A Status Report on Hunger and Homelessness in America's Cities: 1989" (Washington, D.C.: U.S. Conference of Mayors, December 1989).

6. Select Committee on Children, Youth and Families, *U.S. Children and Their Families,* p. 189.

7. Frank F. Furstenberg, Jr., and Kathleen Mullan Harris, "The Disappearing American Father? Divorce and the Waning Significance of Biological Parenthood," draft, Department of Sociology, University of Pennsylvania, March 1990, p. 4. See also Frank F. Furstenberg, Jr., and Christine Winquist Nord, "Parenting Apart: Patterns of Childbearing after Marital Disruption," *Journal of Marriage and the Family* 47, no. 4 (November 1985): 874.

8. Telephone interview, Vance Grant, National Center for Educational Statistics, U.S. Department of Education, May 31, 1990.

9. Select Committee on Children, Youth and Families, *Children's Well-Being: An International Comparison* (Washington, D.C.: U.S. House of Representatives, July 25, 1990).

10. *Children 1990: A Report Card, Briefing Book and Action Primer* (Washington, D.C.: Children's Defense Fund, 1990), p. 4.

11. *Breaking the Cycle of Dependency,* Annual Report (New York: New York City Human Resource Administration, 1988), p. 19. The reports of child abuse in New York City went from 22,000 to 66,000 between 1981 and 1989.

12. There were 60,000 reported cases in 1975 and 2.4 million in 1989. See U.S. Advisory Board on Child Abuse and Neglect, "Child Abuse and Neglect: Critical First Steps in Response to a National Emergency" (Washington, D.C.: U.S. Department of Health and Human Services, August 1990), p. 15.

13. *A Vision for America's Future, An Agenda for the 1990s: A Chil-*

dren's Defense Budget (Washington, D.C.: Children's Defense Fund, 1989), p. xvi.

14. National Center for Health Statistics, *Health: United States, 1989* (Hyattsville, Md.: Public Health Service, 1990).

15. Dialogue excerpted from ABC News, "Burning Questions: America's Kids: Why They Flunk," October 3, 1988.

16. Telephone interview, Fred Beamer, U.S. Department of Education, Office of Educational Research and Improvement, National Center for Education Statistics, July 26, 1990.

17. ABC News, "Burning Questions: America's Kids."

18. Telephone interview, Mary Futrell, October 17, 1990. According to Futrell, only 25 percent of parents visit the school after the child is enrolled. The participation rate of parents is considerably higher in elementary schools than in high schools. Other than parent/teacher night, parent involvement is almost nonexistent in high school. See also the P.T.A./Dodge National Parent Survey, "A Study of Parental Involvement in Children's Education," commissioned by *Newsweek,* 1990.

19. See Susan Tifft, "A Crisis Looms in Science," *Time,* September 11, 1989, p. 68, and Alison L. Sprout, "Do U.S. Schools Make the Grade?" *Fortune,* special issue, Spring 1990, pp. 50–51.

20. Richard Zoglin, "Is TV Ruining Our Children?" *Time,* October 15, 1990, p. 75. According to Yale University's Dr. Victor Strasburger: "The average child between 6 and 11 years of age spends 25 hours per week—roughly one third of non-school hours—watching television . . . By the time they graduate from high school, children will have spent 15,000 hours camped in front of a TV set . . . During this time they will have witnessed some 18,000 murders and countless robberies, bombings, assaults, beatings and tortures. They will also have been exposed to some 350,000 commercial messages." See William J. Bennett, *First Lessons: A Report on Elementary School Education in America* (Washington, D.C.: U.S. Government Printing Office, September 1986), p. 14.

21. National Center for Education Statistics, *A Profile of the American Eighth Grader* (Washington, D.C.: U.S. Department of Education, Office of Education Research and Improvement, June 1990), p. 3.

22. David Popenoe, Department of Sociology, Rutgers University, "For the Children's Sake: Family Decline and Child Well-Being," unpublished book manuscript, September 1990, p. 16.

23. In 1987 federal outlays totaled $1,003.8 billion; $48.3 billion, or 4.8 percent, was spent on children, and $230.4 billion, or 22.9 percent, was spent on the elderly. Telephone interview, Richard Krop, Congressional Budget Office, November 21, 1990. Similar estimates can be found in Timothy M. Smeeding, "The Debt, the Deficit, and Disadvantaged Children: Generational Impacts and Age, Period, and Cohort Effects," in *The Debt and the Twin Deficits Debate,* ed. James M. Rock (Mountain View, Calif.: Bristlecone Books/Mayfield, 1991), p. 47.

24. Peter G. Peterson, "An American Dream: We Must 'Do Better' for Our Children," *New York Times,* July 16, 1989, p. B2.

25. John Coder, Lee Rainwater, and Timothy Smeeding, "Inequality Among Children and Elderly in Ten Modern Nations: The United States in an International Context," *American Economic Review* 79, no. 2 (May 1989): 320–24.

26. Victor R. Fuchs, *Women's Quest for Economic Equality* (Cambridge, Mass.: Harvard University Press, 1988), p. 111.

27. Nancy Gibbs, "Has America Run Out of Time?" *Time*, April 24, 1989, p. 59. See also discussion in Rosabeth Moss Kanter, *When Giants Learn to Dance: Mastering the Challenges of Strategy, Management, and Careers in the 1990s* (New York: Simon & Schuster, 1989), p. 293.

28. See J. L. Richardson et al., "Substance Use Among Eighth Grade Students Who Take Care of Themselves After School," *Pediatrics* 84, no. 3 (September 1989): 556–66, and Sheila Fitzgerald Krein and Andrea H. Beller, "Educational Attainment of Children from Single-Parent Families: Differences by Exposure, Gender and Race," *Demography* 25, no. 2 (May 1988): 221–33.

29. Statement by Roseann Bentley, co-chair of Code Blue. Quoted in the *New York Times,* June 9, 1990, p. A1.

30. Bruce Nussbaum, "Needed: Human Capital," *Business Week,* September 19, 1988, p. 102.

31. Ibid., p. 104.

32. Howard B. Fullerton, Jr., "New Labor Force Projections, Span-

ning 1988 to 2000," *Monthly Labor Review* 112, no. 11 (November 1989): 4; and *Employment and Earnings* (Washington, D.C.: U.S. Department of Labor, Bureau of Labor Statistics, January 1990), p. 160.

33. Committee for Economic Development, *Children in Need: Investment Strategies for the Educationally Disadvantaged* (Washington, D.C.: CED, 1987), p. 4.

34. David Whitman et al., "The Forgotten Half," *U.S. News & World Report,* June 26, 1989, p. 47.

35. Fullerton, "New Labor Force Projections," p. 11. Other studies have come up with even lower figures: *Time* estimates that only 9 percent of new workers in the 1990s will be white males. See Janice Castro, "Get Set: Here They Come!" *Time,* special issue, Fall 1990, p. 52.

36. William B. Johnston and Arnold H. Packer, *Workforce 2000: Work and Workers for the 21st Century* (Indianapolis: Hudson Institute, 1987), pp. 102–3.

37. Commission on Workforce Quality and Labor Market Efficiency, *Investing in People: A Strategy to Address America's Workforce Crisis* (Washington, D.C.: U.S. Department of Labor, 1989), p. 2.

38. Whitman et al, "The Forgotten Half," p. 46.

39. Johnston and Packer, *Workforce 2000,* pp. 97–98.

40. For a description of the 1851 exhibition, see Christopher Hobhouse, *1851 and the Crystal Palace* (New York: Dutton, 1937), pp. 62–69, 134–37.

41. Quoted in Nussbaum, "Needed: Human Capital," p. 101.

42. *America in Transition: The International Frontier* (Washington, D.C.: National Governors' Association, 1989); and Thomas P. Rohlen, *Japan's High Schools* (Berkeley: University of California Press, 1983), p. 3.

43. Steven Schlossstein, *The End of the American Century* (New York: Congdon & Weed, 1989), p. 232.

44. Ibid., pp. 229, 308–9.

45. James S. Coleman, U.S. Department of Health, Education and Welfare, National Institute of Education, "Effects of School on Learning: The IEA Findings," presented at a Conference on Educational Achievement, Harvard University, November

1973, p. 40. See also James S. Coleman, E. Campbell, et al., *Equality of Educational Opportunity* (Washington, D.C.: U.S. Department of Health, Education and Welfare, Office of Education, 1966); and James S. Coleman and Thomas Hoffer, *Public and Private High Schools: The Impact of Communities* (New York: Basic Books, 1987), pp. 90–91. Later studies by Coleman have found that if mathematics is looked at, the relative effect of school is somewhat greater. Family background remains dominant, however.

46. Daniel Patrick Moynihan, *Family and Nation* (New York: Harcourt Brace Jovanovich, 1986), p. 133.

47. Edward F. Denison, *Trends in American Economic Growth, 1929–1982* (Washington, D.C.: The Brookings Institution, 1985), p. 31.

48. Sylvia Ann Hewlett, "Family Support Policy? Consult the Bottom Line," *Management Review,* January 1989, p. 56.

49. Ibid.

50. Telephone interview, Dana E. Friedman, co-president, Families and Work Institute, November 10, 1990.

51. Kathleen Teltsch, "Business Sees Aid to Schools as a Net Gain," *New York Times,* December 4, 1988, p. A1. See also Nancy J. Perry, "Saving the Schools: How Business Can Help," *Fortune,* November 7, 1988, p. 50.

52. Teltsch, "Business," p. A50.

53. Cathy Trost, "Corporate Prenatal-Care Plans Multiply, Benefiting Both Mothers and Employers," *Wall Street Journal,* June 24, 1988, p. B1.

54. Christopher Lasch, *Haven in a Heartless World: The Family Besieged* (New York: Basic Books, 1979).

55. Interview, David Blankenhorn, president of the Institute of American Values, New York City, October 13, 1988.

56. Committee for Economic Development, *Children in Need,* pp. 3, 1.

57. Hearing before the Select Committee on Children, Youth and Families, April 27, 1989, "Born Hooked: Confronting the Impact of Prenatal Substance Abuse" (Washington, D.C.: U.S. House of Representatives, 1989), p. 1. For educational data see discussion in chapter 3.

58. Andrew Stein, "Children of Poverty: Crisis in New York," *New York Times Magazine,* June 8, 1986, p. 39.

59. As of year-end 1987, 37.3 percent of children in New York City were living below the poverty line. Telephone interview, Kevin Athaide, director, Office of Program Planning, Analysis and Development, New York State Department of Social Services, August 1, 1990.

60. Susan Cotts Watkins, Jane A. Menken, and John Bongaarts, "Demographic Foundations of Family Change," *American Sociological Review* 52, no. 3 (1987): 346–58.

61. *Money* magazine, using Department of Agriculture figures, estimated that the average family earning $50,000 or more a year will spend $265,249 to feed, clothe, and shelter a child up to age twenty-two (see Andrea Rock, "Can You Afford Your Kids?" *Money,* July 1990, pp. 88–99) while sociologist Thomas Espenshade arrives at an estimate of $117,000 per child up to age eighteen (estimate based on an average family with two children; telephone interview, July 23, 1990).

62. Viviana A. Zelizer, *Pricing the Priceless Child: The Changing Social Value of Children* (New York: Basic Books, 1985), p. 3.

63. Peter G. Peterson, "An American Dream," p. B2.

64. Committee for Economic Development, *Children in Need,* p. 9.

65. Aaron L. Friedberg, *The Weary Titan: Britain and Experience of Relative Decline, 1895–1905* (Princeton, N.J.: Princeton University Press, 1988), p. 86.

Chapter 2. Disadvantaged Kids and the Resource Deficit

1. Douglas Martin, "A Heavy Burden: Burying Eileen, Sam, Liz and F/C," *New York Times,* March 28, 1990, p. B1.

2. Ibid.

3. "Fact Sheet" prepared for hearing before the Select Committee on Children, Youth and Families, U.S. House of Representatives, "Caring for New Mothers: Pressing Problems, New Solutions," October 24, 1989.

4. United Nations Statistical Office, *Population and Vital Statistics Report,* April 1989. A recent United Nations Children's Fund (UNICEF) report looked at thirty-nine countries and found that

in this larger group the United States ranked twenty-third in low-birthweight births, behind such countries as Hong Kong, Romania, and the Soviet Union. See the Report of the Task Force on Children, *America in Transition: The International Frontier* (Washington, D.C.: National Governors' Association, 1989).

5. National Commission to Prevent Infant Mortality, "Infant Mortality: Care for Our Children, Care for Our Future" (Washington, D.C., January 1988), p. 13.

6. National Commission to Prevent Infant Mortality, "Troubling Trends: The Health of America's Next Generation" (Washington, D.C., February 1990), p. 34.

7. National Commission to Prevent Infant Mortality, "Death Before Life: The Tragedy of Infant Mortality," appendix (Washington, D.C., August 1988), p. 34.

8. National Commission to Prevent Infant Mortality, "International Infant Mortality Comparisons: Briefing Paper," February 1, 1988.

9. From "Opening Remarks" at the National Commission to Prevent Infant Mortality's "International Infant Mortality Comparisons," United Nations, February 1, 1988.

10. "The cost of 'graduating' a sick infant from neonatal intensive care ranges from $20,000 to $100,000 per infant. Overall lifetime health and custodial care for a handicapped child may cost as much as $300,000 to $400,000 per child." (National Commission to Prevent Infant Mortality, "Infant Mortality: Care for Our Children, Care for Our Future," p. 6.)

11. Institute of Health estimate, contained in ibid., p. 6.

12. "In 1985, the Institute of Medicine calculated that each dollar spent on prenatal care for low-income, poorly educated women could save $3.38 in direct medical expenses." Cited in Carol Cronin and Rebecca Hartman, "The Corporate Perspective on Maternal and Child Health: A Background Paper" (Washington, D.C.: Washington Business Group on Health, October 1989), p. 21.

13. "Money, Income and Poverty Status in the United States: 1989" (U.S. Bureau of the Census, Current Population Reports Series P-60, No. 168, September 1990, p. 59, table 20.

14. *A Vision for America's Future, An Agenda for the 1990s: A Children's Defense Budget* (Washington, D.C.: Children's Defense Fund, 1989), pp. 16–17.

15. National Center for Children in Poverty, *Five Million Children: A Statistical Profile of Our Poorest Young Citizens* (New York: Columbia University, School of Public Health, 1990), pp. 16–18.

16. Daniel Patrick Moynihan, *Family and Nation* (New York: Harcourt Brace Jovanovich, 1986), p. 96. See also discussion in Eugene Smolensky, Sheldon Danziger, and Peter Gottschalk, "The Declining Significance of Age in the United States: Trends in the Well-Being of Children and the Elderly Since 1939," in *The Vulnerable,* ed. John L. Palmer, Timothy Smeeding, and Barbara Boyle Torrey (Washington, D.C.: Urban Institute Press, 1988), p. 42.

17. Select Committee on Children, Youth and Families, *Children's Well-Being: An International Comparison* (Washington, D.C.: U.S. House of Representatives, July 25, 1990), pp. 37–38.

18. John Coder, Lee Rainwater, and Timothy Smeeding, "Inequality Among Children and Elderly in Ten Modern Nations: The United States in an International Context," *American Economic Review* 79, no. 2 (May 1989): 323. See also Timothy M. Smeeding, "Poverty, Affluence, and the Income Costs of Children: Cross-National Evidence from the Luxembourg Income Study (LIS)," *Journal of Post-Keynesian Economics* 11, no. 2 (Winter 1988–89): 233.

19. David Whitman et al., "America's Hidden Poor," *U.S. News & World Report,* January 11, 1988, p. 19.

20. Erol R. Ricketts and Isabel V. Sawhill, "Defining and Measuring the Underclass," *Journal of Policy Analysis and Management* 7, no. 2 (1988): 316–24. See also Erol R. Ricketts and Ronald B. Mincy, "Growth of the Underclass: 1970–80," *Journal of Human Resources* 25, no. 1 (Winter 1990): 137–45.

21. Telephone interview, Mark Littman, Bureau of the Census, January 15, 1991. Source: "Money, Income and Poverty Status in the United States: 1989," p. 65, table 22.

22. Whitman et al., "America's Hidden Poor," p. 22.

23. Ibid., p. 21.

24. Telephone interview, Jim Markey, Bureau of Labor Statistics, Division of Labor Force Statistics, August 12, 1990. (Sources: Unpublished data and data derived from January 1986 *Current Population Survey;* Francis W. Horvath, "The Pulse of Economic Change: Displaced Workers of 1981–1985," *Monthly Labor Review* 110, no. 6 (June 1987): 3–12.

25. Telephone interview, Bob Cleveland, U.S. Bureau of the Census, April 30, 1990, May 2, 1990, and September 22, 1990.

26. Ibid.

27. Susan Champlin Taylor, "A Promise at Risk," *Modern Maturity,* August–September 1989, p. 36.

28. Cited in David T. Ellwood, *Poor Support: Poverty in the American Family* (New York: Basic Books, 1988), pp. 53–54.

29. William B. Johnston and Arnold H. Packer, *Workforce 2000: Work and Workers for the 21st Century* (Indianapolis: Hudson Institute, 1987), p. 103.

30. Greg J. Duncan and Saul D. Hoffman, "A Reconsideration of the Economic Consequences of Marital Dissolution," *Demography* 22, no. 4 (November 1985): 485–97.

31. Frank F. Furstenberg, Jr., and Christine Winquist Nord, "Parenting Apart: Patterns of Childrearing after Marital Disruption," *Journal of Marriage and the Family* 47, no. 4 (November 1985): 874.

32. National Commission on the Role of the School and the Community in Improving Adolescent Health, *Code Blue: Uniting for Healthier Youth* (Washington, D.C.: National Association of State Boards of Education and the American Medical Association, 1990), p. 2.

33. *A Vision for America's Future,* p. 91. See also discussion in Leon Dash, *When Children Want Children: The Urban Crisis of Teenage Childbearing* (New York: Morrow, 1989), p. 25.

34. Moynihan, *Family and Nation,* p. 168.

35. William Julius Wilson, *The Truly Disadvantaged: The Inner City, the Underclass, and Public Policy* (Chicago: University of Chicago Press, 1987), pp. 84–89.

36. Telephone interview, Jim Markey, August 12, 1990. About two-thirds (65.8 percent) of black men age twenty to twenty-four were employed in 1989. Source: *Employment and Earnings*

(Washington, D.C.: U.S. Department of Labor, Bureau of Labor Statistics, January 1990), pp. 162, 164.

37. Arthur N. Applebee, Judith A. Langer, and Ina V. S. Mullis, *Crossroads in American Education: A Summary of Findings* (Princeton, N.J.: Educational Testing Service, February 1989), p. 17.

38. "Teenage Pregnancy and Too-Early Childbearing: Public Costs, Personal Consequences" (Washington, D.C.: Center for Population Options, September 1989), pp. 8–9. See also *A Vision for America's Future*, pp. 90–92.

39. "Teenage Pregnancy," pp. 5–6.

40. Alex Kotlowitz, "Tough Students: Inner-City Schools Must Teach Kids Traumatized by Violence, Family Woes," *Wall Street Journal,* March 31, 1989, special education section, p. R11.

41. This program is described in Committee for Economic Development, "Investment Strategies for the Educationally Disadvantaged" (Washington, D.C.: CED, 1987), p. 30.

42. Lisbeth B. Schorr with Daniel Schorr, *Within Our Reach: Breaking the Cycle of Disadvantage* (New York: Anchor, 1988), p. xx.

43. Ellwood, *Poor Support,* p. 200.

44. Telephone interview, Richard Krop, Congressional Budget Office, November 21, 1990. See also Timothy M. Smeeding, "The Debt, the Deficit, and Disadvantaged Children: Generational Impacts and Age, Period and Cohort Effects," in *The Debt and the Twin Deficits Debate,* ed. James M. Rock (Mountain View, Calif.: Bristlecone Books/Mayfield, 1991), pp. 46–47.

45. According to the Partnership for the Homeless, "the most recent estimates differ widely, varying from 600,000 by a research institute to 3 million by an advocacy group. . . . Most attempts at estimating the homeless by cities and localities have concluded that the homeless comprise from .7 to 1.1% of their respective populations. If this range is reasonably accurate, there may be as many as 2 million homeless across the nation." *Moving Forward: A National Agenda to Address Homelessness in 1990 and Beyond and a Status Report on Homelessness in America, a 46-City Survey, 1988–1989* (New York: Partnership for the Homeless, 1989), p. 3.

46. As of April 1989 homelessness among families with children stood at 31 percent. Ibid., p. 7.

47. Jonathan Kozol, *Rachel and Her Children: Homeless Families in America* (New York: Crown, 1988), pp. 4–9.

48. Interview, Gretchen Buchenholz, executive director of the Association to Benefit Children, New York City, January 21, 1989.

49. *S.O.S. America! A Children's Defense Budget* (Washington, D.C.: Children's Defense Fund, 1990), p. 111.

50. Carol F. Steinbach and Neal R. Peirce, "Picking Up Hammers," *National Journal,* June 6, 1987, p. 1465.

51. Paul A. Leonard, Cushing N. Dolbeare, and Edward B. Lazere, "A Place to Call Home: The Crisis in Housing for the Poor" (Washington, D.C.: Center on Budget and Policy Priorities, and Low Income Housing Information Service, April 1989), p. xiv. This report defines "low-income" housing as the number of units renting for $250 or less a month—which is 30 percent of a household's income at the $10,000 income level. See also Edward B. Lazere and Paul A. Leonard, "The Crisis in Housing for the Poor: A Special Report on Hispanics and Blacks," (Washington, D.C.: Center on Budget and Policy Priorities, July 1989), p. x.

52. Leonard, Dolbeare, and Lazere, "A Place to Call Home," pp. xvi, 28–31.

53. Ibid., p. 63. For these figures this report relies on a national study prepared by the Joint Center for Housing Studies at Harvard University. See also *A Vision for America's Future,* p. 101.

54. Leonard, Dolbeare, and Lazere, "A Place to Call Home," p. 1. See also Lazere and Leonard, "The Crisis in Housing for the Poor," pp. 1–2.

55. Leonard, Dolbeare, and Lazere, "A Place to Call Home," pp. 38–39. See also National Housing Forum, "Working Toward a Consensus: Final Report" (Washington, D.C.: U.S. Conference of Mayors, 1988), p. 12.

56. Jack A. Meyer and Marilyn Moon, "Health Care Spending on Children and the Elderly," in *The Vulnerable,* ed. Palmer, Smeeding, Torrey, p. 179. See also *A Vision for America's Future,* p. 6.

57. Kevin Sack, "New York Health Care: A Big Step for Children," *New York Times,* July 11, 1990, p. B1.

58. See discussion in Meyer and Moon, "Health Care Spending on Children and the Elderly," pp. 182–84.

59. Edmund Faltermayer, "How to Close the Health Gap," *Fortune,* May 21, 1990, p. 130.

60. *A Vision for America's Future,* p. 10.

61. Select Committee on Children, Youth and Families, *U.S. Children and Their Families: Current Conditions and Recent Trends* (Washington, D.C.: U.S. House of Representatives, September 1989), p. 282.

62. Telephone interview, Patty Cunningham, Food Program Specialist at the Program Analysis and Monitoring Branch, Department of Agriculture, Food & Nutrition Service, Supplementary Food Program, October 25, 1990.

63. Select Committee on Children, Youth and Families, *Children and Families: Key Trends in the 1980s* (Washington, D.C.: U.S. House of Representatives, 1988), p. 9.

64. Robert Pear, "Many States Cut Food Allotments for Poor Families," *New York Times,* May 29, 1990, p. A1.

65. Ibid., pp. A1, A16.

66. Select Committee on Children, Youth and Families, *U.S. Children and Their Families,* pp. 194–95.

67. B. D. Cohen, "A Growing Measles Problem," *Newsday,* July 3, 1990, p. 7.

68. "Support Spreading for Child Care Aid," *National Journal,* June 25, 1988, p. 1722.

69. Edward F. Zigler and Mary E. Lang, *Child Care Choices: Balancing the Needs of Children, Families and Society* (New York: The Free Press, 1991), p. 22. See also discussion in Select Committee on Children, Youth and Families, *U.S. Children and Their Families,* pp. 96–97.

70. "Changes in American Family Life" (U.S. Bureau of the Census, Current Population Reports Series P-23, No. 163, August 1989), p. 17.

71. *Mothers in the Workplace,* 1987 study conducted by the Center for the Child, National Council of Jewish Women, New York, N.Y.

72. In the late 1980s the Bureau of the Census estimated that 36 percent of the 9.1 million preschool children of working

women were looked after in someone else's home. See *Who's Minding the Kids? Child Care Arrangements: 1986–87* (U.S. Bureau of the Census, Current Population Reports Series P-70, No. 20, 1990).

73. Quoted in Sylvia Ann Hewlett, *A Lesser Life: The Myth of Women's Liberation in America* (New York: Morrow, 1986), p. 120.

74. Interview, February 4, 1989.

75. The United States General Accounting Office estimates the average cost of early education for a four-year-old at $4,797 in 1988. On average, 69 percent of that cost was paid by parents, with 15 percent more coming from other private sources like churches, colleges, and fund raisers. Only 16 percent was covered with public funds. Source: Fred M. Hechinger, "About Education," *New York Times,* April 11, 1990, p. B9. See also discussion in National Center for Children in Poverty, *Five Million Children,* pp. 70–73.

76. Telephone interview, Helen Blank, Children's Defense Fund, October 25, 1990. See also *A Vision for America's Future,* pp. 62–63.

77. "$1 investment in preschool education returns $6 in savings because of lower special education costs, lower welfare and higher worker productivity, and lower costs of crime. . . . Researchers estimate that program benefits yield a six-fold return on one-year program and three-fold return on two-year programs. For a cost of $5000 per participant, total benefits to taxpayers from the program were calculated at $28,000 per participant." (Select Committee on Children, Youth and Families, *Children and Families,* pp. 32–39.)

78. Zigler and Lang, *Child Care Choices,* p. 122.

79. *A Vision for America's Future,* p. 58.

80. Lynette and Thomas Long, *The Handbook for Latchkey Children and Their Parents* (New York: Arbor House, 1983), p. 174.

81. Gwen Morgan, *The National State of Child Care Regulations, 1989* (Watertown, Mass.: Work/Family Directions, 1989). According to the Children's Defense Fund, only twenty-nine states and the District of Columbia have infant-to-worker staffing requirements that meet the four-to-one ratio recommended by the

National Association for the Education of Young Children. See *Children 1990* (Washington, D.C.: Children's Defense Fund, 1990), p. 108.

82. The Child Care Employees Project, a nonprofit group in Oakland, Calif., says, "The average hourly wage for child-care workers in 1988 was $5.35, amounting to an annual income of $9,431, placing them near the poverty line. It is not surprising that every year about 40 percent of these workers quit their jobs." See discussion in Susan Chira, "Preschool Aid for the Poor: How Big a Head Start," *New York Times,* February 14, 1990, p. A1.

83. *A Vision for America's Future,* p. 59.

84. Ibid., pp. 49–60. See also discussion in Sunny Harris, Loretta S. Robinson, and Terrence B. Atkin, *Social Services in the States: Profiles on State Use of Federal Title XX Social Services Block Grant Funds* (Silver Spring, Md.: National Association of Social Workers, 1989).

85. National Center for Children in Poverty, *Five Million Children,* p. 71.

86. Steven A. Holmes, "Day Care Bill Marks a Turn Toward Help for the Poor," *New York Times,* April 8, 1990, p. E4.

87. *A Vision for America's Future,* p. 62.

88. Sara Rimmer, "A School in the Bronx That Is Somehow Making It," *New York Times,* March 12, 1990, pp. A1, B6.

89. Felicia R. Lee, "Altering 'Dismal State' of School Libraries," *New York Times,* November 2, 1989, p. B1.

90. Joseph Berger, "Choosing $90 Million in School Cuts: Layoffs or Attrition, It's Class Chaos," *New York Times,* November 21, 1990, p. B3.

91. Robert Hanley, "The New Math of Rich and Poor," *New York Times,* June 10, 1990, p. E6.

92. *A Vision for America's Future,* pp. 74–75.

93. Schorr, *Within Our Reach,* p. x (from preface by Judith Viorst).

94. Quoted in ibid., p. xxvii.

95. Ibid., p. xix.

96. Valerie Gladstone and James Kamp, "The Littlest Victim," *Life,* October 1989, pp. 16–17.

97. *A Vision for America's Future,* p. xix.

Chapter 3. Mainstream Kids and the Time Deficit

1. Story and interview quotes from ABC News, "20/20": "Palisades High: To Bring the Children Home," April 21, 1989.
2. National Commission on the Role of the School and the Community in Improving Adolescent Health, *Code Blue: Uniting for Healthier Youth* (Washington, D.C.: National Association of State Boards of Education and the American Medical Association, 1990), p. 3.
3. Ibid., p. 4.
4. Edward B. Fiske, "Why Do American Students Keep Stumbling in Last in the Academic Derby?" *New York Times,* February 15, 1989, p. B6.
5. Ellen Hoffman, "The 'Education Deficit,' " *National Journal,* March 14, 1987, p. 618.
6. Fiske, "Academic Derby," p. B6. See also Howard M. Leichter and Harrell R. Rodgers, Jr., *American Public Policy in a Comparative Context* (New York: McGraw-Hill, 1984), p. 232.
7. Irwin S. Kirsch and Ann Jungeblut, National Assessment of Educational Progress, *Literacy: Profiles of America's Young Adults* (Princeton, N.J.: Educational Testing Service, 1985), p. 232.
8. Telephone interview, Robert Barnes, statistician, Office of Planning, Budget and Evaluation, U.S. Department of Labor, August 8, 1990. The most recent comprehensive study of literacy is Kirsch and Jungeblut, *Literacy: Profiles of America's Young Adults.*
9. National Commission on Excellence in Education, *A Nation at Risk: The Imperative for Educational Reform* (Washington, D.C.: U.S. Government Printing Office, April 1983), p. 8.
10. Quoted in National Assessment of Educational Progress, *Learning to Be Literate in America* (Princeton, N.J.: Educational Testing Service, March 1987).
11. Elizabeth Ehrlich, "America's Schools Still Aren't Making the Grade," *Business Week,* September 19, 1988, p. 132. See also National Assessment of Educational Progress, *Learning to Be Literate,* and National Assessment of Educational Progress, *The Reading Report Card, 1971–1988* and *The Writing Report Card,*

1984–1988 (Princeton, N.J.: Educational Testing Service, January 1990).

12. Ehrlich, "America's Schools," p. 129.

13. Joseph Berger, "Companies Step in Where Schools Fail," *New York Times,* September 26, 1989, p. A1.

14. Edwin Newman, "Illiteracy: Death in Life," op-ed, *New York Times,* September 8, 1988, p. A29.

15. Lewis J. Lord et al., "The Brain Battle," *U.S. News & World Report,* January 19, 1987, p. 59.

16. National Commission on Excellence in Education, *A Nation at Risk,* p. 11.

17. Telephone interview, Fred Beamer, Office of Educational Research and Improvement, National Center for Education Statistics, U.S. Department of Education, July 26, 1990. See National Center for Education Statistics, *Digest of Education Statistics: 1989* (Washington, D.C.: U.S. Department of Education, Office of Educational Research and Improvement, December 1989), p. 20, table 108.

18. See discussion in Victor R. Fuchs, *Women's Quest for Economic Equality* (Cambridge, Mass.: Harvard University Press, 1988), pp. 104–6.

19. National Assessment of Educational Progress, *Crossroads in American Education* (Princeton, N.J.: Educational Testing Service, February 1989).

20. Ibid., p. 5.

21. "They Can Add, But . . ." editorial, *Washington Post,* May 18, 1988, p. A22.

22. National Assessment of Educational Progress, *Crossroads in American Education,* pp. 20–21.

23. James J. Kilpatrick, "Lost in Geography," *Washington Post,* April 2, 1987, p. A19.

24. Ibid.

25. Ibid.

26. Telephone interview, Vance Grant, Statistical Services, National Center for Education Statistics, U.S. Department of Education, May 31, 1990.

27. According to the Report of the Task Force on International Education, 90 percent of high school students graduate. *America*

in Transition: The International Frontier (Washington, D.C.: National Governors' Association, 1989). See also Thomas P. Rohlen, *Japan's High Schools* (Berkeley: University of California Press, 1983), p. 3.

28. Gary Putka, "College-Completion Rates Are Said to Decline Sharply," *Wall Street Journal,* July 28, 1989, p. B1.
29. Select Committee on Children, Youth and Families, *U.S. Children and Their Families: Current Conditions and Recent Trends, 1989* (Washing-ton, D.C.: U.S. House of Representatives, 1989), pp. 188–89. See also National Commission on the Role of the School . . . , *Code Blue,* p. 3.
30. Janet E. Gans and Dale A. Blyth, *America's Adolescents: How Healthy Are They?* (Chicago: American Medical Association, 1990), p. 40.
31. John Kass, "Psychiatrists Get Rich, But Do Patients Profit?" *Chicago Tribune,* May 29, 1989, p. 1.
32. Study by E. Mavis Hetherington reported in Jane E. Brody, "Divorce's Stress Exacts Long-Term Toll," *New York Times,* December 13, 1983, p. C5.
33. Fuchs, *Woman's Quest for Economic Equality,* p. 106.
34. Select Committee on Children, Youth and Families, *Eating Disorders: The Impact on Children and Families* (Washington, D.C.: U.S. House of Representatives, July 31, 1987), p. 3.
35. Testimony of Laurel M. Mellin, Director, Center for Adolescent Obesity, School of Medicine, University of California, San Francisco, before the Select Committee on Children, Youth and Families, in *Eating Disorders,* p. 19.
36. Ibid.
37. Sharon Johnson, "Anorexia As Family Problem," *New York Times,* April 20, 1987, p. C12.
38. Gans and Blyth, *America's Adolescents: How Healthy Are They?* p. 17.
39. Select Committee on Children, Youth and Families, *U.S. Children and Their Families,* pp. 230–31.
40. Gans and Blyth, *America's Adolescents: How Healthy Are They?* p. xi.
41. Fuchs, *Woman's Quest for Economic Equality,* p. 111.
42. Information on labor force participation rate of mothers with

children under eighteen from telephone interview, Jim Markey, August 12, 1990, Bureau of Labor Statistics. Source: *Handbook of Labor Force Statistics* (Washington, D.C.: U.S. Department of Labor, Bureau of Labor Statistics, August 1989), table 57 (mothers), calculated from tables 4 and 5.

43. William R. Mattox, Jr., "The Family Time Famine," *Family Policy* 3, no. 1 (1990): 2. See also William R. Mattox, Jr., "The Parent Trap: So Many Bills, So Little Time," *Policy Review* no. 55 (Winter 1991), pp. 6–13.

44. Deborah Fallows, *A Mother's Work,* cited by Megan Rosenfeld in "Thanks a Bunch," *Washington Post,* November 9, 1986, p. H3.

45. "The Changing American Vacation," *Newsweek,* August 28, 1989, p. 8.

46. *Mass. Mutual Family Values Study* (Washington, D.C.: Mellman & Lazarus Inc., 1989).

47. Telephone interview, Bob Cleveland, U.S. Bureau of the Census, April 30, 1990, and May 2, 1990.

48. Subrata N. Chakravarty and Katherine Weisman, "Consuming Our Children?" *Forbes,* November 14, 1988, p. 228.

49. Kirsten Downey, "Typical Buyer: A Vanishing Breed," *Washington Post,* February 10, 1990, p. E1.

50. John Tierney, "Wired for Stress," *New York Times Magazine,* May 15, 1988, p. 49.

51. Ibid., pp. 49–51.

52. Quoted in ibid., p. 82. See also Robert Karasek and Töres Theorell, *Healthy Work: Stress, Productivity, and the Reconstruction of Working Life* (New York: Basic Books, 1990), p. 9.

53. Quoted in "Wired for Stress," p. 82.

54. Cited in Arlie Hochschild with Anne Machung, *The Second Shift: Working Parents and the Revolution at Home* (New York: Viking, 1989), p. 3.

55. Ibid., p. 9.

56. Gina Kolata, "Mothers with Dark Circles," *New York Times Book Review,* June 25, 1989, p. 3.

57. Nancy Gibbs, "How America Has Run Out of Time," *Time,* April 24, 1989, p. 59.

58. Ibid., p. 58.

59. Rosabeth Moss Kanter, *When Giants Learn to Dance: Mastering the Challenges of Strategy, Management, and Careers in the 1990s* (New York: Simon & Schuster, 1989), p. 268 (from a Harris poll).

60. Amanda Bennett, "Early to Bed . . . A Look at the CEO Workweek," *Wall Street Journal,* March 20, 1987, p. 22D. See also Ford S. Worthy, "You're Probably Working Too Hard," *Fortune,* April 27, 1987, pp. 135–40; and Sally Solo, "Stop Whining and Get Back to Work," *Fortune,* March 12, 1990, pp. 49–50.

61. Pamela Mendels, "Eyes Are Off the Clock," *Newsday,* August 19, 1990, p. 58.

62. David E. Pitt, "Metro-North Reports a Rise in Riders," *New York Times,* August 17, 1989.

63. Kanter, *When Giants Learn to Dance,* p. 271.

64. Telephone interview, Jim Markey, August 12, 1990. (Sources: Unpublished data and data derived from January 1986 *Current Population Survey;* Francis W. Horvath, "The Pulse of Economic Change: Displaced Workers of 1981–1985," *Monthly Labor Review* 110, no. 6 (June 1987), pp. 3–12.

65. Kanter, *When Giants Learn to Dance,* p. 270.

66. Ibid., p. 271.

67. Ibid., p. 279.

68. Interview, November 15, 1989.

69. Kanter, *When Giants Learn to Dance,* p. 285.

70. Ibid., p. 273.

71. Ibid., p. 274.

72. Ibid., p. 268.

73. William H. Whyte, Jr., *The Organization Man* (New York: Simon & Schuster, 1956).

74. Quoted in Walter Kiechel III, "The Workaholic Generation," *Fortune,* April 10, 1989, p. 51.

75. J. L. Richardson et al., "Substance Use Among Eighth-Grade Students Who Take Care of Themselves After School," *Pediatrics* 84, no. 3 (September 1989): 556–66.

76. Linda Albert and Michael Popkin, *Quality Parenting* (New York: Random House, 1987), p. 4.

77. This list owes much to the work of Andrée Aelion Brooks; see

Children of Fast-Track Parents (New York: Viking, 1989), pp. 29–30.

78. Brian O'Reilly, "Why Grade 'A' Execs Get an 'F' as Parents," *Fortune,* January 1, 1990, pp. 36–37.

79. Quoted in ibid., p. 38.

80. Walter Kiechel III, "The Workaholic Generation," pp. 52–53.

81. Telephone interview, February 1, 1991.

82. *Studies in Marriage and the Family* (U.S. Bureau of the Census, Current Population Reports Series P-23, No. 162, 1989), p. 5.

83. Ibid.

84. Judith S. Wallerstein and Sandra Blakeslee, *Second Chances: Men, Women and Children a Decade After Divorce* (New York: Ticknor & Fields, 1989), p. 12.

85. *Child Support and Alimony: 1987* (U.S. Bureau of the Census, Current Population Reports Series P-23, No. 167, June 1990), p. 3, table B.

86. Lucy Marsh Yee, "What Really Happens in Child Support Cases: An Empirical Study of the Establishment and Enforcement of Child Support Orders in the Denver District Court," *Law Journal of Denver* 57 (1980): 21–36.

87. *Child Support and Alimony: 1987,* p. 7, table E.

88. Ibid., pp. 5–6, tables C and D.

89. Sylvia Ann Hewlett, *A Lesser Life: The Myth of Women's Liberation in America* (New York: Morrow, 1986), p. 82.

90. Greg J. Duncan and Saul D. Hoffmann, "A Reconsideration of the Economic Consequences of Marital Dissolution," *Demography* 22, no. 4 (November 1985): 485–97. In California, Weitzman comes up with some even more startling figures, she finds that, in this state, divorced women experience a 73 percent decline in their standard of living after divorce, while men experience a 42 percent rise. See Lenore J. Weitzman, *The Divorce Revolution* (New York: The Free Press, 1985), p. 323.

91. Peter T. Kilborn, "For Many Women, One Job Isn't Enough," *New York Times,* February 15, 1990, p. A22.

92. Frank F. Furstenberg, Jr., and Kathleen Mullan Harris, "The Disappearing Father? Divorce and the Waning Significance of Biological Parenthood," draft, Department of Sociology, University of Pennsylvania, March 1990. See also Frank F. Furstenberg, Jr., and Christine Winquist Nord, "Parenting Apart: Pat-

terns of Childrearing After Marital Disruption," *Journal of Marriage and the Family* 47, no. 4 (November 1985): 874.

93. Quoted in Tamar Lewin, "Father's Vanishing Act Called Common Drama," *New York Times,* June 4, 1990, p. A18.

94. Wallerstein and Blakeslee, *Second Chances,* p. 149.

95. Cited in Nicholas Davidson, "Life Without Father," *Policy Review* no. 51 (Winter 1990): 40–44.

96. Wallerstein and Blakeslee, *Second Chances,* p. 238.

97. Carmen Noemi Velez and Patricia Cohen, "Suicidal Behavior and Ideation in a Community Sample of Children: Maternal and Youth Reports," *Journal of the American Academy of Child and Adolescent Psychiatry* 27, no. 3 (May 1988): 349–56.

98. Helen S. Merskey and G. T. Swart, "Family Background and Physical Health of Adolescents Admitted to an Inpatient Psychiatric Unit: 1, Principal Caregivers," *Canadian Journal of Psychiatry* 34, no. 2 (March 1989): 79–83.

99. Cited in Davidson, "Life Without Father," p. 42.

100. Robert H. Coombs and John Landsverk, "Parenting Styles and Substance Use During Childhood and Adolescence," *Journal of Marriage and the Family* 50, no. 2 (May 1988): 473–82.

101. Wallerstein and Blakeslee, *Second Chances,* p. 55.

102. Interviews, September and October 1988.

103. National Association of Elementary School Principals (NAESP), Staff Report, "One-Parent Families and Their Children," *Principal* 60, no. 1 (September 1980): 31–37.

104. Cited in Davidson, "Life Without Father," p. 41.

105. Sheila Fitzgerald Krein and Andrea H. Beller, "Educational Attainment of Children from Single-Parent Families: Differences by Exposure, Gender and Race," *Demography* 25, no. 2 (May 1988): 221–33.

106. Norma Radin, "The Role of the Father in Cognitive, Academic, and Intellectual Development," in *The Role of the Father in Child Development,* ed. Michael E. Lamb (New York: Wiley, 1981), pp. 410–11.

107. Lyn Carlsmith, "Effect of Early Father Absence on Scholastic Aptitude," *Harvard Educational Review* 31, no. 1 (1964): 3–21.

108. "1990 Nielsen Report on TV" (Nielsen Media Research, 1990).

109. Bernice Anderson, Nancy Mead, and Susan Sullivan, "Televi-

sion: What Do National Assessment Results Tell Us?" (Princeton, N.J.: NAEP, December 1986). See also Richard Zoglin, "Is TV Ruining Our Children?" *Time,* October 15, 1990, pp. 75–76.

110. See, for example, Karl Zinsmeister, "Brave New World," *Policy Review,* no. 44 (Spring 1988): 40–48.

111. See, for example, Claire Etaugh, "Effects of Nonmaternal Care on Children: Research Evidence and Popular Views," *American Psychologist* 35, no. 4 (April 1980): 309–19.

112. See discussion in Zinsmeister, "Brave New World," p. 42.

113. David Eggebeen and Peter Uhlenberg, "Changes in the Organization of Men's Lives: 1960–1980," *Family Relations* 34 (April 1985): 255.

114. Jerome Kagan, *The Nature of the Child* (New York: Basic Books, 1984), p. 108.

115. Davidson, "Life Without Father," p. 41.

116. David Gutmann, *Reclaimed Powers: Toward a New Psychology of Men and Women in Later Life* (New York: Basic Books, 1987), p. 198.

117. Nick Stinnett and John DeFrain, *Secrets of Strong Families* (Boston: Little, Brown, 1985), p. 81.

Chapter 4. Private Choices: Looking Out for Number One

1. Garrison Keillor, *We Are Still Married: Stories and Letters* (New York: Viking, 1989), pp. 55–56.

2. Timothy M. Smeeding, "The Debt, the Deficit, and Disadvantaged Children: Generational Impacts and Age, Period, and Cohort Effects," in *The Debt and the Twin Deficits Debate,* ed. James M. Rock (Mountain View, Calif.: Bristlecone Books/ Mayfield, 1991), p. 47, table 2-7.

3. Robert N. Bellah, Richard Madsen, William M. Sullivan, Ann Swidler, and Steven M. Tipton, *Habits of the Heart: Individualism and Commitment in American Life* (New York: Perennial Library, 1986).

4. Ibid., p. 101.

5. Christopher Lasch, *The Culture of Narcissism: American Life in An Age of Diminishing Expectations* (New York: Warner, 1979), pp. 42–43, 30.

6. Daniel Yankelovich, *New Rules: Searching for Self-Fulfillment in a*

World Turned Upside Down (New York: Random House, 1981), p. 91.

7. Bellah et al., *Habits of the Heart,* p. 109.

8. Yankelovich, *New Rules,* p. 8.

9. Arthur Miller, *Death of a Salesman* (New York: Viking, 1949), p. 22.

10. Betty Friedan, *The Feminine Mystique* (New York: Dell, 1984), p. 256.

11. Ibid., p. 305.

12. Mary Ann Glendon, *Abortion and Divorce in Western Law: American Failures, European Challenges* (Cambridge, Mass.: Harvard University Press, 1987), p. 66.

13. The concept of "no-responsibility" divorce was first developed by Glendon. See Mary Ann Glendon, *State, Law and Family* (Amsterdam: North Holland, 1977), p. 233; Mary Ann Glendon, *The New Family and the New Property* (Toronto: Butterworths, 1981), pp. 4–5; and Mary Ann Glendon, *The Transformation of Family Law* (Chicago: University of Chicago Press, 1989), p. 149.

14. Glendon, *The Transformation of Family Law,* p. 189.

15. Glendon, *Abortion and Divorce in Western Law,* p. 81.

16. *Child Support and Alimony: 1987* (U.S. Bureau of the Census, Current Population Reports Series P-23, No. 167, June 1990), pp. 8, 11, tables J and K.

17. Cited in Sylvia Ann Hewlett, *A Lesser Life* (New York: Morrow, 1986), p. 411n21. See also New Jersey Supreme Court Task Force, *Women in the Courts,* June 1984, p. 80.

18. Beverly Stephen, "In Pursuit of Justice for Women in the Courts," *New York Daily News,* August 11, 1984, p. 10.

19. "Usual Weekly Earnings of Wage and Salary Workers; Third Quarter 1990," News Release, Bureau of Labor Statistics (US DL 90-557, October 29, 1990).

20. National Center for Health Statistics, "Advance Report of Final Divorce Statistics, 1987." Monthly Vital Statistics Report 38, no. 12, supplement 2 (Hyattsville, Md.: Public Health Service, 1990).

21. Lenore J. Weitzman and Ruth B. Dixon, "The Alimony Myth: Does No-Fault Divorce Make a Difference?" *Family Law Quarterly* 14 (Fall 1980): 185.

22. Cited in Hewlett, *A Lesser Life,* p. 56. See also Marilyn Chase, "Single Trouble: The No-Fault Divorce Has a Fault of Its Own, Many Women Learn," *Wall Street Journal,* January 21, 1985, p. 1.

23. Greg J. Duncan and Saul D. Hoffman, "A Reconsideration of the Economic Consequences of Marital Dissolution," *Demography* 22, no. 4 (November 1985): 485–97.

24. Interview, April 3, 1989.

25. Judith S. Wallerstein and Sandra Blakeslee, *Second Chances: Men, Women and Children a Decade After Divorce* (New York: Ticknor & Fields, 1989), pp. 18, 156–57.

26. Ibid., p. 157.

27. Glendon, *Abortion and Divorce in Western Law,* p. 105.

28. Ibid., p. 84.

29. Ibid., p. 85.

30. Ibid., p. 86. The generosity of the Swedish benefit-service package is described in S. Kamerman and A. Kahn, *Income Transfers for Families with Children: An Eight-Country Study* (Philadelphia: Temple University Press, 1983), pp. 60, 71.

31. Quoted in Lenore J. Weitzman, *The Marriage Contract* (New York: Free Press, 1981), p. 152.

32. Ibid.

33. Glendon, *Abortion and Divorce in Western Law,* p. 109. See also Glendon, *The New Family and the New Property* and *The Transformation of Family Law.*

34. These themes are developed in Alan Wolfe, *Whose Keeper?* (Berkeley: University of California Press, 1989), pp. 27–107.

35. Cathy Trost, "How Children's Safety Can Be Put in Jeopardy by Day-Care Personnel," *Wall Street Journal,* October 18, 1988, p. A1.

36. Ibid.

37. "The Status of Some of the Major Pieces of Legislation Before Congress," *New York Times,* October 17, 1990, p. A25. Included in the budget package finally agreed upon by Congress and the White House in October 1990 was a child-care bill that offered a measure of regulation. Licensing, registration, and training regulations for child-care providers were to be tightened, but Congress—under pressure from the White House—

backed off requiring that states set up child-care committees to oversee and coordinate child care activities. Thus, it is unclear whether the new standards will be enforced.

38. Peter Applebone, "Toddler Is Rescued After 2½ Days in a Texas Well," *New York Times,* October 17, 1989, p. A1.

39. Lynette Friedrich Cofer and Robin Smith Jacobvitz, "The Loss of Moral Turf: Mass Media and Family Values," in *Rebuilding the Nest: A New Commitment to the American Family,* ed. David Blankenhorn, Steven Bayme, and Jean Bethke Elshtain (Milwaukee: Family Service America, 1990), p. 185. My analysis of the deregulation of the television industry relies substantially on Cofer and Jacobvitz.

40. Ibid., p. 188.

41. Ibid.; see also Aletha Stein and Lynette Friedrich, "Impact of Television on Children and Youth," in *Review of Child Development Research,* vol. 5, ed. E. M. Hetherington (Chicago: University of Chicago Press, 1975), pp. 183–256.

42. Cited in Fred M. Hechinger, "About Education," *New York Times,* February 28, 1990, p. 1.

43. Ibid.

44. Combined viewing audience calculations based on figures from telephone interview, Chris Tardio, publicist at Harpo, Inc., November 1, 1990; telephone interview, "Donahue" production office, November 1, 1990; and telephone interview, Rikki Leopold, publicist at "Geraldo," November 1, 1990. According to the Nielsen Reports, 35 percent of this viewing audience are teens and children. See *1990 Nielsen Report on TV* (Nielsen Media Research, 1990), p. 8. It should be noted that as of January 1991, CBS moved "Geraldo" back to its 9:00 A.M. slot. This move was prompted by public criticism of the program.

45. Verne Gay, "A Makeover for 'Geraldo,' " *Newsday,* January 10, 1990, part II, p. 3.

46. Nan Signorelli, "Children and Adolescents on Television: A Consistent Pattern of Devaluation," *Journal of Early Adolescence* 7, no. 3 (1987): 255–68.

47. Cofer and Jacobvitz, "The Loss of Moral Turf: Mass Media and Family Values," p. 198.

48. *1990 Nielsen Report on TV,* p. 8.

49. Cofer and Jacobvitz, "The Loss of Moral Turf: Mass Media and Family Values," p. 192.

50. Dorothy G. Singer and Jerome L. Singer, "Introductory Comments," *Journal of Early Adolescence* 7, no. 3 (1987): 5.

51. Richard A. Easterlin and Eileen M. Crimmins, "Recent Social Trends: Changes in Personal Aspirations of American Youth," *Sociology and Social Research* 72, no. 4 (July 1988): 217–23.

52. Bill Moyers, *Bill Moyers: A World of Ideas* (New York: Doubleday, 1989), p. 66.

53. Lois A. Weithorn, "Mental Hospitalization of Troublesome Youth: An Analysis of Skyrocketing Admission Rates," *Stanford Law Review* (February 1988): 819–20.

54. John Kass, "Psychiatrists Get Rich, But Do Patients Profit?" *Chicago Tribune,* May 29, 1989, p. 1. See also Kass, "Social Scientists Discover They've Built a Monster," *Chicago Tribune,* June 4, 1989. In 1971 private hospital admissions accounted for 37 percent of juvenile mental hospitalizations; in 1980 the proportion had risen to 61 percent. See National Center for Health Statistics, *Health, United States, 1989* (Hyattsville, Md.: Public Health Service, 1990), p. 200.

55. Kass, "Psychiatrists Get Rich," p. 5.

56. Ira M. Schwartz, "Hospitalization of Adolescents for Psychiatric and Substance Abuse Treatment: Legal and Ethical Issues," *Journal of Adolescent Health Care* 10, no. 6 (1989): 473–78.

57. John Kass, "Enough Is Enough, Youth Psychiatry Critics Say," *Chicago Tribune,* May 31, 1989, p. 14.

58. Kass, "Psychiatrists Get Rich," p. 1.

59. Kass, "Enough Is Enough," p. 14.

60. Ibid.

61. Weithorn, "Mental Hospitalization of Troublesome Youth," pp. 808, 781.

62. Ibid., p. 809.

63. Kass, "Enough Is Enough," p. 14; and "Psychiatrists Get Rich," p. 5.

64. John Kass, "Psychiatric Ads Bring Patients and Protests," *Chicago Tribune,* May 30, 1989.

65. Kass, "Psychiatrists Get Rich," p. 5.

66. "Born Hooked: Confronting the Impact of Perinatal Substance Abuse," Hearing Before the Select Committee on Children, Youth and Families, April 27, 1989 (Washington, D.C.: U.S. House of Representatives, 1989), p. 1.

67. Ibid., p. 89.

68. Ibid., p. 1.

69. Ibid.

70. Andrea Stone, "Drug Epidemic's Tiny Victims: Crack Babies Born to Life of Suffering," *USA Today,* June 8, 1989, p. 3A.

71. Douglas J. Besharov, "Crack Babies: The Worst Threat Is Mom Herself," *Washington Post,* August 6, 1989, p. B1. See also Douglas J. Besharov, "The Children of Crack: Will We Protect Them?" *Public Welfare* 47 (Fall 1989): 7.

72. *New York Times,* "AIDS Is Reported as No. 9 Cause of Death Among Children 1 to 4," December 20, 1988, p. A18. According to Dr. Antonia Novello, deputy director of the National Institute of Child Health and Human Development, "however tragic, sorely underestimate the true scope of pediatric AIDS." She noted that the official figures reflected only those cases that were reported to the Centers for Disease Control, and that for every child who meets the Centers' definition of AIDS, there are probably two to ten others who are infected with HIV.

    Information on symptoms of crack-addicted babies from "Congressional Testimony" by Dr. Ira J. Chasnoff, president, National Association for Perinatal Addiction Research and Education (NAPARE), associate professor, Pediatrics & Psychiatry, Northwestern University Medical School, July 31, 1989.

73. "Born Hooked," p. 112. Statement by Dr. Wendy Chavkin.

74. Barry Bearak, "One Mother's Story: Hooked and Pregnant: A Time Bomb," *Los Angeles Times,* August 22, 1989, p. 1.

75. Susan Diesenhouse, "Drug Treatment Is Scarcer than Ever for Women," *New York Times,* January 7, 1990, p. E26. According to Mr. Vuppala, of the Health Systems Agency, a public planning group, hospital care for drug-addicted infants costs two or three times more than that for normal low-weight infants, because of repeated hospitalizations. Telephone interview, January 22, 1990.

76. "Cost of Caring for 'Drug Babies,'" memorandum to Van McMurtry, staff director, Senate Finance Committee, from Senator Lloyd Bentsen, November 15, 1989, p. 1.

77. Adam Smith, *Wealth of Nations* (New York: Modern Library, 1937), p. 423.

78. John Stuart Mill, "On Liberty," in *Utilitarianism, Liberty, and Representative Government* (New York: Dutton, 1951), p. 85.

79. Robert Lekachman, *A History of Economic Ideas* (New York: Harper & Row, 1959), p. 95.

80. Mill, "On Liberty," pp. 95–96.

81. Ibid., p. 216.

82. Cary L. Moss, staff attorney, American Civil Liberties Union, Women's Rights Project, New York. Quoted in "Punishing Pregnant Addicts: Debate, Dismay, No Solution," *New York Times,* September 10, 1989, p. E5.

83. Martin E. P. Seligman, "Boomer Blues," *Psychology Today,* October 1988, pp. 50–55.

84. Jean Bethke Elshtain, "The Family and Civic Life," in *Rebuilding the Nest: A New Commitment to the American Family,* ed. Blankenhorn, Bayme, and Elshtain, p. 131.

85. Gunnar Myrdal developed the concept of cumulative causation in *Economic Theory and Underdeveloped Regions* (London: Duckworth, 1957), p. 123.

86. These themes are elaborated on in Alan Wolfe, *Whose Keeper? Social Science and Moral Obligation* (Berkeley: University of California Press, 1989), pp. 51–78, 107–32.

87. Andrew Cherlin, *Marriage, Divorce, Remarriage* (Cambridge, Mass.: Harvard University Press, 1982), pp. 47–48.

88. Samuel H. Preston, "Children and the Elderly: Divergent Paths for America's Dependents," *Demography* 21, no. 4 (November 1984): 445.

89. Ibid.

90. Sue Miller, *The Good Mother* (New York: Harper & Row, 1986).

91. Ibid., p. 122.

92. Ibid., p. 124.

93. Ibid., p. 10.

Chapter 5. Public Choices: Shortchanging the Future

1. Mary Augusta Rodgers, "Medicare Paid $65 to Do Mom's Toenails," op-ed, *New York Times,* July 18, 1989.
2. Daniel Patrick Moynihan, *Family and Nation* (New York: Harcourt Brace Jovanovich, 1986), p. 96.
3. Michael D. Hurd, "The Economic Status of the Elderly," *Science* 244 (May 12, 1989): 660.
4. Robert W. Kasten, Jr., "Yes, Cut Social Security Taxes," op-ed, *New York Times,* February 15, 1990, p. A31.
5. Ibid.
6. Ibid. More than 74 percent of taxpayers pay more in combined payroll taxes than they do in income taxes.
7. Subrata N. Chakravarty and Katherine Weisman, "Consuming Our Children?" *Forbes,* November 14, 1988, p. 228.
8. Ibid., p. 225.
9. Ibid. See also Phillip Longman, "Justice Between Generations," *Atlantic Monthly,* June 1985, p. 40.
10. Fabian Linden, *Midlife and Beyond* (New York: Consumer Research Center, Conference Board, Inc., 1985), pp. 5–8.
11. Telephone interview, Mark Littman, Bureau of the Census, August 30, 1990. Source: *Money, Income and Poverty Status in the United States: 1988* (U.S. Bureau of the Census, Current Population Reports Series P-60, No. 166, October 1989).
12. Meredith Minkler, "The Politics of Generational Equity," *Social Policy* 17, no. 3 (Winter 1987): 49.
13. Chakravarty and Weisman, "Consuming Our Children?" p. 230.
14. Stephen Crystal, *America's Old Age Crisis* (New York: Basic Books, 1984), p. x.
15. Minkler, "The Politics of Generational Equity," p. 48. See also Richard J. Margolis, *Risking Old Age in America* (Boulder, Colo.: Westview Press, 1990), pp. 3–53.
16. Telephone interview, Ed Welniak, Bureau of the Census, August 29, 1990. Source: (U.S. Bureau of the Census, Current Population Reports Series P-60, No. 162, February 1989), table 33, p. 129.

17. John Tierney, "Old Money, New Power," *New York Times Magazine,* October 23, 1988, p. 103.
18. Simmons Market Research, Inc., conducted a survey among members of AARP for *Modern Maturity* magazine which showed that 37.1 percent took foreign trips within the last three years.
19. In 1987 federal outlays totaled $1,003.8 billion; $48.3 billion or 4.8 percent was spent on children and $230.4 billion or 22.9 percent was spent on the elderly. Telephone interview, Richard Krop, Congressional Budget Office, November 21, 1990. Similar estimates can be found in Timothy M. Smeeding, "The Debt, the Deficit, and Disadvantaged Children: Generational Impacts and Age, Period and Cohort Effects," in *The Debt and the Twin Deficits Debate,* ed. James M. Rock (Mountain View, Calif.: Bristlecone Books/Mayfield, 1991). For poverty figures, see Bureau of the Census, *Money, Income and Poverty Status in the United States: 1988;* and National Center for Children in Poverty, *Five Million Children: A Statistical Profile of Our Poorest Young Citizens* (New York: Columbia University School of Public Health, 1990).
20. Chakravarty and Weisman, "Consuming Our Children?" p. 228.
21. Sylvia Ann Hewlett, "Running Hard Just to Keep Up," *Time,* special issue, Fall 1990, p. 54.
22. Ibid.
23. Telephone interview, Jim Markey, Bureau of Labor Statistics, August 17, 1990. Source: *Handbook of Labor Statistics* (Washington, D.C.: U.S. Department of Labor, Bureau of Labor Statistics, August 1989), table 57.
24. Chakravarty and Weisman, "Consuming Our Children?" p. 230. See also James R. Wetzel, "American Families: 75 Years of Change," *Monthly Labor Review* 113, no. 3 (March 1990): 9.
25. Telephone interview, David Kellerman, Bureau of the Census, September 13, 1990.
26. National Center for Health Statistics, *Health, United States, 1989* (Hyattsville, Md.: Public Health Service, 1990), p. 256, table 127.

27. Lee Smith, "What Do We Owe to the Elderly," *Fortune,* March 27, 1989, pp. 54–62.
28. Ibid., p. 55.
29. Peter G. Peterson, "The Morning After," *Atlantic Monthly,* October 1987, pp. 63–64. These arguments are expanded in Peter G. Peterson and Neil Howe, *On Borrowed Time: How the Growth in Entitlement Spending Threatens America's Future* (San Francisco: Institute for Contemporary Studies, 1988).
30. *A Vision for America's Future, An Agenda for the 1990s: A Children's Defense Budget* (Washington, D.C.: Children's Defense Fund, 1989), p. 42.
31. A. E. Benjamin, Paul W. Newacheck, and Hannah Wolfe, "Intergenerational Equity and Public Spending." Paper presented at the 115th meeting of the American Public Health Association in New Orleans, October 21, 1987.
32. Smith, "What Do We Owe the Elderly?" p. 55.
33. Ibid.
34. Ernest F. Hollings, "America: Ronald Reagan's Washington Is Crippled and Broke," op-ed, *Washington Post.*
35. Allan R. Gold, "The Struggle to Make Do Without Health Insurance," *New York Times,* July 30, 1990, p. A1.
36. Ibid.
37. Peterson, "The Morning After," p. 62.
38. Lars-Erick Nelson, "The Dark, Costly Side of 'Gray Power,'" *Daily News,* October 22, 1990.
39. Telephone interview, Mark Desautels, Press Liason Office, Congressional Budget Office, February 28, 1991. Source: "Economic and Budget Outlook, Fiscal Years 1991–96" (Washington, D.C.: Congressional Budget Office, January 1991).
40. John Bickerman, "Our Military Pensions *Are* a Scandal," *Washington Post,* March 10, 1985, p. C1.
41. Telephone interview, Richard Krop, Congressional Budget Office, November 21, 1990. See also Smeeding, "The Debt, the Deficit, and Disadvantaged Children," p. 47.
42. Peterson, "The Morning After," p. 62.
43. Smeeding, "The Debt, the Deficit, and Disadvantaged Children," p. 47.

392 NOTES

44. Peter G. Peterson, "The Budget, from Comedy to Tragedy," *New York Times,* September 16, 1990, p. E23.

45. See discussion in Samuel H. Preston, "Children and the Elderly in the U.S.," *Scientific American* 251, no. 6 (December 1984): 47.

46. See discussion in Samuel H. Preston, "Children and the Elderly: Divergent Paths for America's Dependents," *Demography* 21, no. 4 (November 1984): 446.

47. Ibid.

48. Tierney, "Old Money, New Power," pp. 52ff.

49. Ibid.

50. Ibid., pp. 103, 99.

51. Ibid., p. 69.

52. Longman, "Justice Between Generations," p. 39.

53. Linden, *Midlife and Beyond,* p. 3.

54. See *Profile of the* Modern Maturity *Reader 1989,* and Linden, *Midlife and Beyond,* p. 9.

55. Linden, *Midlife and Beyond,* p. 10.

56. Longman, "Justice Between Generations," p. 78.

57. National Center for Health Statistics, *Health, United States, 1989,* p. 256, table 157.

58. Preston, "Children and the Elderly: Divergent Paths," p. 446.

59. Wetzel, "American Families," pp. 8–9, chart 3.

60. Ibid., p. 9.

61. Telephone interview, Steve Rawlings, U.S. Bureau of the Census, August 29, 1990.

62. Preston, "Children and the Elderly: Divergent Paths," p. 447.

63. Ibid.

64. Peterson, "The Budget, from Comedy to Tragedy."

65. Peterson, "The Morning After," p. 62.

66. Ibid., p. 64.

67. Ibid.

68. Ibid., p. 68.

69. Ibid.

70. Annetta Miller with Mary Hager and Betsy Roberts, "The Elderly Duke It Out," *Newsweek,* September 11, 1989, p. 42.

71. Eleanor Clift with Mary Hager, "A Victory for the Haves?" *Newsweek,* October 16, 1989, p. 38.

72. Miller et al., "The Elderly Duke It Out," p. 42. See also Steven Findlay, "Finally, a Health-Cost Cap," *U.S. News & World Report,* June 13, 1988, pp. 63–64.
73. Julie Kosterlitz, "Catastrophic Coverage a Catastrophe?" *National Journal,* November 19, 1988, p. 2949. See also Miller et al., "The Elderly Duke It Out," p. 43.
74. Kosterlitz, "Catastrophic Coverage a Catastrophe?" p. 2952.
75. Helen Dewar, "Bentsen Opposes Rollback of Medicare Surcharges," *Washington Post,* January 12, 1989, p. A5.
76. James Tobin, from a 1964 essay, quoted in Longman, "Justice Between Generations," p. 76.
77. William Baumol, quoted in ibid.
78. Merrill Lynch, "Our Neglected Infrastructure," *Weekly Economic and Financial Commentary,* May 19, 1989, p. 3.
79. Alfred L. Malabre, Jr., "Economic Roadblock: Infrastructure Neglect," *Wall Street Journal,* July 30, 1990, p. A1.
80. Joan C. Szabo, "Our Crumbling Infrastructure," *Nation's Business* 77, no. 8 (August 1989): 16.
81. Lynch, "Our Neglected Infrastructure," pp. 6–8; and Szabo, "Our Crumbling Infrastructure," p. 16.
82. James E. Lebherz, "U.S. Must Face Infrastructure Problem," *Washington Post,* October 30, 1988, p. H4.
83. "New York Is Falling Apart," CBS News, "60 Minutes," September 10, 1989.
84. Malabre, "Economic Roadblock," p. A1.
85. Ibid.
86. Benjamin M. Friedman, "The Campaign's Hidden Issue," *The New York Review of Books,* October 13, 1988, p. 26.
87. Peterson, "The Morning After," p. 48.
88. Ibid., pp. 47–48.
89. Richard G. Darman, "Beyond the Deficit Problem: 'Now-now-ism' and 'The New Balance,' " address to the National Press Club, Washington, D.C., July 20, 1989, p. 7.
90. Ibid., p. 3.
91. Ibid.
92. Alan Murray, "The Outlook: Dick Darman Wants His Maypo!" *Wall Street Journal,* July 31, 1989.
93. Robert N. Bellah, Richard Madsen, William M. Sullivan, Ann

Swidler, and Steven M. Tipton, *Habits of the Heart: Individualism and Commitment in American Life* (New York: Perennial Library, 1986).

94. *John F. Kennedy,* Public Papers of the President of the United States (Washington, D.C.: U.S. Government Printing Office), p. 3.

95. David E. Rosenbaum, "Prof. Moynihan Wakes the Class with Truth About Taxes," *New York Times,* January 21, 1990, p. E4. See also Kasten, "Yes, Cut Social Security Taxes."

96. Joe Klein, "Fussbudgetry," *New York,* February 12, 1990, p. 12.

97. David Wessel, "Social Security: Myths and Moynihan," *Wall Street Journal,* January 15, 1990, p. 1.

98. Longman, "Justice Between Generations," p. 41.

99. Preston, "Children and the Elderly: Divergent Paths," p. 451.

Chapter 6. Government Policy and the Beginnings of Life

1. Diana Hembree and Julie Scheff, "The Preventable Tragedy," *Parenting* (August 1989): 69–70.

2. National Commission to Prevent Infant Mortality, "Infant Mortality Fact Sheet," January 1990.

3. Ibid. See also Milt Freudenheim, "In Pursuit of the Perfect Baby," *New York Times,* December 28, 1988, p. A9.

4. The Alan Guttmacher Institute, "15 Million Women of Reproductive Age Have No Maternity Insurance," press release, December 15, 1987; Rachel Benson Gold, Asta M. Kenney, and Susheela Singh, "Paying for Maternity Care in the United States," *Family Planning Perspectives* 19, no. 5 (September/October 1987): 202; and Philip Hilts, "Life Expectancy for Blacks in U.S. Shows Sharp Drop," *New York Times,* November 29, 1990, p. A1.

5. Sonia L. Nazario, "High Infant Mortality Is a Persistent Blotch on Health Care in US," *Wall Street Journal,* October 19, 1988, p. A1.

6. Institute of Medicine, "Prenatal Care: Reaching Mothers, Reaching Infants" (Washington, D.C.: National Academy Press, 1988).

7. Maternal and Child Health Program, "The Campaign for Healthier Babies" (New York: March of Dimes Birth Defects Foundation, March 1989), pp. 10–11; "New Jersey's Good Deal for MOMS," editorial, *New York Times,* December 11, 1989, p. A22.

8. Hilts, "Life Expectancy For Blacks," p. A1.

9. Interview with Mary Ann Glendon in Bill Moyers, *Bill Moyers: A World of Ideas* (New York: Doubleday, 1989), p. 470.

10. Carol Cronin and Rebecca Hartman, "The Corporate Perspective on Maternal & Child Health: A Background Paper" (Washington, D.C.: Washington Business Group on Health, October 1989), p. 7.

11. "Cost of Caring for 'Drug Babies,' " memorandum to Van McMurtry, Staff Director, Senate Finance Committee, from Senator Lloyd Bentsen, November 15, 1989, p. 1.

12. Telephone interview with Allen Kott, New York State Division of Substance Abuse Services, New York City, February 5, 1990.

13. The examples contained in the following paragraphs are obtained from C. Arden Miller, *Maternal Health and Infant Survival* (Washington, D.C.: National Center for Clinical Infant Programs, July 1987).

14. Telephone interview, Richard Coorish, Health Insurance Association of America (HIAA), December 1, 1990. See "The Cost of Maternity Care and Childbirth in the United States" (Washington, D.C.: HIAA, 1989), p. 1.

15. "Caring for New Mothers: Pressing Problems, New Solutions," prepared for a hearing before the Select Committee on Children, Youth and Families, October 24, 1989.

16. Marcia Levine's story is excerpted from Betty Holcomb, "Pregnant? You're Fired," *Working Mother,* March 1990, p. 41.

17. Ibid.

18. Quoted in ibid., pp. 42, 46.

19. Quoted in ibid.

20. Quoted in ibid.

21. The discussion in the following paragraphs on maternity and parenting benefits is based on data presented in Sylvia Ann Hewlett, *A Lesser Life: The Myth of Women's Liberation in America* (New York: Morrow, 1986), pp. 70–109. See also Sheila B.

Kamerman, Alfred J. Kahn, and Paul Kingston, *Maternity Policies and Working Women* (New York: Columbia University Press, 1983).

22. Steven A. Holmes, "Bush Vetoes Bill on Family Leave," *New York Times,* June 30, 1990, p. A9.

23. Steven A. Holmes, "Senate Sends Parental Leave Bill to White House," *New York Times,* June 15, 1990, p. A13.

24. Telephone interview, Howard Hawghe, economist, Bureau of Labor Statistics, December 1, 1990. In 1989 50.3 percent of mothers of children under one year old were in the labor force; in 1975 the figure was 31.4 percent.

25. Steven A. Holmes, "Senate Sends Parental Leave Bill to White House," *New York Times,* June 15, 1990, p. A13.

26. Lawrence Perlman, "Family Leave—It's Good Business," op-ed, *Washington Post,* July 25, 1990, p. A21.

27. Marge Roukema, "Mr. Bush, Keep Your Promise to American Families," op-ed, *New York Times,* June 20, 1990, p. A25.

28. Gilbert Steiner, *The Children's Cause* (Washington, D.C.: The Brookings Institution, 1976), p. 115.

29. Sue Tolleson Rinehart, "Maternal Health Care Policy: Britain and the United States," *Comparative Politics* 19, no. 2 (January 1987): 197.

30. William H. Chafe, *The American Woman: Her Changing Social, Economic and Political Roles, 1920–1970* (New York: Oxford University Press, 1972), p. 187.

31. Marian Wright Edelman, "A Political-Legislative Overview of Federal Child Care Proposals," in *Raising Children in Modern America: Problems and Prospective Solutions,* ed. Nathan B. Talbot (Boston: Little, Brown, 1974), p. 316.

32. James J. Kilpatrick's column, "A Conservative View," reprinted in the *Congressional Record,* vol. 117, part 34: December 2, 1971 to December 7, 1971 (Washington, D.C.: U. S. Government Printing Office, 1971), p. 44, 137.

33. Edelman, "A Political-Legislative Overview," p. 316.

34. Dr. Benjamin Spock, *Baby and Child Care,* 2d ed. (New York: Simon & Schuster, 1967), p. 570. A subsequent edition of the book was kinder to working mothers, but even in the later edition Spock still argues that the best caretakers in the first three years of life are the parents. Group care is not considered

a good alternative until the child is at least three years old. See Dr. Benjamin Spock, *Baby and Child Care,* 3d ed. (New York: Pocket Books, 1976).

35. Selma H. Fraiberg, *Every Child's Birthright: In Defense of Mothering* (New York: Basic Books, 1977). In this book Fraiberg stresses the dire consequences of maternal deprivation before eighteen months of age.

36. Burton White, "Should You Stay Home with Your Baby?" *Young Children* 37, no. 1 (November 1981): 11.

37. Burton L. White, *The First Three Years of Life* (New York: Avon, 1975), p. 134.

38. Interview, Burton White, March 1, 1983.

39. Daniel Patrick Moynihan, *Family and Nation* (New York: Harcourt Brace Jovanovich, 1986), pp. 4–5.

40. Brigitte Berger and Peter Berger, *The War Over the Family: Capturing the Middle Ground* (London: Penguin, 1983), p. 26.

41. Hewlett, *A Lesser Life,* p. 15.

42. Gloria Steinem, quoted in Martha Smiley's "The Dilemmas of Childlessness," *Time,* May 2, 1988, p. 88.

43. Berger and Berger, *The War Over the Family,* pp. 26–28.

44. Barrington Moore, Jr., "Thoughts on the Future of the Family," in *The Family and Change,* ed. John Edwards (New York: Knopf, 1969), p. 456.

45. Berger and Berger, *The War Over the Family,* p. 27.

46. Steven A. Holmes, "House Backs Bush Veto of Family Leave Bill," *New York Times,* July 26, 1990, p. 116.

47. Betty Friedan, "On Prodigal Parents," *New Perspectives Quarterly* 7, no. 2 (Spring 1990): 66.

48. Berger and Berger, *The War Over the Family,* pp. 71–75.

49. Quoted in Letty Cottin Pogrebin, *Family Politics: Love and Power on an Intimate Frontier* (New York: McGraw-Hill, 1983), p. 60.

50. *A Vision for America's Future, An Agenda for the 1990s: A Children's Defense Budget* (Washington, D.C.: Children's Defense Fund, 1989), p. xvii.

51. Mary Ann Glendon, *Abortion and Divorce in Western Law* (Cambridge, Mass.: Harvard University Press, 1987), p. 142. See also Clifford Geertz, *Local Knowledge: Further Essays in Interpretive Anthropology* (New York: Basic Books, 1983), p. 175.

52. Testimony of Dr. Lenora Cole Alexander, director of the

Women's Bureau, U.S. Department of Labor, before the Joint Economic Committee of the U.S. Congress, April 3, 1984, p. 9.

53. See discussion in June E. Hahner, *Emancipating the Female Sex: The Struggle for Women's Rights in Brazil, 1850–1940* (Durham, N.C.: Duke University Press, 1990).

54. Gus W. Haggstrom, Linda J. Waite, David E. Kanouse, and Thomas J. Blaschke, "Changes in the Life Styles of New Parents" (Santa Monica, Calif.: Rand Corporation, December 1984), p. 61.

55. Vance Packard, *Our Endangered Children: Growing Up in a Changing World* (New York: Little, Brown, 1983), p. 56.

56. Hewlett, *A Lesser Life*, p. 374.

Chapter 7. The Private Sector and Win-Win Scenarios

1. Louis V. Gerstner, Jr., "The Work Force Challenge." Remarks at the American Express Company Senior Management Conference, Tucson, Arizona, October 13, 1988, p. 1. Gerstner is now CEO of R. J. Reynolds.

2. Ibid., p. 3.

3. Ibid., p. 4.

4. James D. Robinson III, remarks, Senior Management Conference, Palm Springs East, March 1990.

5. Gerstner, "The Work Force Challenge," p. 4.

6. Interview, Rennie Roberts, senior vice president of human resources, and Jean Fraser, vice president of employee relations, American Express, January 31, 1990.

7. "Human Resource Communique" (American Express, Summer 1989), p. 2.

8. Ibid.

9. *Becoming the Best Place to Work* (American Express Travel Related Services, 1990).

10. *Philanthropy at American Express* (American Express, 1990).

11. Ibid.

12. Interview, Rennie Roberts and Jean Fraser.

13. GE Company, "People Power: The Global Human Resource Challenge for the Nineties," company position prepared by

Frank P. Doyle, senior vice president, corporate relations staff, September 23, 1989.

14. William B. Johnston and Arnold H. Packer, *Workforce 2000: Work and Workers for the 21st Century* (Indianapolis: Hudson Institute, June 1987), p. xix. Projections updated with data obtained from Howard B. Fullerton, Jr., "New Labor Force Projections, Spanning 1988 to 2000," *Monthly Labor Review* 112, no. 11 (November 1989): 3.

15. Fullerton, "New Labor Force Projections," p. 4.

16. Ibid., p. 11. Other analysts have come up with even lower figures. In 1990 *Time* magazine estimated that only 9 percent of net incoming workers would be white males. See Janice Castro, "Get Set: Here They Come!" *Time,* special issue, Fall 1990, p. 52.

17. David E. Bloom and Neil G. Bennett, "Future Shock: America's Dismal Demographic Future," *The New Republic,* June 19, 1989, p. 20.

18. Fullerton, "New Labor Force Project Projections," pp. 10–11.

19. Ibid.

20. Lee A. Daniels, "Experts Foresee a Social Gap Between Sexes Among Blacks," *New York Times,* February 5, 1989, p. 30.

21. Albert Shanker, "European vs. U.S. Students: Why Are We So Far Behind?" *New York Times,* April 23, 1989, p. E7.

22. See, for example, Curtis McKnight et al., *The Underachieving Curriculum: Assessing U.S. School Mathematics from an International Perspective* (Champaign, Ill.: International Association for the Evaluation of Education Achievement, Stipes Publishing, 1987).

23. Ellen Graham, "Retooling the Schools: The System Needs a Complete Overhaul, Not Just More Tinkering," *Wall Street Journal,* March 31, 1989, p. R3; and Julie Amarano Lopez, "System Failure: Businesses Say Schools Are Producing Graduates Unqualified to Hold Jobs," *Wall Street Journal,* p. R12.

24. Telephone interview, February 27, 1991.

25. Reported in Edward B. Fiske, "Impending U.S. Jobs 'Disaster': Workforce Unqualified to Work," *New York Times,* September 25, 1989, p. A1. For more recent analysis, see William B. Johnston and Arnold H. Packer, *Screening In* (Indianapolis:

Hudson Institute, January 1991). The Labor Department sees it this way:

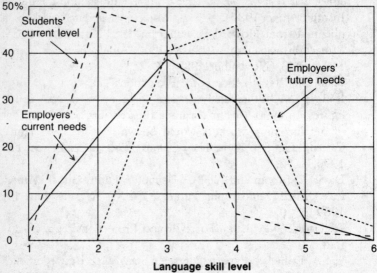

Language skill level

Source: Labor Department

Percentage of students and jobs available at each level of verbal skill, ranked from 1 to 6.
The scale is prepared by the Labor Department, Level 6 signifies the ability to read technical journals. Rudimentary communication skills required in manual labor jobs fall into level 1. Level 3 is typical of retail salespeople or skilled construction workers.

26. Johnston and Packer, *Workforce 2000,* pp. 97–98.
27. Graham, "Retooling the Schools," p. R3.
28. Johnston and Packer, *Workforce 2000,* pp. 98–99.
29. Ibid.
30. Fiske, "Impending U.S. Jobs 'Disaster,' " *New York Times,* September 25, 1989, p. B6.
31. Telephone interview, Howard Hawghe, Economist, Bureau of Labor Statistics, December 1, 1990. See also Fran Sussner Rodgers and Charles Rodgers, "Business and the Facts of Family Life," *Harvard Business Review* 67, no. 6 (November–December 1989): 121.

32. Sandra L. Burud, Pamela R. Aschbacher, and Jacquelyn McCroskey, *Employer Supported Child Care: Investing in Human Resources* (Dover, Mass.: Auburn House, 1984), pp. 22–26.

33. Nationwide, mothers of preschool children have a very high absentee rate—11.5 percent, compared to 5.8 percent for married women with no children. See Joseph R. Meisenheimer II, "Employee Absences in 1989: A New Look at Data from the CPS," *Monthly Labor Review* 113, no. 8 (August 1990): 29.

34. Union Bank's story and figures from Cynthia Ransom, Pamela R. Aschbacher, and Sandra L. Burud, "The Return in the Child-Care Investment," *Personnel Administrator,* October 1989, pp. 54–58.

35. Honeywell's story and figures from Lynne M. Warne, "News Release" (Minneapolis, Minn.: Honeywell, Inc., August 3, 1989). See also "The Honeywell Sick Child Care Program User's Guide."

36. Marilyn Gardner, "Family-Friendly Corporations: They Help Balance Demands of Home and Work," *Christian Science Monitor,* June 30, 1988, p. 32.

37. J. Douglas Phillips, "Employee Turnover and the Bottom Line," working paper, Merek & Co., Inc., February 1989, p. 2.

38. Ibid., p. 6.

39. Glenn Collins, "Wooing Workers in the '90s: New Role for Family Benefits," *New York Times,* July 20, 1988, p. A14; and telephone interview, J. Douglas Phillips, December 18, 1990.

40. Sunbeam's story reported in telephone interview, David Adams, health services administrator at the Sunbeam Appliance Company's Coushatta, La., plant, May 2, 1990. See also Milt Freudenheim, "In Pursuit of the Punctual Baby," *New York Times,* December 28, 1988, p. D1.

41. Carol Lawson, "For Working Parents, Some Hope of Help," *New York Times,* March 15, 1990, p. C10. See also Aaron Bernstein, "Business Starts Tailoring Itself to Suit Working Women," *Business Week,* October 6, 1986, p. 51.

42. Quoted in Sylvia Hewlett, "Family Support Policy? Consult the Bottom Line," *Management Review* 78, no. 1 (January 1989): 57.

43. "IBM Writes the Book on Liberal Leave," *U.S. News & World Report,* October 31, 1988, p. 13.

44. Rodgers and Rodgers, "Business and the Facts of Family Life," p. 127. See also "IBM Work and Personal Life Balance Programs" booklet. In late 1990 IBM announced it would spend $3 million next year to build five child-care centers near its offices and plants around the country. *New York Times,* December 12, 1990, p. D1.

45. NCNB's story and figures from Letters to the editor of *Harvard Business Review,* January–February 1990, pp. 194–95. See also Rodgers and Rodgers, "Business and the Facts of Family Life," p. 127.

46. Examples from: *Work and Family Program Overview* (New Brunswick, N.J.: Johnson & Johnson, October 1988); Pamela Mendels, "Family Plan at AT&T," *Newsday,* May 31, 1989, p. 47; Celestine Bohlen, "Unions Say AT&T Pact Sets New Standard for Family Benefits," *New York Times,* May 30, 1989, p. A14; Elizabeth Ehrlich with Susan B. Garland, "For American Business, a New World of Workers," *Business Week,* September 19, 1988, p. 114; program information, Apple Computer Inc., Cupertino, California; Allstate Insurance Company, Corporate Human Resources, *Work & Family Connections* (Northbrook, Ill.: Allstate Insurance, 1989); program information from E.I. DuPont de Nemours & Company, Wilmington, Delaware.

47. Rodgers and Rodgers, "Business and the Facts of Family Life," p. 127.

48. Letters to the editor, *Harvard Business Review* 68, no. 1 (January–February 1990): 195–96.

49. "Employer Supports for Child Care," *Mothers in the Workplace Study* (National Council of Jewish Women, Center for the Child, August 1988).

50. Rodgers and Rodgers, "Business and the Facts of Family Life," p. 125.

51. Bureau of National Affairs, "Second Annual Conference on Work & Family: New Directions for the 1990s," November 2–3, 1989, Washington, D.C. Only 4,177 U.S. employers, about 10 percent of companies with 100 or more employees, provided some form of child-care assistance in 1989.

52. Rosabeth Moss Kanter, *When Giants Learn to Dance: Mastering the Challenges of Strategy, Management, and Careers in the 1990s* (New York: Simon & Schuster, 1989), p. 29. See also Aaron

Bernstein, "Where the Jobs Are Is Where the Skills Aren't," *Business Week,* September 19, 1988, p. 108.

53. Carl S. Kaplan, "Employee Child-Care in the Spotlight," *Newsday,* April 12, 1989, p. 43.

54. Peter F. Drucker, *The New Realities* (New York: Harper & Row, 1989), p. 190.

55. Kathleen Teltsch, "Business Sees Aid to Schools as a Net Gain," *New York Times,* December 4, 1988, p. A50.

56. Quotes and information on Pat Taylor and the Taylor Plan come from the following sources: George Melloan, "A Louisiana Wildcatter Shines His Point of Light," *Wall Street Journal,* May 2, 1989, p. A19; Allan Katz, "Metropolitan View: The Lone Wolf," *The Times-Picayune,* July 30, 1989, p. B7; and David Foster and Ronnie Virgets, "I'll Do It My Way," *New Orleans Magazine,* December 1988, p. 89.

57. Milwaukee's figures and quotes from Dirk Johnson, "Milwaukee Plans a College Guarantee for Pupils," *New York Times,* February 7, 1990, p. B6.

58. GE Foundations Annual Report 1988; Kathleen Teltsch, "Business Sees Aid to Schools as a Net Gain," *New York Times,* December 4, 1988, p. 1.

59. Information on Nabisco, Chicago, and Eastman Kodak obtained from Steven A. Holmes, "School Reform: Business Moves In," *New York Times,* February 1, 1990, p. D1.

60. Committee for Economic Development, *Investing in Our Children: Business and the Public Schools* (New York: CED, 1985).

61. Committee for Economic Development, Research and Policy Committee, *Children in Need: Investment Strategies for the Educationally Disadvantaged* (New York: CED, 1987), p. 21.

62. Ibid., p. 3.

63. Interview, October 24, 1989.

64. Merrill McLouglin with Jeannye Thornton, Pamela Ellis-Simons, Lynn Adkins, and Tracy L. Shryer, "The Children's Hour," *U.S. News & World Report,* November 7, 1988, p. 36.

65. CED, *Children in Need,* pp. ix, 5–8, 21.

66. Ibid., pp. 15, 16.

67. Kathleen Teltsch, "Helping Steer the Deprived Young," *New York Times,* April 10, 1988, p. A30.

68. Information on the Beethoven Project obtained from Judy

Langford Carter, acting executive director, Ounce of Prevention Fund, Chicago, testimony before the National Commission on Infant Mortality, Atlanta, January 11, 1988; "What Can We Do to Prevent the Cycle of Poverty?" 1987 Clifford Beers Lecture, delivered by Irving B. Harris, president, Ounce of Prevention Fund, March 24, 1987, Child Study Center, Yale University; Barbara Vobejda, "From Cradle to Grades: A Chicago Program Starts Before Birth to Help the Neediest Children," *Washington Post National Weekly Edition,* February 17, 1988, pp. 10–11; *The Ounce of Prevention Fund Magazine,* published quarterly by Ounce of Prevention Fund, 188 W. Randolph St., Suite 2200, Chicago 60601; Ounce of Prevention Fund, "Ideas in Action: The Ounce of Prevention Fund Annual Report, 1988–1989" (Chicago: Ounce of Prevention Fund); Kathleen Teltsch, "A Cradle-to-Kindergarten Aid Plan in Chicago," *New York Times,* December 28, 1986, p. A1; Teltsch, "Helping Steer the Deprived Young," p. A30; Teltsch, "11 Infants in Chicago Child Aid Program," *New York Times,* March 29, 1987, p. A20; Deborah L. Cohen, "Reform at 5: The Unfinished Agenda—'We Became the Hopes and Dreams' of All," *Education Week* 8, no. 19 (February 1, 1989), p. 1; and *New York Times,* editorial, "Head Start on Head Start," January 13, 1987, p. A26.

69. Carol Lawson, "7 Employers Join to Provide Child Care at Home in a Crisis," *New York Times,* September 7, 1989, pp. A1, C12.

70. Rodgers and Rodgers, "Business and the Facts of Family Life," p. 126.

71. Glen Collins, "Wooing Workers in the 90's: New Role for Family Benefits," *New York Times,* July 20, 1988, pp. A1, A14.

72. Betty Holcomb, senior editor of *Working Mother,* Letters to the Editor, *Harvard Business Review* 68, no. 1 (January–February 1990): 195.

73. Rodgers and Rodgers, "Business and the Facts of Family Life," p. 125. See also Stephanie L. Hyland, "Helping Employees with Family Care," *Monthly Labor Review* 113, no. 9 (September 1990): 22–26.

74. Telephone interview, Jules Lichtenstein, Chief Applied Policy

Branch, Small Business Administration. Data from *Current Population Survey,* unpublished data.

75. As I demonstrate in *A Lesser Life,* approximately one-half of the wage gap between male and female earnings is due to discrimination and one-half to family burdens. See Sylvia Ann Hewlett, *A Lesser Life: The Myth of Women's Liberation in America* (New York: Morrow, 1986), pp. 70–109.

76. Gus W. Haggstrom, Linda J. Waite, David E. Kanouse, and Thomas J. Blaschke, "Changes in the Life Styles of New Parents" (Santa Monica, Calif.: Rand Corporation, December 1984), p. 61.

77. Hewlett, *A Lesser Life,* p. 82.

78. Interview, January 23, 1990.

79. Quoted in Lawson, "7 Employers."

80. Cathy Trost, "Creative Child-Care Programs Aid Employees Who Work Odd Hours," *Wall Street Journal,* March 18, 1988, p. B1.

81. Telephone interview, Frank Sorbino, New York City Department of Education, May 16, 1990.

82. David T. Kearns, "Help to Restructure Public Education from the Bottom Up," *Harvard Business Review* 66, no. 6 (November–December 1988): 70; and Fiske, "Impending U.S. Jobs 'Disaster,' " p. A1.

83. Interview, Alda Dolch, coordinator, Academy of Finance, John Dewey High School, Brooklyn, New York, February 27, 1990.

84. CED, *Children in Need,* pp. 2–3.

Chapter 8. A Call to Action

1. Committee for Economic Development, *Children in Need: Investment Strategies for the Educationally Disadvantaged* (New York: CED, 1987), p. 3.

2. Timothy M. Smeeding, "The Debt, the Deficit, and Disadvantaged Children: Generational Impacts and Age, Period and Cohort Effects," in *The Debt and the Twin Deficits Debate,* ed. James M. Rock (Mountain View, Calif.: Bristlecone Books/Mayfield, 1991), p. 47.

3. National Governor's Association, *America in Transition: Report of*

the Task Force on Children (Washington, D.C.: Government Printing Office, 1989).

4. See discussion in Edward F. Zigler and Meryl Frank, eds., *The Parental Leave Crisis: Toward a New National Policy* (New Haven: Yale University Press, 1988), p. xix.

5. Edward F. Zigler and Mary E. Lang, *Child Care Choices: Balancing the Needs of Children, Family and Society* (New York: The Free Press, 1991), p. 111.

6. *New York Times,* September 3, 1984, as cited in Sylvia Ann Hewlett, *A Lesser Life: The Myth of Women's Liberation in America* (New York: Morrow, 1986), p. 276.

7. Steven A. Holmes, "House, 265–145, Votes to Widen Day Care Programs in the Nation," *New York Times,* March 30, 1990, p. A1.

8. Ibid.

9. "The Status of Some of the Major Pieces of Legislation Before Congress," *New York Times,* October 17, 1990, p. A25.

10. Steven A. Holmes, "Tentative Accord Reached on Child Care for Low-Income Families," *New York Times,* October 27, 1990, p. 8.

11. Karen DeWitt, "U.S. Plan on Child Care Is Reported to Be Stalled," *New York Times,* January 27, 1991, p. 18.

12. Steven A. Holmes, "Day Care Bill Marks a Turn Toward Help for the Poor," *New York Times,* April 8, 1990, p. E4; and Jaclyn Fierman, "Child Care: What Works—And Doesn't," *Fortune,* November 21, 1988, pp. 166–76.

13. *Facts About Child Care,* Child Care Action Campaign Information Guide No. 7 (New York: Child Care Action Campaign, 1990).

14. Edward F. Zigler and Mary E. Lang, *Child Care Choices: Balancing the Needs of Children, Families and Society* (New York: The Free Press, 1991), pp. 199–214.

15. Fierman, "Child Care: What Works," p. 170.

16. Calvin Sims, "Body Heat," *New York Times Education Supplement,* April 8, 1990, p. 29.

17. Alex Kotlowitz, "Tough Students: Inner-City Schools Must Teach Kids Traumatized By Violence, Family Woes," *Wall Street Journal,* March 31, 1989, special education section, p. R11.

18. Kathleen Teltsch, "Helping Steer the Deprived Young," *New York Times,* April 10, 1988, p. A30.

19. M. Edith Rasell and Lawrence Mishel, "Shortcoming Education: How U.S. Spending on Grades K–12 Lags Behind Other Industrial Nations," briefing paper (Washington, D.C.: Economic Policy Institute, 1989), pp. 1–2.

20. Ibid., p. 2.

21. Committee for Economic Development, *Children in Need,* p. 21.

22. *A Vision for America's Future,* p. 62.

23. Data on the Ypsilanti project obtained from Lisbeth B. Schorr, *Within Our Reach: Breaking the Cycle of Disadvantage* (New York: Doubleday, 1988), pp. 192–200.

24. Committee for Economic Development, *Investing in Our Children: Business and the Public Schools* (New York: CED, 1985).

25. Robert Reinhold, "School Reform: 4 Years of Tumult, Mixed Results," *New York Times,* August 10, 1987, p. A1.

26. Jack Beatty, "A Post Cold War Budget," *Atlantic Monthly,* February 1990, p. 76.

27. Ibid.

28. Ibid.

29. See Jonathon Kozol, *Rachel and Her Children: Homeless Families in America* (New York: Crown, 1988); and Paul A. Leonard, Cushing N. Dolbeare, and Edward B. Lazere, "A Place to Call Home: The Crisis in Housing for the Poor" (Washington, D.C.: Center on Budget and Policy Priorities and Low Income Housing, April 1989).

30. Kirsten Downey, "Typical Buyer: A Vanishing Breed," *Washington Post,* February 10, 1990, p. E1.

31. Joint Center for Housing Studies, Harvard University, "The State of the Nation's Housing, 1990," p. 16.

32. "A Mother's Choice," *Newsweek,* March 31, 1986, p. 51.

33. Jonathan Rauch, "Out of Reach," *National Journal,* April 16, 1988, p. 1039.

34. Eric Schmitt, "Collapsing Housing Market Is Taking an Emotional Toll," *New York Times,* April 13, 1990, p. B1.

35. Rauch, "Out of Reach," p. 1039; see also *Time,* special issue, fall 1990, p. 54.

36. Leonard, Dolbeare, and Lazere, "A Place to Call Home," pp. 32–33.

37. Louis S. Richman, "Housing Policy Needs a Rehab," *Fortune,* March 27, 1989, p. 92.

38. Ibid.; and Leonard, Dolbeare, and Lazere, "A Place to Call Home," p. 29.

39. Sara Rimer, "New York Pulling Out of 13 More Welfare Hotels," *New York Times,* March 3, 1989, p. B3.

40. Iver Peterson, "Prospects Rise for Housing Legislation," *New York Times,* June 11, 1989, p. R1.

41. *VA History in Brief: What It Is, Was, and Does* (Washington, D.C.: Veterans Administration, May 1986), pp. 5–8.

42. Leon H. Keyserling, "Homes for All—and How," *Survey Graphic* 35, no. 2 (February 1946): 37.

43. See discussion in chapter 5.

44. See discussion in Zigler and Lang, *Child Care Choices,* p. 215. See also Peter G. Peterson, "The Morning After," *Atlantic Monthly,* October 1987, p. 65.

45. Zigler and Lang, *Child Care Choices,* p. 215.

46. For an analysis of the Wisconsin model, see Irwin Garfinkel and Marygold S. Melli, "The Use of Normative Standards in Family Law Decisions: Developing Mathematical Standards for Child Support," *Family Law Quarterly* 24, no. 2 (Summer 1990): 157–78.

47. Telephone interview, December 12, 1990.

48. Andrew Cherlin, *Marriage, Divorce, Remarriage* (Cambridge, Mass.: Harvard University Press, 1982), pp. 47–48.

49. Michael Prowse, "When the Cornflake Bowl is Empty," *Financial Times* (London), August 8, 1990, p. 13.

50. *Fortune* magazine has made a similar argument. See Lee Smith, "What Do We Owe the Elderly?" *Fortune,* March 27, 1989, p. 60.

51. Michael Marriott, "For Fledgling Teacher Corps, Hard Lessons," *New York Times,* December 5, 1990, p. A1. See also Susan Chira, "Princeton Student's Brainstorm: A Peace Corps to Train Teachers," *New York Times,* June 20, 1990, p. A1.

52. *Keeping Faith in New York City: A Partnership for Our Children* (New York: Inter-Faith Coalition of 200 Clergy and Congregations, January 17, 1991).

53. David E. Rosenbaum, "Peace Dividend: A Dream for Every Dollar," *New York Times,* February 18, 1990, p. E1.

54. "$150 Billion a Year: How to Spend It," editorial, *New York Times,* March 9, 1990, p. A34.
55. Rosenbaum, "Peace Dividend," p. E1.
56. Ibid.
57. "Bat Plane Dodges Flak at the Capitol," *U.S. News & World Report,* July 31, 1989, p. 10.
58. Peterson, "The Morning After," p. 65. See also Peter G. Peterson and Neil Howe, *On Borrowed Time* (San Francisco: Institute for Contemporary Studies, 1988), p. 188.
59. William Safire, "The Opposition Stirs," *New York Times,* January 1, 1990.

Chapter 9. Saving Our Children, Saving Ourselves

1. Quoted in Roger Wilkins, "The Black Poor Are Different," *New York Times,* op-ed, August 22, 1989, p. A23.
2. Quoted by Peter G. Peterson, "We Must 'Do Better' for Our Children," *New York Times,* July 16, 1989.
3. James C. McKinley, Jr., "Killings in '89 Set a Record in New York," *New York Times,* March 31, 1990, p. 27; Jonathan Greenberg, "All About Crime," *New York,* September 3, 1990, pp. 26–27.
4. Michael Prowse, "The Not So Great Society," *Financial Times* (London), April 20, 1990.
5. Ronald D. White, "Uneasy Street," *Washington Post,* op-ed, August 30, 1985, p. A23.
6. Central Park story and quotes compiled from: Michael Stone, "What Really Happened in Central Park," *New York,* August 14, 1989, pp. 29–43; David E. Pitt, "More Crimes Tied to Gang in Park Rape," *New York Times,* April 24, 1989, p. B1; James C. McKinley, Jr., "Official Says Youths Admit Role in Attack," *New York Times,* April 24, 1989, p. B1; Michael T. Kaufman, "Park Suspects: Children of Discipline," *New York Times,* April 26, 1989, p. A1; "None of Us Is Safe," *New York Post,* April 24, 1989, p. 1; and Ray Kerrison, "Message from Central Park," *New York Post,* April 24, 1989, p. 4.
7. David E. Pitt, "Gang Attack: Unusual for Its Viciousness," *New York Times,* April 25, 1989, p. B1; see also Don Terry, "A Week of Rapes: The Jogger and 28 Not in the News," *New York Times,* May 29, 1989, p. 25.

8. John Tierney, "New Yorkers Trying to Outwit Shrub Rustlers," *New York Times,* May 24, 1990, p. A1.

9. Daniel Patrick Moynihan, *Family and Nation* (New York: Harcourt Brace Jovanovich), p. 192.

10. "What Can We Do to Prevent the Cycle of Poverty?" 1987 Clifford Beers Lecture, delivered by Irving B. Harris, president, Ounce of Prevention Fund, March 24, 1987, Child Study Center, Yale University.

11. Jimmy Breslin, "A Sorry Christmas List: One Million Behind Bars," *Newsday,* December 17, 1989, p. 7. In 1990 we spent $13 billion on AFDC; see "Economic and Budget Outlook, Fiscal Years 1991–96" (Washington, D.C.: Congressional Budget Office, January 1991).

12. Colman McCarthy, "The High Cost of Confinement," *Washington Post,* June 6, 1987, p. A23.

13. Ibid.

14. Vincent Schiraldi, "Prisons Don't Really Get Tough on Crime," *Los Angeles Times,* December 9, 1987, p. 7.

15. McCarthy, "The High Cost of Confinement," p. A23.

16. Quoted in Jonathan E. Gradess, "Execution Does Not Pay," op-ed, *Washington Post,* February 28, 1988, p. C5.

17. Martin Weston, "The Poverty That Can Lead to Crime," *Newsday,* September 27, 1990, p. 61.

18. Commission on Workforce Quality and Labor Market Efficiency, *Investing in People: A Strategy to Address America's Workforce Crisis* (Washington, D.C.: U.S. Department of Labor, 1989), p. 1.

19. Paul Kennedy, "Can the U.S. Stay Number One?" *New York Review of Books* 36, no. 4 (March 16, 1989), p. 36.

20. Robert B. Reich, "Who Is Us?" *Harvard Business Review* 68, no. 1 (January–February 1990): 59.

21. Commission on Workforce Quality, *Investing in People,* p. 7.

22. Japanese examples taken from: Jane Condon, *A Half Step Behind: Japanese Women of the '80s* (New York: Dodd, Mead, 1985), pp. 120–39.

23. Lisbeth Schorr, *Within Our Reach: Breaking the Cycle of Disadvantage* (New York: Doubleday, 1988), p. xix.

24. Interview, "60 Minutes," CBS-TV, October 22, 1989.

Epilogue. The Limits of Freedom

1. Quoted in Roger Rosenblatt, "Coming to America," *Life,* February 1990, p. 40.
2. Michael Prowse, "The Not So Great Society," *Financial Times* (London), April 20, 1990, p. 26.
3. Rosenblatt, "Coming to America," p. 41.
4. Francis Fukuyama, "The End of History," *The National Interest* no. 16 (Summer 1989): 3.
5. Martin E. P. Seligman, "Boomer Blues," *Psychology Today,* October 1988, p. 50.
6. Bill Moyers, *Bill Moyers: A World of Ideas* (New York: Doubleday, 1989), p. 60.
7. Tom Wolfe, *The Bonfire of the Vanities* (New York: Bantam, 1988), p. 58.
8. Alexis de Tocqueville, *Democracy in America,* vol. 11 (New York: Vintage, 1945), pp. 209, 219.
9. Carol Gilligan, *In a Different Voice: Psychological Theory and Women's Development* (Cambridge, Mass.: Harvard University Press, 1982), pp. 149, 129.
10. Germaine Greer, *Sex and Destiny: The Politics of Human Fertility* (New York: Harper & Row, 1984), p. 7.
11. Primarily as a result of elaborate programs of family support, women earn 86 percent of the male wage in Italy, and 78 percent of it in France. In contrast, women earn only 70 percent of the male wage in the United States, where there are very few social supports for families. See discussion in Sylvia Ann Hewlett, *A Lesser Life: The Myth of Women's Liberation in America* (New York: Morrow, 1986), pp. 70–109.
12. 1st Corinthians 13.

Permissions

Apart." © CBS Inc. 1989. All Rights Reserved. Originally broadcast on September 10, 1989, over the CBS Television Network. *Parenting,* for "The Preventable Tragedy" by Diana Hembree and Julie Scheff. Penguin Books, for *We Are Still Married: Stories and Letters,* by Garrison Keillor. Copyright © 1982, 1983, 1985, 1986, 1987, 1988, 1989, by Garrison Keillor. Used by permission of Viking Penguin, a division of Penguin Books USA, Inc. *The New York Daily News,* for "The Dark, Costly Side of 'Gray Power,' " by Lars-Erick Nelson. Copyright © New York News Inc. Reprinted with permission. Combine Music Corp., for "Me and Bobby McGee," by Kris Kristofferson and Fred Foster. © 1969 Temi Combine Inc. All rights controlled by Combine Music Corp. and administered by Emi Blackwood Music Inc. All rights reserved. International Copyright Secured. Used by Permission. Steven Guarnaccia, for the illustration on p. 351. King Features Syndicate, for cartoon by Ed Gamble. Reprinted with special permission of King Features Syndicate. Copley News Service, for "Oprah Winfrey" cartoon by Steve Kelley, on p. 151. Los Angeles Times Syndicate, for cartoon by Dan Wasserman, on p. 238. Copyright © 1987, Boston Globe. Distributed by Los Angeles Times Syndicate. Reprinted with permission.

Index

Gang rape, in Central Park, 336–337
Garfinkel, Irwin, 322
Gearity, Stefanie, 248–249
General Electric: education and, 269, 274, 275, 291; family supports of, 27, 251
General Motors, 269
Geography, American students and, 85–86
George Washington Preparatory High School, 278
"Geraldo," 129, 130, 151–152, 333
Germany, family supports in, 221, 229
Gilligan, Carol, 252–253
Ginzberg, Eli, 284
Giving-getting compact: child and, 167; "Now-now-ism" and, 206–208; Yankelovich on, 133, 134
Glaser, David, 315
Glendon, Mary Ann, 136–137, 142, 145, 217, 239
Gol, Jean, 286
Golden Valley, 174
Good Mother, The (Miller), 170–173
Government: child care and, 70; *Children in Need* and, 279; cost-effectiveness of programs and, 301; crack babies and, 165; debt, 204–206, 348; divorce reform and, 129–130, 135–147; education and, 20, 25, 73, 187; family-friendly workplaces encouraged by, 302; family support and, 230–242, 292 (*see also* Action Plan for Children); health care spending, 61–63 (*see also* Catastrophic health care); housing and, 58–59; infrastructure and, 199–203; parenting leave and, 224–236, 240, 304–305, 321, 354; prenatal care and, 61–62, 217–225, 305; responsibility for children and, 34–35; self-absorption and, 129, 146, 165–167; spending on young, 17–18, 36, 130, 187, 191–193, 198–199, 301, 346; television and, 129, 130, 149–156, 167, 302. *See also* Congress; Elderly, government spending on
G.I. Bill, loan provisions of, 318
Grace Commission, 187
Gramm, Phil, 330

Greer, Germaine, 355
Guba, Martha, 147
Gurian, Craig, 224
Guttmacher, Alan, Institute, 43
Guzman, Carina, 212–214
Guzman, Cinde, 212–214, 216, 219

Habits of the Heart (Bellah), 131
Halfon, Neal, 162
Hallmark cards, 110
Harris, Edith, 59
Harris, Irving, 280–281, 292, 339
Harris, Kathleen Mullan, 113
Harris, Louis, Associates, 268
Hart Island, 41–43
Harvard Preschool Project, 232
Hastings Center, 183
Head Start, 25, 67, 178, 181, 187, 311, 313; Beethoven Project and, 281; Congress and, 306; cost of, 300, 301
Health care: as birthright, 51; for children, 15, 59–63, 182, 187, 192; government and, 61–63. *See also* Catastrophic health care; Medicare; Prenatal care
Health insurance: inadequacy of, 59–63; uninsured pregnant women and, 213–216, 394n4
Henley, Robert, 309
Heritage Foundation, 330
Hernandez, Nellie, 248–249
Higgins, Larry, 278
High-school dropouts, 14, 20, 30, 31, 86–87
Hiller, Lynn, 72
Hispanics: education and, 20; unemployment among, 52–53; in work force, 253–254, 257
Hochschild, Arlie, 97
Homeless, 349; children as, 14, 35, 57–59, 360–361n5; government programs and, 316–317; numbers of, 57, 370n45; in welfare hotels, 2–6, 359n1
Homework, decline in, 118
Honeywell, 260–261
Houghton, James P., 27
Housing: cuts in, 210; elderly and, 178–179; lack of, 57–59, 371n51; neglect of children and, 238; rent

ABOUT THE AUTHOR

Sylvia Ann Hewlett is an economist and former director of the Economic Policy Council, a labor-management think tank. She is also the author of *A Lesser Life: The Myth of Women's Liberation in America* (1986). A consultant to major corporations, Hewlett lectures widely throughout the country and writes frequently for such publications as *Time, Family Circle,* the *New York Times,* and the *Harvard Business Review.*